See the WIDER picture

Giant's Causeway, County Antrim, Northern Ireland

Hot volcanic lava created this beautiful and strange place 50-60 million years ago. About 40,000 columns of rock make up the Giant's Causeway. Most columns have six sides and some are 12 metres tall. People once believed a giant built it because he wanted to build a bridge from Ireland to Scotland to fight another giant. The Giant's Causeway is very popular with tourists.

Is there a place like this in your country?

Course Map

Your Student's Book comes with access to:

▶ The Student's eBook

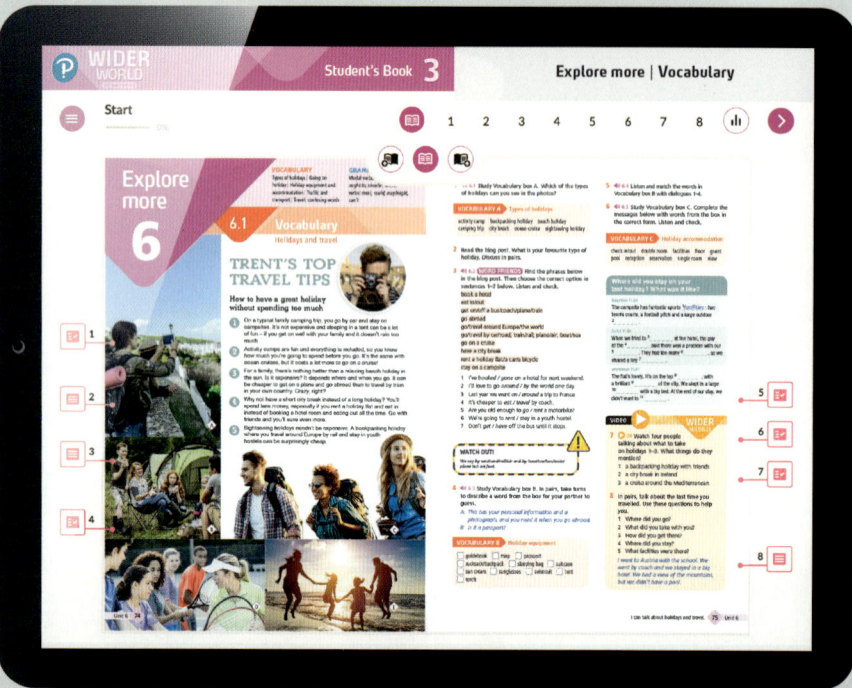

Audio, video and interactive activities with instant marking bring the content of the Student's Book to life in the eBook. It includes everything you need to participate in online lessons.

Wider World Second Edition is fully accessible on your computer, tablet and mobile phone. You can enjoy the full functionality of your course wherever you are.

You can access your digital components through the Pearson English Portal. See the inside front cover for access details.

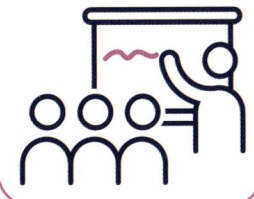

Classroom Lessons

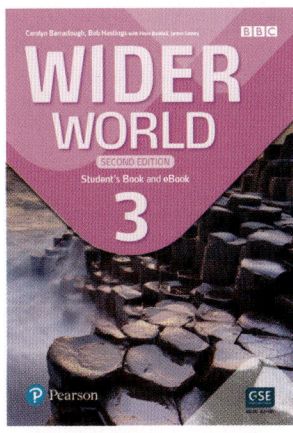

Student's Book

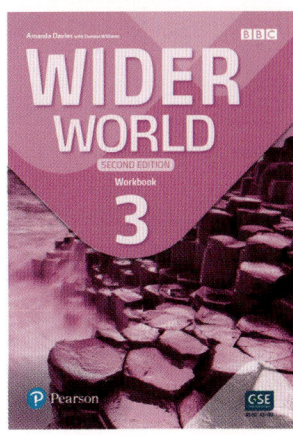

Workbook

Online Lessons

eBook

Homework

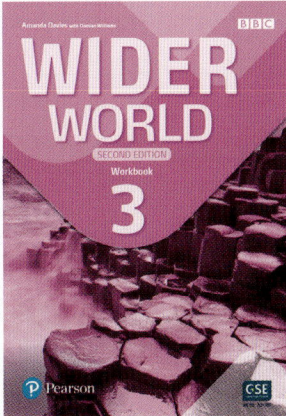

Workbook

Contents

		Vocabulary	Grammar	Reading and Vocabulary	Grammar
Welcome to New Park 0		**0.1 Introducing Abe** — Activities and interests	Home and furniture	*There is/are* with *some/any*	Possessive adjectives and possessive *'s* — pp. 6–7		**0.2 Introducing Bea** — Jobs	Everyday activities	Present Simple with adverbs of frequency — p. 8		
Tech check 1		Lifestyle: • Technology • Using technology • Social media — BBC VIDEO Wider World — pp. 12–13	• Present Simple and Present Continuous, state verbs — BBC VIDEO Wider World — p. 14	Science competitions and projects — Short texts about Science competitions and projects — p. 15	Verb + *-ing*, verb + *to*-infinitive — VIDEO *The video call* — p. 16
		BBC CULTURE *Screenagers*	VIDEO *Disconnecting*	Visual Thinking: What makes you say that?	
Wild and beautiful 2		Weather and climate: • Word building: weather • Weather • Climate — pp. 24–25	• Past Simple: regular and irregular verbs — p. 26	*A dangerously hot place* — An article about Death Valley, USA — p. 27	• Past Continuous and Past Sim — VIDEO *A crazy day* — BBC VIDEO Wider World — p. 28
		SET FOR LIFE Self-Management Keep calm when things go wrong Stay positive and carry on pp. 34–35			
Tasty treats 3		Food and drink: • Food • Cooking • Flavours — pp. 36–37	• Present Perfect with *ever, never, just, already* and *yet* — VIDEO *An English breakfast* — BBC VIDEO Wider World — p. 38	*Five superfoods – they're tasty and healthy!* — An article about the health benefits of five foods — p. 39	• Present Perfect with *for* and *since* • Present Perfect and Past Simp — p. 40
		BBC CULTURE *Fantastic food*	VIDEO *Indian food, Liverpool style*	Visual Thinking: Think, Puzzle, Explore	
Entertain us! 4		Film and TV: • Types of film • Word building: entertainment • Film and TV — BBC VIDEO Wider World — pp. 50–51	• Comparatives and superlatives • *Too/(not) enough, (not) as ... as* — BBC VIDEO Wider World — p. 52	*What's the best way to listen to music?* — A blog post about listening to music — p. 53	• Quantifiers: *some, any, much, many, (a) few, (a) little, a lot of, lots of* — VIDEO *The short video challer* — p. 54
		SET FOR LIFE Leadership Lead a team Team up! pp. 60–61			
To the limit 5		Sport: • Sports equipment • Sporting events • Sports collocations — pp. 62–63	• Future forms: *will, be going to,* Present Continuous, Present Simple — VIDEO *The fitness class* — p. 64	*Competitive sport or just a hobby?* — An article about different attitudes to sport — BBC VIDEO Wider World — p. 65	• First Conditional with *if* and *unless* — BBC VIDEO Wider World — p. 66
		BBC CULTURE *Sporting tradition*	VIDEO *The Highlands Games*	Visual Thinking: Connect, Extend, Challenge	
Explore more 6		Holidays and travel: • Types of holidays • Going on holidays • Holiday equipment and accommodation — BBC VIDEO Wider World — pp. 74–75	• Modal verbs: *must, have to, ought to, should* — VIDEO *A weekend break* — BBC VIDEO Wider World — p. 76	*Getting around Venice* — An article about transport in Venice, Italy — p. 77	• Modal verbs: *must, could, ma might, can't* (speculation) — p. 78
		SET FOR LIFE Social responsibility Be an eco-friendly traveller Eco-friendly travel pp. 84–85			
People power 7		Family and friends: • Word building: family • Phrasal verbs • Collocations: relationships — pp. 88–89	• Second Conditional — VIDEO *A dilemma* — BBC VIDEO Wider World — p. 90	*Five steps to friendship* — An article about making and keeping friends — p. 91	• Relative clauses — p. 92
		BBC CULTURE *From generation to generation*	VIDEO *Arctic life*	Visual Thinking: Concept, Challenge, Change	
Just justice 8		Crime: • Crimes and criminals • Crime collocations • Solving crimes • The law — pp. 100–101	• Present and Past Simple passive — p. 102	*A fair punishment* — An article about youth courts — p. 103	• Have/get something done — VIDEO *A new look* — p. 104
		SET FOR LIFE Critical thinking Make a decision You decide! pp. 110–111			
Lessons in life 9		Education: • School subjects • Describing students • Learning and assessment — pp. 112–113	• Reported speech: statements — p. 114	*How to train your brain!* — An article about becoming a confident student — p. 115	• Word order in questions — VIDEO *An interview* — p. 116
		BBC CULTURE *Different forms of education*	VIDEO *Learning goals*	Visual Thinking: Your viewpoint, The writer's viewpoint, What do you think now	

GRAMMAR TIME pp. 126–135   **IRREGULAR VERBS** p. 136   **STUDENT ACTIVITIES** pp. 137, 142–143

0.3 Introducing Eren Clothes and accessories | Present Continuous p. 9	**0.4 Introducing Carla** Countries and languages | Was/were | there was/there were | Past Simple: regular verbs p. 10	**0.5 Revision** p. 11		
Listening and Vocabulary	**Speaking**	**Writing**	**Revision**	**Progress Check**
A radio programme about using technology p. 17	VIDEO *Let's give it a try* Problem-solving SET FOR LIFE Creativity p. 18	A description of your daily routine and online hobbies • Connectors p. 19	Vocabulary Activator p. 20 Revision p. 21	**1–3** pp. 48–49 • **Vocabulary and Grammar:** multiple choice, open cloze, transformations • **Speaking:** role play • **Listening:** matching • **Reading:** multiple choice, open questions • **Writing:** an email to a friend
Project: a digital presentation about an app pp. 22–23				
A conversation about an adventure camp p. 29	VIDEO *I can explain* Criticising and explaining BBC VIDEO Wider World SET FOR LIFE Self-management p. 30	An article describing your local area and climate • Indefinite pronouns p. 31	Vocabulary Activator p. 32 Revision p. 33	
An advert for a cake competition BBC VIDEO Wider World p. 41	VIDEO *Are you ready to order?* Ordering food SET FOR LIFE Collaboration p. 42	An email to a friend • Giving instructions p. 43	Vocabulary Activator p. 44 Revision p. 45	
Project: a digital poster of a menu pp. 46–47				**1–6** pp. 86–87
An interview about a festival p. 55	VIDEO *I'd rather not dance* Talking about preferences SET FOR LIFE Self-management p. 56	A review on a blog • Adverbs p. 57	Vocabulary Activator p. 58 Revision p. 59	• **Vocabulary and Grammar:** multiple choice, transformations, word formation • **Speaking:** role play • **Listening:** gap-fill • **Reading:** matching • **Writing:** a review of a film or documentary
A conversation about a sports award p. 67	VIDEO *What are you up to today?* Talking about plans SET FOR LIFE Social Responsibility p. 68	Short messages • Prepositions + -ing form p. 69	Vocabulary Activator p. 70 Revision p. 71	
Project: a video podcast about a traditional sport pp. 72–73				
An interview about holidays for visually impaired people p. 79	VIDEO *Can you say that again?* Understanding a conversation SET FOR LIFE Communication p. 80	An email about travel arrangements • Future time clauses p. 81	Vocabulary Activator p. 82 Revision p. 83	
Two monologues about assistance dogs BBC VIDEO Wider World p. 93	VIDEO *Who's this girl on the right?* Identifying people in a group SET FOR LIFE Communication p. 94	A short story • Sequencers p. 95	Vocabulary Activator p. 96 Revision p. 97	**1–9** pp. 124–125 • **Vocabulary and Grammar:** word formation, open cloze, multiple-choice cloze • **Speaking:** role play • **Listening:** multiple choice • **Reading:** gapped text • **Writing:** an opinion essay
Project: a presentation about how people in remote places collect food pp. 98–99				
A podcast about a burglary BBC VIDEO Wider World p. 105	VIDEO *Is something wrong?* Keeping a conversation going SET FOR LIFE Social Responsibility p. 106	An opinion essay • Connectors of purpose and result p. 107	Vocabulary Activator p. 108 Revision p. 109	
Classroom conversations between teachers and students BBC VIDEO Wider World p. 117	VIDEO *What a coincidence!* Exchanging information SET FOR LIFE Social Responsibility p. 118	A formal letter asking for information • Talking about learning goals p. 119	Vocabulary Activator p. 120 Revision p. 121	
Project: a website for a new school pp. 122–123				

CLIL SCIENCE p. 138 MUSIC p. 139 GEOGRAPHY p. 140 SCIENCE p. 141

Welcome to New Park

0

VOCABULARY
Activities and interests | Home and furniture | Jobs | Everyday activities | Clothes and accessories | Countries and languages

GRAMMAR
There is/are with *some/any* | Possessive adjectives and possessive *'s* | Present Simple with adverbs of frequency | Present Continuous | *Was/were, there was/were* | Past Simple: regular verbs

This is Abe. His name's Abel Kerr, but his friends and family call him Abe. He's fifteen and he's from the USA. But now his new home is in the UK. His dad's name is Will and he is British. He's a scientist and he's got a new job in London. Abe's mum is American. She's a dentist. She hasn't got a job in the UK, so she's staying in the USA at the moment.

Abe's new house in the UK is nice, but it's a bit small. There are three bedrooms and there's a small garden too.

Abe's favourite hobby is photography. He's got a blog with lots of his photos. He likes reading, watching movies and making videos too.

He hasn't got any brothers or sisters, but he's got a British cousin. Her name's Bea. Bea's mum is Abe's aunt. She's his dad's sister. They all get on very well.

0.1 Introducing Abe

Activities and interests | Home and furniture | *There is/are* with *some/any* | Possessive adjectives and possessive *'s*

1 ▶ 1 🔊 0.1 Watch or listen and answer the questions.
1 What's the boy's name?
2 Where is he from?
3 Where is his new home?
4 What's his favourite hobby?

2 In pairs, read the text about Abe again and mark the sentences T (true) or F (false). Correct the false sentences.
1 ☐ Abe's dad is a dentist.
2 ☐ Abe's mum has got a job in the UK.
3 ☐ Abe's new home isn't very big.
4 ☐ Abe's interested in films.
5 ☐ Abe's got a sister called Bea.
6 ☐ Abe's dad and Bea's mum are brother and sister.

3 Write Abe's answers to the questions.
1 What's your name? *My name's Abe.*
2 Where are you from?
3 What's your house like?
4 Have you got any brothers or sisters?

4 In pairs, ask and answer the questions in Exercise 3 about you.

5 🔊 0.2 **I KNOW!** Study Vocabulary box A. In pairs, add as many words as you can to the box.

VOCABULARY A — Activities and interests

going to the cinema   listening to music
playing computer games   reading books   taking photos

6 Study the Speaking box. In pairs, talk about what you and the people in your family like/don't like.

I love reading comic books, but my sister doesn't like reading.

SPEAKING — Likes and dislikes

I like/love …   He likes/loves …
I don't like …   She doesn't like …
I don't mind …   He doesn't mind …
I can't stand …   She can't stand …

7 🔊 0.3 **I KNOW!** Study Vocabulary box B. In pairs, add as many words as you can to the box.

VOCABULARY B — Home and furniture

bath bathroom bed bedroom ceiling cupboard
dining room floor garage garden kitchen mirror roof
shower wall window

8 Find the words from Vocabulary box B in the messages.

Abe

Your photo of your house in the USA on your blog is amazing. How many rooms are there? *Bea*

There are four bedrooms and three bathrooms. There's a big dining room, but we usually eat in the kitchen. *Abe*

What's your bedroom like? *Bea*

It's nice. I like bright, comfortable rooms. *Abe*

Yes, me too! *Bea*

I've got my own bathroom. *Abe*

Really? That's fantastic! I can't stand waiting to use the bathroom in my house. Is there a bath in your bathroom? *Bea*

No, there isn't, but there's a shower. I don't mind having a bath, but I prefer showers. *Abe*

Yes, me too! *Bea*

There are trees outside my bedroom window so my room never gets hot in the summer. *Abe*

That's cool! Do you like your new house in the UK? *Bea*

Yeah, it's nice but … *Abe*

But what? *Bea*

There isn't a wood nearby and I love walking or cycling there. *Abe*

Yes, me too. *Bea*

9 Study Grammar box A. Look at the dialogue and the photo in Exercise 8 and complete the sentences below with *there is/are* or *there isn't/aren't*.

GRAMMAR A — *There is/are* with *some/any*

	Singular	Plural
+	There's a bed.	There are some books.
–	There isn't a desk.	There aren't any mirrors.
?	Is there a table?	Are there any chairs?

1 *There are* four bedrooms.
2 _____ a big dining room.
3 _____ a bath in Abe's bathroom.
4 _____ some trees next to the house.
5 _____ any chairs in front of the house.

10 In pairs, make more sentences about Abe's house in the USA using *there is/are* and the prepositions below.

between in near next to on
opposite under

11 Study Grammar box B. Complete the sentences below with possessive adjectives or the possessive *'s*.

GRAMMAR B — Possessive adjectives and possessive *'s*

's = singular	Bea's mother is my dad's sister.
s' = plural	My friends' homes are near my house.
Possessive adjectives	my/your/his/her/its/our/their bedroom

1 A: Whose photo is it?
   B: It's Abe*'s* photo.
2 A: Is Abe Bea_____ brother?
   B: No, he's _____ cousin.
3 A: Is that Abe_____ room?
   B: No. It's _____ dad _____ room.
4 A: Is that _____ house?
   B: No, it's not mine.
      It's my friend_____ house.

YOUR WORLD

12 Write sentences about your home. Use *there is/are* and the prepositions in Exercise 10.

0.2 Introducing Bea

Present Simple with adverbs of frequency | Jobs | Everyday activities

This is Bea. Her name's Bea Barker and she's fifteen. Penny is her mum. She's a Drama teacher and she works in a college. Bea's mum is funny and kind, and she likes gardening.

On school days Bea always gets up early. She doesn't usually eat much for breakfast, but at weekends she usually gets up late and has a big breakfast.

She spends a lot of time with her friends: cousin Abe, Carla and Eren.

Carla is Bea's best friend. Bea never feels sad when she talks to Carla. She chats to her almost every day.

In her free time Bea does sport. She enjoys walking in the park with her mum and she writes a nature blog. She wants to be a scientist or a journalist.

1 ▶ 2 ◀) 0.4 Watch or listen and find these things in the text.
   1 a surname   2 three jobs   3 a meal
   4 a place you can go to in your free time

2 Study the Grammar box. Find examples of the Present Simple in the text.

GRAMMAR	Present Simple with adverbs of frequency
+	**−**
I live in a small town. She works in a school.	I don't live in a big city. She doesn't teach Maths.
?	
Do you read a lot? Does she get up early?	Yes, I do./No, I don't. Yes, she does./No, she doesn't.
Always, usually, often, sometimes and *never* go before most verbs but after the verb *to be*. I usually get up early. I'm never late for school.	

3 Choose the correct option. Then write Bea's answers to the questions.
   1 What do / **does** your mum do?
      She's a Drama teacher – she works in a college.
   2 How do / does your mum spend her free time?
   3 Do / Does you get up early at weekends?
   4 Who do / does you like spending time with?
   5 How often do / does you chat with your best friend?
   6 What do / does you do in your free time?

4 In pairs, ask and answer the questions in Exercise 3.

5 Complete the sentences with the Present Simple form of the verbs in brackets.
   1 We *don't go* (not go) to school on Saturdays.
   2 Bea and Carla _____ (often/be) together.
   3 Bea's mum _____ (never/get up) after 8 a.m.
   4 _____ (you/live) in a big house?
   5 Bea _____ (not see) Eren every day.
   6 Bea _____ (always/write) her blog in her room.

6 ◀) 0.5 Study the Vocabulary box. In pairs, add as many words as you can to the box.

VOCABULARY	Jobs
chef farmer hairdresser mechanic nurse scientist	

7 In pairs, describe a job from the Vocabulary box. Your partner has to guess what job it is.
   A: *This person works in a hospital with doctors.*
   B: *A nurse.*

8 ◀) 0.6 **WORD FRIENDS** Find examples of the phrases below in the text in Exercise 1. Can you add more everyday activities?

chat to/meet/see/spend time with friends   do homework get dressed   get home   get up early/late   go out go to school   have a shower   have breakfast/lunch/dinner

9 In pairs, describe a school day. Use the phrases in Exercise 8 to help you.
   I always wake up at six o'clock.

10 In pairs, describe the people in your house. What do they do? What's their routine?   **YOUR WORLD**

0.3 Introducing Eren

Clothes and accessories | Present Continuous

This is Eren King. He lives near his new best friend, Abe. And this is Eren's grandad, Frank. He's staying with Eren and his family at the moment. They get on really well. Eren loves his other grandparents too, but they live in Turkey, so he doesn't see them often.

Eren's grandad has got a great sense of style! They're both wearing similar colours today. Grandad's wearing his favourite bright shirt and grey jumper. Eren's wearing his favourite hoodie and his dad's watch. At the moment, Grandad's feeling relaxed because he's watching TV.

Tennis is one of Eren's favourite sports. He is planning to enter a tennis competition soon, so he's practising nearly every day at the moment. He's a bit nervous about it. He really wants to win!

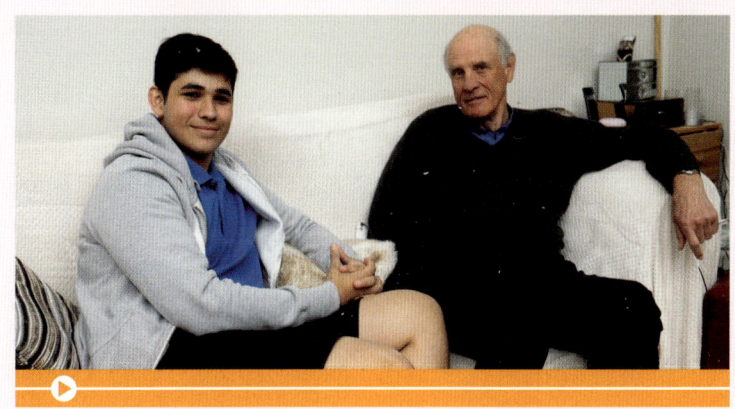

1 Look at the photo. Do you think these two people get on well? Why?/Why not?

2 ▶ 3 🔊 0.7 Watch or listen and mark the sentences T (true) or F (false).
1 ☐ The man in the photo is Eren's father.
2 ☐ Both people in the photo are wearing their favourite clothes.
3 ☐ The watch belongs to Eren.
4 ☐ Eren doesn't live in Turkey.
5 ☐ Eren is planning to play more online games.
6 ☐ Eren often plays tennis.

3 🔊 0.8 Study the Vocabulary box. Which clothes and accessories from the box can you see in the photo?

VOCABULARY > **Clothes and accessories**

baseball cap   earrings   hoodie   jacket   jumper
school uniform   watch

4 **I KNOW!** In pairs, add as many words as you can to the Vocabulary box.

5 Study the Grammar box. Find examples of the Present Continuous in the text.

GRAMMAR > **Present Continuous**

+	−
I'm wearing a watch.	I'm not wearing a cap.
He's watching TV.	He isn't watching a film.
They're staying with us.	They aren't staying in the UK.
?	
Are you feeling relaxed?	Yes, I am./No, I'm not.
Is she wearing a skirt?	Yes, she is./No, she isn't.

6 Order the words to make questions. Then answer the questions about you.
1 you / are / sleeping / ?
2 are / wearing / trainers / you / ?
3 the students / are / working hard / ?
4 sending / text messages / your friend / is / ?

7 Study the Speaking box. In pairs, add as many words to describe feelings as you can to the box.

SPEAKING > **Talking about feelings**

How do you feel?
I'm annoyed/bored/excited/frightened/nervous/relaxed/tired.

8 🔊 0.9 Listen to a dialogue and answer the questions.
1 How does Max feel about the tennis match?
2 What is Max's problem?

9 In pairs, talk about how you feel before an exam/on your birthday/on holiday/after a party.

0.4 Introducing Carla

Countries and languages | *Was/were* | *There was/were* | Past Simple: regular verbs

This is Carla Silva. She's Bea's best friend.

Carla's dad's from Brazil and her mum's half Spanish. Carla was born in the UK, so she speaks English most of the time. And she talks a lot, by the way! She speaks Spanish well and last summer she visited her mum's family in Spain. Carla can understand Portuguese, but she doesn't speak it very well, so she's having lessons. Carla is really into keeping fit. At the moment she's doing an online fitness class with Bea. She was surprised the first time she did a fitness class because she didn't think online lessons were hard work. Luckily, the classes are great fun.

Carla loves trying new things. She likes singing, so she tried singing lessons, but the lessons weren't easy and they didn't help her! She loves acting and she wants to be an actor.

1 🔊 0.10 Copy the Vocabulary box. Add the words below to the correct groups in the box. Listen and check.

China	Chinese	France	French	German
Germany	Italian	Italy	Poland	Polish
Spain	Spanish	Turkey	Turkish	

VOCABULARY Countries and languages

Countries	Languages
Brazil/Portugal	Portuguese

2 **I KNOW!** In pairs, name as many countries as you can.

3 ▶ 4 🔊 0.11 Watch or listen. Find three countries and three languages in the text.

4 What languages do you and your family speak? Tell the class.

My dad speaks Spanish and a little French.

5 Read the text again, then cover it. Write three things about Carla.

6 Study Grammar box A. Complete the sentences below with *was/were* or *wasn't/weren't*.

GRAMMAR A Was/were, there was/were

+	–
She was on holiday.	She wasn't on holiday.
We were on holiday.	We weren't on holiday.
There was a party.	There wasn't a party.
There were lots of people.	There weren't lots of people.

?	
Was it fun?	Yes, it was./No, it wasn't.
Were they at home?	Yes, they were./No, they weren't.
Was there a party?	Yes, there was./No, there wasn't.
Were there many people?	Yes, there were./No, there weren't.

1 The weather *was* terrible when we _____ in Spain.
2 A: _____ you at the cinema last night?
   B: No, I _____ .
3 The film festival _____ fun and there _____ lots of films to watch. It was great!
4 _____ your parents angry when you _____ late home?
5 A: _____ the English test difficult?
   B: Yes, it _____ . There _____ lots of difficult exercises.

7 🔊 0.12 Study Grammar box B. Listen and answer the questions.

GRAMMAR B Past Simple: regular verbs

+	–
She lived in Rio.	They didn't invite him.

?	
Did they like the film?	Yes, they did./No, they didn't.

1 Which country did the girl visit last year?
2 Who did she stay with?
3 What did they do on the beach?
3 What language did the girl learn?

YOUR WORLD

8 In pairs, tell your partner about three or four things that were true for you last year but are not true now.

Unit 0   10

0.5 Revision

1 In pairs, describe the photo. Make as many sentences as you can. How do you think the friends are feeling?

2 🔊 0.13 Listen and mark the sentences T (true) or F (false).
 1 ☐ The friends are sitting in the garden because the weather is nice.
 2 ☐ New Park has lots of things for young people to do.
 3 ☐ Bea is planning to visit her family in Bath.
 4 ☐ Eren's got a Maths test that he isn't happy about.

3 Complete the quiz questions with one word in each gap.

4 In groups, do the quiz in Exercise 3. Use the texts in Lessons 1–4 to help you. How much can you remember?

YOUR WORLD

5 In pairs, write two similar quiz questions about you. Give the questions to your teacher and have a class quiz with two teams.

The big character QUIZ

1 Where _____ Abe, Bea, Eren and Carla live?
2 Who _____ staying with Eren?
3 Where _____ Carla's dad come from?
4 _____ Abe's dad British?
5 What _____ Bea's mum's name?
6 _____ lived in America last year?
7 _____ is Eren's favourite sport?
8 _____ Carla born in the UK?
9 Who _____ Bea chat to almost every day?
10 _____ did Carla travel to last year?
11 _____ Bea write a sports blog?
12 _____ Abe's mum stay in the USA?

Tech check 1

VOCABULARY
Technology | Using technology | Social media | Opposites | Time

GRAMMAR
Present Simple and Present Continuous, state verbs | Verb + -ing, verb + to-infinitive

Grace's tech blog

Everyday essentials?

One of the most important gadgets in our house is the remote control. It's old technology, but in our family everybody wants to choose the channel.

In the shower I listen to music on a waterproof speaker. This is a great gadget, but I want a waterproof bathroom TV so I can watch music videos, too! But is that essential? No.

Then there's the problem of passwords. I have so many, I sometimes forget them. It's a nightmare! So I use a password app to help me remember them all. That's pretty important.

My personal favourites at the moment are my new wireless earbuds. I posted a review and uploaded some pictures of them on my blog, so have a look! I listen to music all the time, so this is the tech I can't live without!

My final choice is for my family. We all love our new smart speaker. Mum uses the voice assistant to ask for food recipes and I enjoy asking it to play music. Luckily, it is connected to the wi-fi router, so we don't have to use our data because my little sister can't stop talking to it. Unfortunately, her favourite command is 'Tell me a joke!'

Do you agree with my choices? Let me know your tech essentials.

1.1 Vocabulary
Lifestyle

1 Look at the photos. What do you think is happening in each one? Find three items of technology in the photos.

2 Read the article. Do you agree with Grace's choices?

Unit 1 12

3 🔊 **1.1** Study the Vocabulary box and check you understand the words. Which is your number one essential item?

> **VOCABULARY** — Technology
>
> charging cable   password app   power bank
> remote control   smart speaker   wi-fi router
> wireless earbuds

4 **I KNOW!** In pairs, add as many words as you can to the Vocabulary box.

5 🔊 **1.2** Listen and guess the objects. Listen again and check.

6 In pairs, think of two gadgets or items of technology for each adjective. Which object would be the best present for you? Why?

> awesome   essential   old-fashioned   terrible   useful

I'd like to have a smart speaker because it's really useful, so my family would like it too.

7 🔊 **1.3** **WORD FRIENDS** Match phrases 1–6 with icons A–F. Listen and check.

1. ☐ connect to the wi-fi router
2. ☐ search for information online
3. ☐ send/share a link
4. ☐ set a new password
5. ☐ take a screenshot
6. ☐ upload pictures

8 🔊 **1.4** Listen to five people talking. Write down the phrases from Exercise 7 you hear.

9 🔊 **1.5** **WORD FRIENDS** Check you understand the phrases below. Then choose the correct option in sentences 1–7 below. Listen and check In pairs, say if the sentences are true for you.

> add someone to a group
> chat with friends
> connect with someone on social media
> delete a post/photo
> follow someone on social media
> message someone
> post on social media
> take a selfie
> update your story

1. I *follow / set* my favourite singers and groups on social media.
2. When I have some great news, I *search / update* my story.
3. I spend a lot of time *chatting / uploading* with friends on social media.
4. I can *update / add* people to groups on my social media.
5. I don't often *connect / delete* posts.
6. My brother *posts / chats* things on social media nearly every day!
7. I probably *take / message* a selfie every week.

10 Complete the text with one word in each gap.

> According to a recent study, over eighty percent of teenagers say that social ¹*media* has a positive effect on their lives. It's a great way to ² _____ with friends, catch up with people's news or connect ³ _____ someone. And it's also incredibly easy. When we search for information ⁴ _____ , we don't often use PCs or laptops any more. Instead, over ninety percent of us use our smartphones to get on the internet. Many people spend three hours a day this way. Think about that next time you want to ⁵ _____ your story. In your life, you might spend about five years online!

VIDEO ▶   **WIDER WORLD**

11 ▶ 5 Watch three people talking about technology. What gadgets do they mention?

12 Who in your family uses technology the most? What do they use it for?

My brother uses it the most. He's got a really good smartphone. He uses it for shopping online, watching films and studying.

I can talk about everyday technology.

1.2 Grammar

Present Simple and Present Continuous, state verbs

Filming in a skate park

**I'm Evy, Way In's lead singer.
People often ask us questions about our lives:**

'Do you write the band's blog?'
I don't normally write it. Ziggy does. But he's busy, so I'm doing it today.

'What do you normally do on Saturdays?'
On Saturday afternoons we often travel from one city to the next. Then, in the evening, we usually play live in concert. We're playing a lot of concerts these days! It's good to be popular!

'What are you doing today?'
We're not playing music and I'm not singing. We're filming our new music video in a skate park. The skateboarders are doing some amazing things. One girl, Sara, knows lots of awesome tricks! I love her style!

1 🔊 **1.6** In pairs, look at the photo and the title of the text. What do you think the text is about? Read it and check your guesses.

2 Study the Grammar box. Find examples of the Present Simple, Present Continuous and state verbs in the text.

GRAMMAR — Present Simple and Present Continuous, state verbs

Present Simple
They usually *travel* on a tour bus.
She *doesn't write* the blog every day.
Do they *speak* English? Yes, they *do*.

Present Continuous
He*'s travelling* a lot these days.
They *aren't recording* a song at the moment.
Is he *skateboarding* now? No, he *isn't*.

State verbs
Some verbs don't normally have a continuous form:
love, like, hate, know, think, see, feel, understand, want, need

GRAMMAR TIME > PAGE 126

---

3 🔊 **1.7** Choose the correct option. Listen and check.
1 Ziggy and Evy *sit / are sitting* on a bench at the skate park at the moment.
2 Evy usually *sings / is singing* in concerts on Saturday evenings.
3 The band members *don't often visit / aren't often visiting* skate parks.
4 The skateboarders *do / are doing* some fantastic skateboard tricks now.
5 Sara *always wears / is always wearing* her lucky helmet.
6 Several people *film / are filming* the skateboarders.

4 Make questions about the text. Use the Present Simple or Present Continuous. Then ask and answer the questions in pairs.
1 Evy / normally / write / the band's blog / ?
2 the band members / usually / travel / on Saturday afternoons / ?
3 the band / play / a lot of concerts / these days / ?
4 the skateboarders / perform / in a competition / today / ?
5 Sara / wear / a helmet in the photo / ?
6 Sara / know / lots of awesome tricks / ?

5 Complete the text with the Present Simple or Present Continuous forms of the verbs in brackets.

My name's Sara. I ¹*love* (love) skateboarding – I'm a real fan. I ² _____ (practise) at a local park every weekend. I ³ _____ (not often/do) competitions because I'm from a small town. I'm very excited today because I ⁴ _____ (perform) in a music video for *Way In*. At the moment we're ⁵ _____ (get) ready. Lots of people ⁶ _____ (come) into the park now. My mum and dad ⁷ _____ (sit) near the front because they ⁸ _____ (want) to take photos and upload them for their friends!

VIDEO — WIDER WORLD

6 ▶ **6** Watch six people talking about the sports and hobbies they enjoy. Write down as many sports/hobbies as you can.

7 In pairs, talk about your favourite sports and hobbies.

1.3 Reading and Vocabulary
Science competitions and projects

A

Help the world, win a prize and have fun!

Our Science and Technology Group (STG) is hoping to win this year's National Science Competition and we need your help.

This is a competition for young people aged 11–16. It takes place every year. The participants look for tech answers to important problems. The winners can get a prize of up to £25,000 for their school or youth group.

Here are some ideas we are thinking about:
- an easy-to-use remote control for older people.
- using technology to help an animal in danger.
- a robot dolphin that cleans plastic from the sea.

If you like Science and Technology, come and join us, and help us win the prize.

Kieran Malone, STG

B

Hi Angie,

I've got an idea for our end-of-term Science project. I'd like to help animals that are in danger – all sorts of animals, not just cute ones. I found some cool activity sheets online. They don't seem complicated. One of them shows how to make bat boxes – safe homes for bats. Yes, bats! They look a bit strange, but they're really interesting animals. I know we're studying for our final exams right now, but I'm really excited about the Science project. So, come on! Let's make a bat box!

Lorraine

C

Hi Lorraine,

That's a fun idea, and it's original, too. You're so clever (but you know that, don't you? 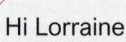)! My grandfather makes bird boxes, so he could help us make an excellent bat box. And we could put a small waterproof camera in the box to film the bats! What do you think?

Angie

1 In groups, discuss the questions.
1. Do you ever do Science projects at your school? What are they like?
2. Would you like to take part in a national Science competition? Why?/Why not?

2 🔊 1.8 Read the texts quickly. Who is writing about:
1. a Science competition?
2. a school Science project?

3 Read the texts and answer the questions.
1. What group is Kieran part of?
2. What does the group want to participate in this year?
3. How old are participants in the competition?
4. What is the maximum prize in the competition?

B and C
5. What animals does Lorraine want to help?
6. What are Lorraine and Angie studying for at the moment?
7. Who is Angie thinking of asking for help?
8. What does Angie suggest putting in the box?

4 🔊 1.9 Complete the Vocabulary box. Find the opposites of the adjectives below in the texts.

VOCABULARY — Opposites

boring	– _cool_, 1_____, 2_____, 3_____
dangerous	– 4_____
easy	– 5_____
normal	– 6_____
stupid	– 7_____
terrible	– 8_____

5 In groups, think of examples of these things.
- a strange animal
- an interesting book
- a fun game
- an original idea
- a complicated game
- a safe place
- an excellent TV show
- a clever person

6 **YOUR WORLD** Complete the entry form for a Science project. Include a short description of the project. Then, in pairs, talk about your project idea.

Science project – Entry form

Name:	School:
Age:	Project:

I can understand a message and an email about Science competitions and projects.

1.4 Grammar

Verb + -ing, verb + to-infinitive

VIDEO **THE VIDEO CALL**

Bea: Hello, Abe. Is now a good time to talk?
Abe: It's fine, but I need to pack while I'm talking. We need to go to the airport soon.
Bea: OK, sooo I just waaanted to cheeeck …
Abe: Bea, I can't see you. And there's something wrong with your sound.
Bea: Hang on. Is that better?
Abe: Yes, that's better. I can see and hear you now.
Bea: Great! That beach background looks amazing!
Abe: Good! My room's a mess at the moment. Look. Do you prefer seeing the beach?
Bea: No, I don't mind seeing your room. Did you remember to … ?
Abe: What's that noise?
Bea: It's Mum. Can you stop vacuuming? Mum? I'm trying to talk to Abe! Sorry about that, Abe.
Abe: No worries. I'm really looking forward to seeing you in person.
Bea: Me too. And don't forget to bring me that basketball shirt.
Abe: Of course. Look, I'm packing it now.
Bea: Fantastic! Thanks, Abe. See you in the UK soon. Safe journey!

1 Look at the photo. What do you think Abe is doing? Why?

2 ▶ 7 🔊 1.10 Watch or listen. What does Bea want Abe to do? What problems does she have?

3 Study the Grammar box. Find more examples of verbs followed by -ing or to-infinitive in the dialogue.

GRAMMAR — Verb + -ing, verb + to-infinitive

Verb + -ing
After: *avoid, can't stand, enjoy, finish, look forward to, (not) mind, miss, practise, stop*; after prepositions
I *don't mind seeing* your room.
She is tired *after driving* the whole night.

Verb + to-infinitive
After: *agree, allow, ask, choose, decide, forget, hope, learn, need, offer, plan, remember, try, want, would like/love*
I'm *trying to talk* to Abe.

Verb + -ing or to-infinitive
After: *like, love, hate, prefer, start*
Do you *prefer seeing/to see* the beach?

GRAMMAR TIME > PAGE 126

4 Choose the correct option. In which sentence are both options correct?
1. Are you planning *getting / to get* a new smartphone soon?
2. I love my Science project and would like *being / to be* a scientist.
3. I like *thinking / to think* of new passwords. I can be creative!
4. We're planning *watching / to watch* a sci-fi film tonight.
5. We're packing to go on holiday. We enjoy *going / to go* to new places.
6. Freddie misses *seeing / to see* his friends from his old school.

5 Complete the text with the correct form of the verbs below.

| ~~chat~~ check look see share use |

Top tips for video calls

Most people love ¹*chatting* to family and friends via video calls, but what about online lessons? You want to make a good impression, so don't forget ²_____ the microphone before you join a new video call. Have the camera at eye level and learn to ³_____ straight at it some of the time.

Maybe you don't mind ⁴_____ untidy rooms, but it's a good idea to check that the room behind you is tidy. Finally, if you enjoy ⁵_____ different backgrounds, make sure you choose them carefully. That's especially important if you plan ⁶_____ your screen during the call.

6 In pairs, write some tips on how to use a gadget. **YOUR WORLD**

Unit 1 16 I can use verbs followed by the -ing form and/or the to-infinitive.

1.5 Listening and Vocabulary

Are you technology crazy?

Do you need a digital detox?

1. **When do you first check your phone?**
   a in the evening
   b probably at lunchtime
   c the minute I wake up
2. **When is it too late to message somebody?**
   a after 10 p.m. on a weekday
   b at midnight
   c It's never too late.
3. **What do you do when you have a free moment?**
   a I listen to music.
   b I read a book.
   c I go online.
4. **How often do you check your messages?**
   a Once a day. I don't get many.
   b At school. I check them at break time.
   c I check them all the time.

1 Do you think you spend too much time looking at screens?

2 Do the quiz and compare your results. Then go to page 142 to read what your answers say about you.

3 🔊 1.11 Study the Vocabulary box and complete the gaps with words from the quiz. Listen and check.

> **VOCABULARY** ▸ Time
>
> second, ¹*minute*, hour
> 6 a.m., ² _____
> in the morning/afternoon/³ _____
> on a school day/⁴ _____ /Sunday(s)
> at the weekend/⁵ _____ /mealtimes/lunchtime/
> ⁶ _____
> ⁷ _____ /twice/three times a day/week/
> month/year

4 Ask and answer the questions in pairs. Compare your ideas with the class.
   1 What's your favourite mealtime? Why?
      I love lunchtime because I eat with my friends.
   2 What time do you go to bed at the weekend?
   3 How many seconds are there in five minutes?
   4 What time do you get up on a school day?
   5 What do you normally do at break time?
   6 What do you do 'the minute' you wake up?

5 🔊 1.12 Listen to the first part of a radio programme. What is the programme about? Choose the correct answer.
   a the number of families that use phones or tablets in their free time
   b how much time families spend on their phones or tablets

6 🔊 1.13 Listen to the second part of the programme. Match the people to the way they use the technology.
   1 ☐ Lara
   2 ☐ Mum
   3 ☐ Dad
   4 ☐ Lara's brother
   5 ☐ Everyone

   a looks at funny video clips and laughs.
   b often shares photos.
   c reads the news on a tablet.
   d downloads and uses running apps.
   e uses the phone alarm and checks messages.

YOUR WORLD

7 How important is technology in your life? What technology do you use and what do you like doing with it? Write five sentences.

Technology is important. It's useful because I can go online, do my homework and chat with friends. In my free time I use technology to listen to music, …

I can understand a radio programme about using technology.

1.6 Speaking
Problem-solving

VIDEO ▶ LET'S GIVE IT A TRY

Bea: What's that?
Abe: It's the router! Great, let's install it! Um, where do you think you plug it in?
Bea: By the front door! The same place as in my house. There!
Abe: Right, it should be working now. We could upload that new video on my vlog to see if the router works. Come on!

A few minutes later

Abe: The internet is working, but it's so slow. Look, the page is still loading!
Bea: Maybe the signal's too weak? I know: there are apps … to test the wi-fi. Why don't we download one?
Abe: Yes, let's give it a try.
Bea: Hmm, the signal's really weak in here!
Abe: Yeah, there's no way I can play video games here. Shall we check the other rooms?
Bea: Yes, what about the kitchen?
Abe: That's a good idea.
Bea: The signal's a bit better here. Look, it's getting stronger!
Abe: What about here?
Bea: Not out there! You can't play video games outside!
Abe: But it's not raining … today!

SOUNDS GOOD! Come on! • Not out there!

1 ▶ 8 🔊 1.14 Look at the photo. What are Abe and Bea doing? Watch or listen and check.

2 Study the Speaking box. Find examples of the phrases in the dialogue.

SPEAKING — Problem-solving

Describing the problem
The internet is working, but it's slow.
Where do you think you plug it in?
The signal's really weak in here!

Suggesting solutions
We could upload the video to see if the router works.
Let's install it!   What about looking online?
Why don't we download one?
Shall we check the other rooms?

Accepting or rejecting solutions
(That's a) good/great idea.
Yes, let's give it a try.
You can't play video games outside!

3 🔊 1.15 Listen to four problems and suggest solutions. Use the Speaking box to help you.

SET FOR LIFE

4 What do you usually do when you have a problem with technology?
- Ask your friends for help.
- Search online for solutions.
- Ask an IT specialist for help.

5 In pairs, go to page 142 and follow the instructions.

YOUR WORLD

6 In pairs, think of some problems you can have with technology and suggest solutions.

A: Sometimes it's complicated to download a new app.
B: Yes, I know what you mean, but you can usually find help online.

I can describe a problem, suggest solutions and respond to suggestions.

1.7 Writing

A description of your daily routine and online hobbies

Post

What are your daily routine and online hobbies?

1 In real life I live in a big flat near the centre of Manchester. In my everyday life I go to Belton School on weekdays. I sometimes go for a run before school. I **also** often play football at the weekend. After school I always do my homework, of course, **and** then I usually go on my laptop.

2 My favourite online hobby is building a virtual world. After school and at the weekend I usually spend a few hours in my online world. It has lots of great places, **but** my favourite is a theme park I'm building on an island. It's very different from Manchester! There are loads of amazing rides. As well as a beautiful beach, there are also lots of trees. I design new rides for about an hour a day. At the moment I'm testing the rides to make sure they work.

3 I enjoy my online hobbies. However, I also really like chatting to friends at school about my theme park plans **because** they have good ideas for new rides. I often take screenshots of my virtual world and I enjoy sharing them on social media **too**. Although it's not a real place, my virtual world is very relaxing, so I look forward to spending time there!

Zak Murphy

1 Read the article quickly. What is Zak writing about?

2 Read the article. Which of the things below does Zak write about in paragraph 1? Which are in paragraphs 2 and 3?

a [1] daily routines d [ ] hobbies
b [ ] friends   e [ ] summary
c [ ] an online place

3 Study the Writing box and look at the article again. Complete the sentences to make them true for you.

WRITING — A description of your daily routine and online hobbies

1 **Describe daily routines (real world examples)**
In the morning/Before school ¹_____ .
In the afternoon/On weekdays ²_____ .
I usually/often/sometimes/never ³_____ .

2 **Describe online hobbies (virtual world examples)**
My favourite hobby is ⁴_____ .
After school ⁵_____ .
At the weekend ⁶_____ .

3 **End your article: show contrast and sum up**
I enjoy my online lifestyle. However, I also really like chatting to friends online.
Although it's not a real place, my virtual world is very relaxing.
I look forward to spending time there.

4 Study the Language box. Write the connectors in bold from the article in the correct group.

LANGUAGE — Connectors

Adding similar information: as well (as),
¹_____ , ²_____ , ³_____
Showing contrast: however, although, ⁴_____
Giving reasons: so, ⁵_____

5 Write some true sentences about you. Use connectors from the Language box.

WRITING TIME

6 Write an article for your school website describing your daily routine and online hobbies.

 Find ideas
Make notes about:
• your daily routine and habits.
• your online hobbies.
• how you can combine your daily routine with your online hobbies.

 Plan
Organise your ideas into three paragraphs. Use Zak's article to help you.

 Write and share
• Write a draft article. Use the Language box and the Writing box to help you.
• Share your article with another student for feedback.
• Use the feedback from your partner and write the final version of your article.

 Check
• Check language: did you use connectors correctly?
• Check grammar: did you mostly use the Present Simple and adverbs of frequency?

I can write a description of my daily routine and online hobbies.

Vocabulary Activator

WORDLIST 🔊 1.16

Technology
charging cable (n)
password app (n)
power bank (n)
remote control (n)
smart speaker (n)
wi-fi router (n)
wireless earbuds (n)

Word friends
(using technology)
connect to the wi-fi router
search for information online
send a link
set a new password
share a link
take a screenshot
upload pictures

Word friends
(social media)
add someone to a group
chat with friends
connect with someone on social media
delete a photo
delete a post
follow someone on social media
message someone
post on social media
take a selfie
update your story

Time
6 a.m./6 p.m.
at lunchtime
at mealtimes
at the weekend
hour (n)
in the afternoon
in the evening
in the morning
minute (n)
on a schoolday/Sunday(s)
once/twice/three times a day/week/month/year
second (n)

Opposites
boring – cool, fun, interesting, original
dangerous – safe
easy – complicated
normal – strange
stupid – clever
terrible – excellent

Extra words
awesome (adj)
background (n)
blog (n)
catch up with (v)
channel (n)
charge (v)
choice (n)
choose (v)
command (v)
competition (n)
effect (n)
essential (adj)
gadget (n)
helpful (adj)
icon (n)
impression (n)
install (v)
live in concert
look for (v)
luckily (adv)
microphone (n)
participant (n)
perform (v)
plug in (v)
popular (adj)
practise (v)
pretty (= quite) (adv)
recipe (n)
record a song
robot (n)
Science project (n)
set up (v)
signal (n)
sound (n)
study (n)
style (n)
switch on/off (v)
take place
tech answer (n)
tell a joke
trick (n)
video call (n)
virtual world (n)
vlog (n)
voice assistant (n)
youth group (n)

1 Complete the sentences with words from the wordlist.
  1 I use the *remote control* to turn on the TV.
  2 I can never think of a good password, so I downloaded a useful _____ .
  3 I took a _____ of the picture on that webpage with my smartphone.
  4 You should _____ a new password if you want to keep your information safe.
  5 Please send me the _____ to that useful website – I want to check it out.

2 Tick (✓) the correct column for each gadget. Then, in pairs, say which items are important to you and why.

Gadget	I have this.	I would like one or a new one.
wireless earbuds		
power bank		
smart speaker		
wi-fi router		

3 Complete the phrases with words from the wordlist. Then, in pairs, say which things you do.
  1 *search* for information _____ to help with homework projects
  2 _____ with family or friends abroad
  3 _____ comments with my opinions on blogs
  4 _____ selfies and upload them on social media
  5 _____ famous people on social media

4 Use words from the wordlist to find these things.
  1 four time phrases that use *the*
  2 two time phrases that use *a*
  3 two things you can do with and without a computer or phone
  4 two objects which can help you to listen to music

5 🔊 1.17 **PRONUNCIATION** Listen to the words below and write them in the correct column according to the word stress.

> ~~background~~   connect   earbuds   laptop   online   password   smartphone   upload

1 Oo	2 oO
background	

6 🔊 1.18 **PRONUNCIATION** Listen, check and repeat.

Unit 1 20

Revision

Vocabulary

1 Choose the correct option.
1. I get up early *at / on* a schoolday.
2. Remember to take the *charging / loading* cable for your phone when you go on holiday.
3. Do you *update / follow* any famous people on social media?
4. If there's no electricity, *an energy / a power* bank can charge your phone.
5. I usually eat a sandwich *in / at* lunchtime in school.

2 Write the correct word for each definition.
1. Something you plug into your mobile phone to charge it. <u>charging cable</u>
2. You do this to a photo when you remove it from your smartphone. _____
3. You do this to pictures when you move them from your phone to your computer or the internet. _____
4. Times when you eat breakfast, lunch or dinner. _____
5. Put a message on the internet. _____

3 Complete the conversation with the words below.

> add   chat   message   search   ~~send~~   update

A: Hi, Greg. Can you ¹<u>send</u> me today's Maths homework? I don't have it.
B: Sure. The teacher also says we can use a Maths app to do our homework. Maybe we can ² _____ online for a free app?
A: Well, the app only helps a bit. Maybe we need to ³ _____ Jackie for help. She's good at Maths.
B: That's a good idea. I ⁴ _____ with her on social media sometimes, but not about homework.
A: She has a group where students help each other with homework. Do you want me to ⁵ _____ you to it?
B: Yes, please. I'll check her homepage now. Maybe she's there because she likes to ⁶ _____ her story in the evening.

Grammar

4 Choose the correct option. Then, in pairs, say which sentences true for you.
1. *I'm usually walking / I usually walk* to school.
2. *I'm feeling / I feel* happy when I can stay in bed on Saturday morning.
3. *I'm studying / I study* a lot at the moment.
4. My best friend *needs / is needing* a new phone now.
5. *I learn / I'm learning* how to play a new computer game. It's hard!

5 Complete the dialogues with the Present Simple or Present Continuous form of the verbs in brackets.

A
A: What music ¹<u>does Uncle Ted like</u> (Uncle Ted/like)? It's his birthday next week and I ² _____ (not know) what he ³ _____ (want).
B: He ⁴ _____ (listen) to a lot of music. Maybe some wireless earbuds?

B
A: You ⁵ _____ (not do) much right now. Can you help Grandma with her mobile?
B: What ⁶ _____ (she/try) to do?
A: Use social media, but she ⁷ _____ (not know) how to update her story. She ⁸ _____ (want) to post a selfie.

6 Complete the technology tips with the correct form of the verbs in brackets. Then, in pairs, put the tips in order from most to least important.

Technology tips

1. Don't agree <u>to share</u> (share) a link without knowing it's safe.
2. Avoid _____ (spend) too much time looking at screens.
3. Stop _____ (work) on your laptop and have a screen break when your eyes feel dry and tired.
4. Practise _____ (use) a new app before you really need it.
5. Remember _____ (save) a document when you finish _____ (work) on it.

Speaking

7 In pairs, follow the instructions to role play a dialogue about a problem with technology. Then swap roles.
- Student A: ask Student B what the problem is.
- Student B: describe the problem.
- Student A: suggest a solution to Student B's problem.
- Student B: reject the solution.
- Student A: suggest a different solution.
- Student B: accept Student A's new solution and thank him/her.

Dictation

8 🔊 1.19 Listen. Then listen again and write down what you hear.

21 Unit 1

BBC CULTURE

Screenagers

UK/USA: how do teenagers use their mobile phones?

Most British teenagers own a mobile phone. These 'screenagers' spend a large part of their day online, looking at screens. They can connect when and where they like with their smartphones and tablets. Apparently, UK teenagers avoid using smartphones to call their friends. Instead, they prefer to watch video clips, play games, share photos and stories, and send instant messages. As for social media, teens like keeping in touch via the latest apps and videos. They leave older websites and apps to their mums and dads! The same applies to teenagers in the USA.

Teenagers may be connected all the time, but there is one place where most UK teenagers can't use their digital devices: school! In the UK there is no law about phone use in schools, but teachers can ban devices from students if necessary. However, not all teachers agree and some even try to use smartphones in class.

A recent British report said that banning smartphones from schools will give students more time for their education. It said that smartphones are a distraction, make students less productive and are bad for learning.

However, in the US it's a different story. Recently, some schools across the US decided to allow students to use smartphones at school. They said that smartphones can be an excellent resource in the classroom. We carry a lot of information in our pockets and this information can be really useful. In these schools, smartphones can definitely make you smarter!

distraction (n) something that stops you thinking clearly
ban (v) not allow something

1 Look at the photo. What can you see?

2  1.20 **VISIBLE THINKING** In pairs, follow these steps.
   WHAT MAKES YOU SAY THAT?
   1 Study the discussion questions and give your opinion.
      a Are smartphones a necessary part of our lives?
      b Do you think teenagers use smartphones too much?
   2 Read the article and discuss the questions.
      a Do you think it is a good idea to use phones in class? Why?/Why not?
      b Can smartphones make you smarter? How?

3 Read the article again and answer the questions.
   1 How are teenagers in the UK similar to teenagers in the USA?
   2 How can teachers stop students using mobile phones in the classroom?
   3 Do all teachers in the UK stop students from using their smartphones in class?
   4 Why do some teachers in the US want students to use smartphones in class?

4 In pairs discuss the questions.
   1 Are you a 'screenager'? Do you find it hard not to use your phone?
   2 How do you think mobile phones change how people communicate with each other?

BBC ▶ Disconnecting

5 In pairs, look at the photos. What information do you think they show about phones?

6 ▶ 9 Watch the video. What information are scientists trying to find?

7 ▶ 9 Watch the video again and choose the correct option.
1 The professor secretly sends text messages so she can *contact / see the stress levels in* people.
2 Matt and Natalie take a break from *work / digital devices*.
3 Natalie *wanted / didn't want* her phone back so soon.
4 After the break, Matt and Natalie used their phones *as usual / less*.

8 In pairs, discuss the questions.
1 Do you think using technology is a bad habit? Why?/Why not?
2 Do you think we should take more breaks from technology?

PROJECT TIME

9 In groups of three, prepare a digital presentation about an app. Follow these steps.

1 In groups, choose a learning app. Decide who can find the answers to these questions.
- What can the app help you to do?
- How can you download and use it?
- What are the advantages and disadvantages of using it?

2 Individually, create your part of the presentation.
- Research the information online.
- Create a slide or a few slides to present your information.
- Remember to say where you found the information.

3 In your group, create your presentation.
- Put the slides in order and give each slide a title.
- Write a short summary of your research.
- Check and edit your presentation.
- Practise giving the presentation as a group.

4 Share your presentation with the class.
- Answer other students' questions.
- Listen to the other presentations. Ask questions.

Wild and beautiful

2

VOCABULARY
Word building: weather | Weather and climate | Adverbs of degree | Camping | In the wild

GRAMMAR
Past Simple: regular and irregular verbs | Past Continuous and Past Simple

Rising water

Lorenzo Quinn's sculpture in Venice, Italy, makes us think about the problem of rising sea levels. This isn't because of rain but because of climate change. Rising temperatures have caused ice in the Arctic and Antarctic to melt faster. As a result, more water is entering the oceans. Other cities located near the sea are also affected by global warming. Jakarta in Indonesia and New Orleans in the USA are sinking about five centimetres a year, so they may be under water by 2100. In cities like these, strong winds from storms and hurricanes make flooding worse. Trees can help us to fight climate change. They not only help clean the air, but they also keep places cool during times of drought. When there is heavy rain, tree roots can keep soil in place so that it isn't washed away in floods. For these reasons, we should plant lots of trees each year.

2.1 Vocabulary

Weather and climate

1 Look at the photo of the sculpture in Venice above. What do you know about Venice, Italy? What do you think is happening to the water there?

2 In pairs, read the article above. Answer the questions.
1. What does the sculpture represent?
2. Why are sea levels higher?
3. What problem do Jakarta and New Orleans share?
4. What are the benefits of planting trees?

3 🔊 2.1 Study Vocabulary box A and complete the table with the correct nouns. Listen and check.

VOCABULARY A — Word building: weather

Noun	Adjective
cloud	cloudy
	foggy
	icy
	rainy
	snowy
	stormy
	sunny
	windy

WATCH OUT!
To describe the weather, we use *it's* + adjective.
It's rainy/foggy/windy.
Rain and *snow* can be verbs too.
It's raining/snowing. It rains/snows here every day.

4 In pairs, describe the weather for two days this week.

On Monday it was cold and rainy. Yesterday it was cloudy and warm.

5 🔊 2.2 Study Vocabulary box B and complete the sentences below. Listen and check.

VOCABULARY B — Weather

breeze   drought   flood   gale   hurricane   lightning
shower   sunshine   thunder

1 When the wind isn't very strong, it's a *breeze*.
2 You always hear thunder after you see the _____ .
3 When water from a river covers the roads, there's a _____ .
4 It's a bright, warm day with no clouds. There's lots of _____ .
5 There isn't much rain, just a little bit of a _____ .
6 The wind is really strong. It might be a _____ or a _____ .

6 🔊 2.3 **WORD FRIENDS** Complete the phrases with the words below. Check you understand all the phrases. Listen and check.

bad   climate   cold   dry   ~~low~~   rising

1 The weather forecast for today is for:
 a heavy rain/snow.
 b strong winds.
 c high/*low* temperatures.
2 It will be:
 a ten degrees Celsius (10°C).
 b minus five degrees.
 c wet/_____ .
 d cool/warm.
 e boiling hot.
 f freezing _____ .
3 The temperature is _____/falling.
4 The weather is good/_____/fine.
5 This area has a hot/mild/cold _____ .

7 In pairs, ask and answer questions about the weather.
1 Do you know what the temperature is today?
2 What's the weather like?
3 What's the forecast for this evening/tomorrow/next week?

8 🔊 2.4 Listen to three weather forecasts. Which city is the warmest at the moment?

Krakow   Barcelona   Istanbul

9 🔊 2.4 Listen again to the weather forecasts and complete the gaps. Then, in pairs, compare your answers.
1 Krakow: *cold* , _____ , _____
2 Barcelona: _____ , _____ , _____ , _____
3 Istanbul: _____ , _____ , _____ , _____

YOUR WORLD
10 In pairs, talk about the climate in your country. What kind of weather do you like?

I can talk about the weather and climate.   **25**   Unit 2

2.2 Grammar

Past Simple: regular and irregular verbs

1 Do you enjoy storms? Why?/Why not?

2 🔊 2.5 Read the article. Find three unusual facts about the colour, place and number of lightning strikes it describes.

3 Study the Grammar box. Find the Past Simple forms of the verbs below in the article. Which are regular? Which are irregular? Why is this hard to decide with negatives and questions?

> create   feel   happen   know   look   mean   move
> save   see   spot   stay   take   use   want

GRAMMAR — Past Simple: regular and irregular verbs

Regular verbs
It **looked** pinkish orange.
The storms **didn't move**.
When **did** that **happen**?

Irregular verbs
We **saw** an unusual storm.
I **didn't know** what to do.
Did you **take** any photos? Yes, I **did**./No, I **didn't**.

We use the Past Simple with past time expressions, e.g. *yesterday, last week/year; two hours/days/weeks/years ago, in April, in 1595.*

GRAMMAR TIME ▸ PAGE 127

Venezuela's special storm

You might find storms fascinating or frightening. But can they be positive? If you live in Venezuela, your answer may be yes!

In 1595 a storm in Venezuela saved the country. How did that happen? Foreign sailors wanted to attack, but they saw strange lightning. It looked pinkish orange, so they didn't know what it was. They felt scared. In the bright light of the storm, soldiers on land spotted the ships.

This took place over Lake Maracaibo on the Catatumbo River. It is an area famous for its special storms. Long ago sailors used storms in the same way as lighthouses: to help them find their way. The geography of the high mountains by the lake created unusual but perfect storm conditions. It meant that the storms didn't move – they stayed in the same place.

Nowadays the Catatumbo Lightning holds a Guinness World Record as the place with the most lightning bolts per square kilometre.

4 Rewrite the sentences in the positive form.
  1 The Catatumbo storms didn't happen in Venezuela.
     The Catatumbo storms happened in Venezuela.
  2 The lightning didn't scare the sailors in 1595.
  3 The storms didn't help many sailors to find their way.
  4 The lightning didn't appear in the same place again and again.

5 Rewrite the sentences in the negative form.
  1 The sailors saw green lightning.
     The sailors didn't see green lightning.
  2 The sailors felt excited about the storm.
  3 Sailors thought the Catatumbo storms were normal.
  4 The storms took place over the sea.

6 Complete the sentences with past time expressions to make them true for you.
  1 I saw snow _____ .
  2 We had really bad weather _____ .
  3 We loved the warm weather on our holiday _____ .
  4 I went out in the rain _____ .

7 Make questions in the Past Simple.
  1 who / Mariana / meet / ?
     Who did Mariana meet?
  2 what / Professor Mendes / study / ?
  3 when / Mariana / go / to Lake Maracaibo / ?
  4 how many storms / she / see / ?
  5 where / she / put / the photos / ?

8 🔊 2.6 For each question in Exercise 7, write the beginning of the answer, with the main verb. Then listen to the interview and complete the answers.
  1 *Mariana met …*

YOUR WORLD

9 In pairs, ask and answer the questions about the last storm you saw.
  1 Where were you?
  2 Did you hear thunder and see lightning?
  3 How did you feel?

Unit 2 26 I can use the Past Simple to talk about past events.

2.3 Reading and Vocabulary

Life in a hot place

1 What do you do when it's very hot outside? Add your own ideas.

> go outside   have a cold drink   stay inside   wear cool clothes

2 Look at the photo and read the article. What does Miguel like about the place where he lives?

3 Study the two sentences in red in the article. Which one is a fact and which one is an opinion? Find more facts and opinions in the article.

4 🔊 2.7 Read the whole article again and choose the correct answer.
1 Miguel says that the temperature
   a is the same in Beatty and Death Valley.
   b makes you feel tired.
   c is normal for the time of year.
2 The volcano crater was
   a quite cold.
   b really unusual.
   c not very big.
3 One night in the desert Miguel
   a felt worried about something.
   b slept in the open air.
   c saw something special in the sky.
4 According to Miguel, sand dunes
   a look like mountains.
   b can make noises.
   c can be used for sport.
5 Which of the following is an opinion, not a fact?
   a In March or April it's cooler than in summer.
   b Sand can make a noise.
   c The trip was totally awesome.

5 🔊 2.8 Study the Vocabulary box. Find the highlighted phrases in the article and complete the box with the correct adverbs. Listen and check.

VOCABULARY Adverbs of degree

Adverb + strong adjective	Adverb + regular adjective
¹ *absolutely* boiling	⁴ _____ boring
² _____ different	⁵ _____ strange
³ _____ awesome	⁶ _____ worried

AMAZING WORLD
On this blog we publish articles about the most amazing places on our planet.

This week's article is by Miguel Garcia.
Miguel is from Beatty, USA, a town next to Death Valley National Park, which has record-breaking high temperatures.

A dangerously hot place

What are summer temperatures like where you live? It's August, so it's forty degrees Celsius in Beatty town and forty-five degrees Celsius in Death Valley, which is absolutely boiling. When you wake up in the morning, your eyes feel dry and you don't want to move because it is hot.

Some people think it's really boring in Death Valley, but I really love outdoor adventures in the desert. We usually go on a camping trip in March or April, when it's cooler than in summer. This year we visited a huge volcano crater, about a kilometre wide. It was amazing, completely different from any other place! They filmed some famous science fiction movies there because it looks like another planet.

The night sky is so clear in the desert that you can see thousands of stars. I wanted to sleep outside, but Dad was quite worried about scorpions, so I couldn't do that. I took some great photos of the Milky Way above us, though.

Did you know that sand can make a noise? On the final day of our trip we visited sand dunes at Mesquite and heard the sound of wind blowing the sand. It was very strange. We also tried sandboarding down the dunes. It's like snowboarding down a mountain, but on the sand. It was my favourite activity on a totally awesome trip.

6 Choose the correct option.
1 Wow! The sand dunes are *absolutely / very* amazing!
2 Your photos are *totally / quite* good.
3 Walking in the heat without a drink is *completely / very* ridiculous!
4 The stars in the desert sky look *really / totally* nice.

7 Make sentences about the things below. Use adverbs of degree and adjectives from Exercises 5 and 6.
1 the place where you live
2 an interesting place to visit near you
3 things you do in summer
4 something you did last weekend

YOUR WORLD

8 Write a blog post about something you did or saw recently that is typical of life in your area.

It was really hot yesterday. My sister and I went to the beach and bought ice cream. …

I can understand an article about life in a hot place.

2.4 Grammar

Past Continuous and Past Simple

VIDEO **A CRAZY DAY**

Dad: What's that noise? Abe, is that you?
Abe: It's blowing a gale out there. We had a bit of an adventure.
Dad: Really? Here, have a towel. Now go upstairs and put on some dry clothes.
Abe: But Dad, not now! I've taken a super cool photo for my blog. I just need to download and check it. And then post it.
Dad: OK, fine, but put this hoodie on then. I'll make you a nice warm drink. So, tell me about it …
Abe: I was walking in the park with Bea when we met Eren and Carla. They were playing with a frisbee, so I decided to take some photos. The sun was shining and we were having a great time, so we weren't thinking about the weather. Then I noticed some dark storm clouds were getting closer. Eren was throwing the frisbee when suddenly, lightning hit a tree near us, and I took a photo at the same time!
Dad: Here's your hot chocolate. Great photo!
Abe: Thanks, Dad. It started raining hard then, and the wind got stronger too. We realised we weren't safe, so we all ran home.
Dad: Thank goodness you're home. Are your friends OK?
Abe: They're all fine. Yeah, that was completely crazy! Right, time to upload my work.

1 ▶ 10 🔊 2.9 Look at the photo. What do you think happened to Abe? Watch or listen and check.

2 Find examples of the Past Continuous and the Past Simple in the dialogue.

GRAMMAR — Past Continuous and Past Simple

Past Continuous
It **was raining**.
We **weren't thinking** about the weather.
Were you **running**? Yes, I **was**./No, I **wasn't**.

Past Continuous and Past Simple
Abe **downloaded** his photo **while** his dad **was making** a warm drink.
He **was throwing** the frisbee **when** lightning **hit** a tree.

GRAMMAR TIME > PAGE 127

3 Choose the correct option.
1 We *drank / were drinking* hot chocolate when we *heard / were hearing* the thunder.
2 The rain *started / was starting* while we *sat / were sitting* on the beach.
3 George was travelling on the bus *while / when* he found a phone.
4 I *took / was taking* a lot of photos while I *walked / was walking* in the desert.
5 We were putting up the tent *when / while* the wind got stronger.
6 Daisy *fell / was falling* on the ice while she *skated / was skating* with friends.

4 Complete the extract from an email with the Past Simple or Past Continuous form of the verbs in brackets.

Hi Sara,

How was your History trip? When I was studying History, we ¹*went* (go) on a trip to France. It was spring, but it was freezing cold. One day, the weather suddenly ² _____ (change) while we ³ _____ (walk) in the hills. We soon ⁴ _____ (get) lost in the fog! Our teachers had to phone for help. While we ⁵ _____ (wait), I ⁶ _____ (hear) a strange noise. It was …

VIDEO **WIDER WORLD**

5 ▶ 11 Watch four people talking about holidays. Make notes about weather, family and transport.

6 In pairs, talk about funny things that happened on a school trip or holiday. Use the Past Simple and Past Continuous.

I can use the Past Continuous and the Past Simple to talk about past events.

2.5 Listening and Vocabulary
In the wild

1 Look at the photos. Do you enjoy being outdoors? Why?/Why not? Compare your ideas with the class.

2 🔊 2.10 Listen to an advert for an activity camp and mark the sentences T (true) or F (false).
1 ☐ The camp is a summer camp.
2 ☐ The camp is for families.
3 ☐ The campsites are in different locations.

3 🔊 2.11 **WORD FRIENDS** Complete the phrases with the verbs below. Listen and check.

~~discover~~   listen   look   make (x2)   sleep   watch

1 *discover* unusual plants
2 _____ outside
3 _____ a shelter
4 _____ to the wildlife
5 _____ the stars
6 _____ for wild animals
7 _____ a fire

4 🔊 2.12 Listen to Poppy talking about Wild Adventure camp and complete her diary with activities from Exercise 3.

Monday: ¹*make a shelter*
Tuesday: ² _____
Wednesday: ³ _____
Thursday: ⁴ _____
Friday: ⁵ _____

5 🔊 2.12 Listen again and answer the questions.
1 Why didn't Poppy sleep outside in the end?
2 Why didn't she listen to the wildlife?
3 Why weren't there any spiders in the camp?
4 What did Poppy see in the cave?

6 🔊 2.13 Study the Vocabulary box. Write the words from the box in the correct group below. Listen and check.

VOCABULARY ▸ In the wild

bat   bear   cave   leaf   path   sky   spider   star   sunset   waterfall   wildlife

1 Elements of landscape: *cave* , _____ , _____ , _____ , _____ , _____ , _____ , _____
2 Wild animals: _____ , _____ , _____

7 **I KNOW!** In groups, add more words to each group in Exercise 6. Each word scores a point. Which group wins?

8 Choose the correct option.
1 My favourite season is autumn, when the *stars / leaves* fall off the trees.
2 We walked into the *cave / waterfall* where it was cold and dark.
3 In the distance there was something big and brown. A *bear / spider* was standing and looking at us.
4 At the end of the day, there's an amazing *path / sunset* over the lake.
5 The sun was shining and the *sky / star* was blue – a perfect day to go out on the boat.

YOUR WORLD

9 Choose the correct option to make the sentence true for you. Then write a short paragraph.
I'd love / I'd hate to go to an adventure camp because …

I can understand a conversation about outdoor activities.

2.6 Speaking
Criticising and explaining

VIDEO ▶ **I CAN EXPLAIN**

Abe: Bea? What are you doing?
Bea: Abe, hi! I'm trying to help Mum with the garden. Can you give me a hand?
Abe: Yeah, no problem. I know you know about gardening, but I don't.
Bea: Don't worry. It's easy. You can take the weeds out of this flower bed. Is that OK?
Abe: Sure.
Bea: You put the weeds in here … See? And these are Mum's favourite flowers, OK? So, be careful. Right, I have to cut the grass.
Abe: Weeds bad, flowers good. Flowers, weeds. Got it.
Later …
Bea: What's going on?
Mum: What's going on? My poor flowers!
Bea: What? I didn't realise … Mum, I can explain.
Mum: Honestly! Why did you do that?
Abe: Aunt Penny? It's my fault. I didn't mean to pick your flowers. I was helping Bea and I thought they were weeds.
Mum: I see. Abe, were you really trying to help?

SOUNDS GOOD! Can you give me a hand? • No problem. • Got it.

1 ▶ 12 🔊 2.14 Look at the photo and think of reasons why Bea and Abe are working in the garden. Do you think they are enjoying it? Watch or listen and check.

2 Why do you think Abe did the wrong thing?

SET FOR LIFE

3 In groups, discuss the questions.
1 Why is it important to give clear instructions?
2 Why is it important to look and listen carefully?

4 Study the Speaking box. Find examples of the phrases in the dialogue.

SPEAKING | Criticising and explaining

Criticising
What's going on?
Why did you do that?

Explaining and apologising
I can explain.   I'm so sorry.   I thought …
I didn't mean to …   I didn't realise …

Accepting explanations and apologies
I see.   That's all right.   Never mind.

5 🔊 2.15 Complete the dialogues with phrases from the Speaking box. Listen and check.
1 A: Hey, why did you take my seat?
   B: Oh. I *didn't realise* you were sitting there.
2 A: What's _____ ? This is my phone!
   B: Oh, sorry!
   A: Never _____ . It does look like yours!
3 A: Oh dear! I just shouted at my friends.
   B: _____ that?
   A: I was angry. I _____ to hurt their feelings.

6 In pairs, turn to page 142 and follow the role play instructions.

VIDEO ▶ **WIDER WORLD**

7 ▶ 13 Watch four people talking about problems. Number the problems below in the order the people mention them.
a ☐ climbing a ladder
b ☐ late for work
c ☐ not being serious
d ☐ no money

8 In pairs, tell your partner about a time when you had a problem.

Unit 2 | 30 | I can criticise and explain when things go wrong.

2.7 Writing

An article describing your local area and climate

ARTICLES WANTED Write about your local area and climate. Email your article to us – we'll put the best ones in our magazine.

Is Lima a good place to visit?

1 Everybody knows Peru has lots of mountains, but Lima, where I live, is on the coast. On many days of the year it's very cloudy here, but it doesn't often rain. Sometimes I think it's very cloudy here, but the climate is just right. For example, it's usually between 15 and 25°C, so it's never boiling hot or freezing cold. Don't come here between June and September, though, as many days are very foggy.

2 In Lima you can find great food and music everywhere. There are lots of activities such as adventure sports too. Last year while my little cousin Jorge was staying with us, we went to the beach at Barraca. My cousin looked up and saw a 'big bird'. At first he was quite worried and then he realised that somebody was paragliding. It looked amazing!

3 If you want to visit somewhere outside Lima, the Palomino Islands are about forty-five minutes away by boat. We took my cousin there in November. The sun was shining and the sea was warm. While we were travelling, some big sea lions swam past! To sum it up, you can have a totally fantastic experience here. There isn't anywhere better!

1 Is your local area a good place to visit? Why?/Why not?

2 Read the advert and article. Would you like to visit Lima? Why?/Why not?

3 Read the article again. Which of these things does it mention and in which paragraph?
 a *2* food and music   d ☐ population
 b ☐ location   e ☐ weather and climate
 c ☐ another place nearby   f ☐ activities

4 Study the Writing box. Make similar true sentences about the area where you live.

WRITING An article describing your local area and climate

1 **Describe the area, weather and climate**
   Lima, where I live, is on the coast.
   It doesn't often rain.
   The climate is just right.

2 **Describe typical activities and places**
   You can find great food and music everywhere.
3 There are lots of activities …
   The Palomino Islands are about forty-five minutes away …

Give examples
For example, …   One/An example is …   …, like …
… such as …

5 Study the Language box. Find five indefinite pronouns in the article. Then use indefinite pronouns to write some true sentences about your local area.

LANGUAGE Indefinite pronouns

People	Things	Places
somebody/-one	something	somewhere
everybody/-one	everything	everywhere
anybody/-one	anything	anywhere

WRITING TIME

6 Write an article for the advert in Exercise 2.

1 **Find ideas**
   Make notes about:
   • some facts about the weather, climate and things to do where you live.
   • a trip you went on. Think about the situation and what you did.

2 **Plan**
   Organise your ideas into three paragraphs. Use the article about Lima to help you.

3 **Write and share**
   • Write a draft article. Use the Language box and the Writing box to help you.
   • Share your article with another student for feedback.
   • Use the feedback from your partner and write the final version of your article.

4 **Check**
   • Check language: did you use indefinite pronouns correctly?
   • Check grammar: did you use the Past Simple and Past Continuous to illustrate your points?

I can write an article about my local area and climate.

Vocabulary Activator

WORDLIST 🔊 2.16

Word building (weather)
cloud (n)
cloudy (adj)
fog (n)
foggy (adj)
ice (n)
icy (adj)
rain (n)
rainy (adj)
snow (n)
snowy (adj)
storm (n)
stormy (adj)
sun (n)
sunny (adj)
wind (n)
windy (adj)

Weather
breeze (n)
drought (n)
flood (n)
gale (n)
hurricane (n)
lightning (n)
shower (n)
sunshine (n)
thunder (n)

Word friends (weather and climate)
boiling hot
degrees Celsius
freezing cold
heavy rain
heavy snow
high/low temperature
hot/mild/cold climate
minus five degrees
strong wind
the temperature is rising/falling
the weather is bad/cool/dry/fine/good/warm/wet

Adverbs of degree
absolutely (boiling) (adv)
completely (different) (adv)
quite (worried) (adv)
really (strange) (adv)
totally (awesome) (adv)
very (boring) (adv)

Word friends (camping)
discover unusual plants
listen to the wildlife
look for wild animals
make a fire
make a shelter
sleep outside
watch the stars

In the wild
bat (n)
bear (n)
cave (n)
leaf (n)
path (n)
sky (n)
spider (n)
star (n)
sunset (n)
waterfall (n)
wildlife (n)

Extra words
adventure (n)
Antarctic (n)
Arctic (n)
bright (adj)
camping trip (n)
conditions (n)
degree (n)
desert (n)
find your way
foreign (adj)
freezing (adj)
grow (v)
huge (adj)
lake (n)
land (n)
lighthouse (n)
local (adj)
melt (v)
Milky Way (n)
mountain (n)
ocean (n)
perfect (adj)
planet (n)
record-breaking (adj)
root (n)
sand dune (n)
scared (adj)
scorpion (n)
sea level (n)
sink (v)
sleep in the open air
soil (n)
special (adj)
treetop (n)
volcano (n)
wash away (v)
weather forecast (n)

1 Use the words from the wordlist to find these things.
  1 six pairs of opposite adjectives
  2 two weather words that refer to too much or too little water
  3 three animals
  4 three things you can see in the sky

2 Match words 1–8 with words a–h to make phrases. In pairs, use the wordlist to check your answers. Then make true sentences using four of the phrases.

  1 ☐ low   a a shelter
  2 ☐ absolutely   b the stars
  3 ☐ make   c Celsius
  4 ☐ watch   d weather
  5 ☐ sleep   e snow
  6 ☐ heavy   f boiling
  7 ☐ degrees   g temperature
  8 ☐ warm   h outside

3 Choose the odd one out.
  1 rainy   snowy   sunny   icy
  2 breeze   rain   wind   gale
  3 cloudy   thunder   rainy   foggy
  4 cave   temperature   waterfall   leaf

4 Complete the sentences about the weather with words from the wordlist. Then, in pairs, talk about the type of weather you prefer and the type of weather you don't like.
  1 The roads are *icy* today, so please drive carefully.
  2 It's freezing _____ today, so wear your warmest clothes.
  3 The weather forecast said it will be thirty _____ Celsius today. That's hot!
  4 I can hear _____ . Can you see any lightning?
  5 The river is _____ quickly because of all the rain. I hope there won't be a flood.

5 In pairs, make true sentences using strong adjectives and adverbs of degree from the wordlist.
The weather today is absolutely amazing!

6 🔊 2.17 **PRONUNCIATION** Listen to the words below and write them in the correct column according to the word stress.

absolutely   amazing   completely   perfect   totally

1 Oo	2 oOo	3 oOoo	4 Ooo

7 🔊 2.18 **PRONUNCIATION** Listen, check your answers to Exercise 6 and repeat.

Revision

Vocabulary

1 Choose the word that does NOT go with the noun in bold.
1. dry / cloudy / sunshine / rainy **WEATHER**
2. high / low / rising / fine **TEMPERATURE**
3. absolutely / totally / very / completely **AWESOME**
4. falling / mild / hot / cold **CLIMATE**
5. listen to / discover / sleep / look for **WILDLIFE**

2 In pairs, use phrases from Exercise 1 to say what you like and don't like. Remember: you can make negative sentences too.

3 Complete the words in the email.

Dear students,
This year's Science project is a camping trip. Here are some of the things we want to do:
- look for ¹wi_ld_ animals and birds
- ²di_____ unusual plants
- walk an amazing ³pa_____ around the lake and through the forest
- make a ⁴sh_____ that can keep you dry from falling rain
- listen to the sounds of birds and other ⁵wi_____
- ⁶sl_____ outside and watch the ⁷st_____

Pack clothes for ⁸ra_____, windy and even ⁹st_____ weather. Bring enough clothes to put on dry ones if you get completely wet.
Thank you,
Your Science teachers

4 Complete the definitions with the correct word. Then write two more definitions.
1. _____ weather is when it is difficult to see because clouds are close to the ground.
2. _____ conditions happen when temperatures below 0°C change water.
3. _____ plants and animals don't live with people.
4. A _____ is the green part of a plant that uses sunshine.

Grammar

5 Choose the correct option.
1. A: I *hear / heard* a bat flying in my room last night.
   B: How did you *know / knew* it was a bat?
2. A: I didn't *see / saw* you at school yesterday.
   B: That's because I *go / went* to the doctor.
3. A: Which places did your parents *visit / visited* in Scotland last summer?
   B: Mostly lakes and mountains. They *stay / stayed* away from the cities.
4. A: Why did Dr Sanchez *take / took* photographs of the volcano?
   B: He *want / wanted* to show them to some colleagues.

6 Make questions in the Past Simple. Then ask and answer the questions in pairs.
1. you / go / for a walk / yesterday / ?
2. you / have / dinner with your grandparents / at the weekend / ?
3. you / sing / songs on your birthday / ?
4. where / you / go / on holiday / last year / ?
5. who / you / chat to / on social media / last night / ?

7 Complete the sentences with the Past Simple or Past Continuous form of the verbs in brackets.
1. My mum *saw* (see) a bright star when she _____ (watch) the night sky a short time ago.
2. We _____ (walk) home on rainy weather yesterday when we _____ (hear) thunder.
3. While I _____ (do) my homework, my cat _____ (jump) onto my desk.
4. Dad _____ (find) a scorpion in his shoe once when he _____ (camp) in the desert.
5. I _____ (leave) home with an umbrella this morning because it _____ (rain).

Speaking

8 In pairs, turn to page 142 and follow the instructions to role play a dialogue.

Dictation

9 🔊 2.19 Listen. Then listen again and write down what you hear.

SET FOR LIFE

Stay positive and carry on

A

My phone was new a week ago! Aaarrgh!

B

Whaaat? Who took my wheels?

C

My favourite band are in town, but I can't get a ticket.

D

This is what I got for dinner after football practice finished late!

1 Look at the social media posts. In pairs, discuss the questions.
1 Imagine you are the people in situations A–D. How do you feel? Use the adjectives below to help you.

> angry   annoyed   calm   sad   stressed
> surprised   worried

2 Which do you think is the worst situation? Why?
3 Do similar things ever happen to you? Give examples and describe how you felt.

2 🔊 2.20 Listen to Sam and Jess. Which situation from the posts are they talking about? Do they both keep calm?

3 🔊 2.20 Listen again and answer the questions.
1 How does Jess think Sam can go to school?
2 Does Sam like Jess's idea? Why?/Why not?
3 Why doesn't Sam want to buy new wheels for his bike?
4 Why does he want to leave the bike outside the library?

4 Choose the sentences (a or b) that best describe Sam's attitude.
1 a He focuses on his bad luck.
   b He focuses on things that he can do to improve the situation.
2 a He imagines bad things that aren't likely to happen.
   b He only thinks about the facts and things that are likely to happen.
3 a He remembers that some other people's problems are more serious than his.
   b He can't see that his problem isn't the end of the world.

Keep calm when things go wrong

USEFUL TIPS

When something bad happens, we often feel stressed or sad. It's important to keep calm and control negative feelings.

- Breathe slowly.
- Don't focus on your mistakes or bad luck.
- Focus on things that you can do to improve the situation.
- Don't think about bad things that aren't likely to happen.
- Remember that friends often give good advice.

5 ◆) 2.21 Listen to the next part of Sam and Jess's conversation and answer the questions.
How does Sam decide to:
1 get his bike home?
2 get to school in the morning?
3 try to get money for new wheels?
4 protect his bike in the future?

6 ◆) 2.21 Study the Useful Phrases box. Then listen again and tick (✓) the expressions you hear in Sam and Jess's conversation.

7 What do you think? Which attitudes from Exercise 4 help people to keep calm when bad things happen? Do you have any other advice for keeping calm?

It's a good idea to focus on things that you can do to improve the situation.

8 In pairs, discuss the situations. Think about how you feel at first. Then say what you can do to keep calm.
1 Your family's car breaks down the day before you go on holiday. You have to stay at home until the car is fixed.
2 You love your dog, but he's very naughty. He tries to eat your expensive new trainers and destroys them.
3 You are in a café. Someone near you falls over and their orange juice goes all over you.

9 Read the Useful Tips. Do you usually do what the tips suggest? Which tip is the most useful? Why?

USEFUL PHRASES

Finding something good in a bad situation
☐ It isn't the end of the world.
☐ At least …
☐ It's lucky that …

Being a friend to someone in a bad situation
☐ Bad luck! What are you going to do?
☐ Can you … ?

Finding solutions
☐ I guess I can …
☐ Maybe I can …
☐ Perhaps the best thing is to …

SET FOR LIFE

10 In pairs, role play a situation where something bad happens and you manage to keep calm. Follow these steps.

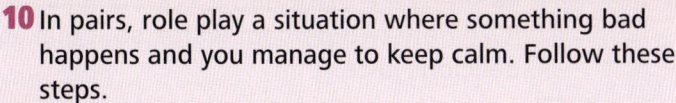

1 Choose a situation from Exercise 1 or 8.

2 Write the dialogue. Use expressions from the Useful Phrases box.
Student A: Describe the bad situation. (You feel sad or stressed about it.)
Student B: Encourage your friend to keep calm.
Student A: Give a positive solution. Remember to stay calm and manage your emotions.

3 Practise your dialogue. Remember to use your body and voice to show how you feel.

4 Present your dialogue to the class or record it on your phone.

Tasty treats

3

VOCABULARY
Food | Cooking | Flavours |
Word building: food |
Collocations about food |
Describing food

GRAMMAR
Present Perfect with *ever, never, just, already* and *yet* | Present Perfect with *for* and *since* | Present Perfect and Past Simple

KNOW YOUR FOOD
Do you know these fascinating facts about everyday food?

1 ☐ You can eat them raw, cooked or in a hot, spicy sauce. In Africa, farmers use them to keep elephants away: they don't like the smell.

2 ☐ It's delicious boiled, roasted or in soup. It has beautiful flowers and you can eat its leaves. It looks like a potato, but it's different.

3 ☐ You can eat this small green or black fruit raw. Its oil is a basic ingredient in Mediterranean cooking. In Spain, they put it on toast instead of butter.

4 ☐ It's green on the outside, red on the inside, its seeds are black and it's good in salads. It's ninety-two percent water, so it makes delicious juice.

5 ☐ It comes in all shapes and sizes and we can eat this for breakfast, lunch and dinner. It's usually baked, but we can fry it too and it's great with butter on it!

6 ☐ This is made from milk and you can buy it in lots of different flavours. When it's frozen, it can make a fantastic dessert, especially when you add some nuts and fresh fruit.

3.1 Vocabulary
Food and drink

1 Look at photos A–F. Do you know any of these foods? Which did you eat yesterday?

2 🔊 3.1 Read the clues in the quiz and match them with photos A–F. Listen and check.

3 🔊 3.2 Study Vocabulary box A and write the words in the correct group below. One word does not belong to any of the groups.

> **VOCABULARY A** ▸ **Food**
>
> chillies   garlic   green pepper   mushroom   nuts   oil   olives
> onion   peach   pear   pepper   pineapple   sausage   seeds
> sweet potato   tuna   vinegar

Vegetables	potato
Fruit	apple
Meat/Fish	chicken
Condiments	salt
Snacks	nuts
Cereals	bread
Dairy products:	milk

4 **I KNOW!** In groups, add more words to each group in Exercise 3. How many can you add in one minute? Compare your ideas with the class.

5 Circle the odd one out. Use the groups in Exercise 3 to help you. Explain your answers.
1 beef   lamb   sausage   (tuna)
   Tuna is a fish, the other three are kinds of meat.
2 chillies   garlic   nuts   onion
3 butter   cream   noodles   yoghurt
4 mushroom   peach   pear   pineapple
5 burger   curry   salad   soup
6 bread rolls   flour   honey   toast
7 ice cream   oil   pepper   vinegar

6 🔊 3.3 Complete the text with the words below. Listen and check. What are your favourite three extra toppings on pizza? Discuss in pairs.

> mushrooms   olives   onions   peppers   pineapple   ~~sausage~~   tuna

FAVOURITE PIZZA TOPPINGS: CLASS SURVEY

Most pizzas have mozzarella cheese and tomato, but what are our school's top ten extra pizza toppings? Well, in our survey, it's clear that we like meat because number one is ¹*sausage*, number four is beef and number five is chicken. Number two isn't a meat, but it isn't a fruit or a vegetable, either. It's ² _____ – in thin slices, of course. Number three is a very useful vegetable that we use in lots of recipes: ³ _____. Number six is extra cheese, number seven is green ⁴ _____. Number eight is ⁵ _____ but black ones, not green. Number nine is a fish: it's ⁶ _____. And finally, number ten is surprising because it's a fruit: ⁷ _____ ! Yes, I know. I think it's strange too.

7 🔊 3.4 Study Vocabulary box B. In pairs, ask and answer the questions below.

> **VOCABULARY B** ▸ **Cooking**
>
> boiled   cooked   flavour   fresh   fried   frozen
> ingredients   raw   recipe   roasted   sauce

1 Do you prefer boiled potatoes or fried potatoes? Raw carrots or cooked carrots? Fresh fruit or frozen yoghurt?
2 How often do you eat roast chicken? How often do you have hot, spicy sauces?
3 Who does the cooking in your house? Do they prefer easy recipes or difficult ones with lots of ingredients?

8 🔊 3.5 Study Vocabulary box C. In pairs, add more words to the box. Then say which flavours of ice cream you love/can't stand.

I love vanilla ice cream, but I can't stand chocolate ice cream.

> **VOCABULARY C** ▸ **Flavours**
>
> chocolate   coconut   coffee   mango
> melon   mint   strawberry   vanilla

> ⚠️ **WATCH OUT!**
> We can use flavours as nouns or as adjectives. When we use them as adjectives, they always appear in singular form.
> *I like **strawberries**.* (noun)
> *I like **strawberry** ice cream.* (adjective)

9 🔊 3.6 Which ice cream flavours do these people mention? Which ones are unusual? Which one is fake?

YOUR WORLD

10 Which of the foods in the lesson do you love eating at these meals or as a snack? Which meal is your favourite? Say why.
• breakfast • lunch • dinner

I love eating toast with olive oil for breakfast. It's my favourite meal.

I can talk about food and drink.   **37**   Unit 3

3.2 Grammar

Present Perfect with *ever, never, just, already* and *yet*

VIDEO ▶ **AN ENGLISH BREAKFAST**

Abe: Good morning. Oh! Am I early?
Bea: No. Sorry, I've just got up. I haven't finished eating yet. Are you hungry?
Abe: No, I've already eaten. What's that?
Bea: Baked beans on toast.
Abe: I've never heard of anyone eating beans for breakfast. It looks kind of strange.
Bea: Have you ever tried it?
Abe: No, I haven't.
Bea: It's really good. Try some.
Abe: I've just eaten. Have you finished yet?
Bea: No. I haven't eaten my fried egg yet.
Abe: You've already eaten a plate of beans!
Bea: So? I love big breakfasts on Saturdays.
Abe: What's that?
Bea: It's brown sauce. It's great with chips.
Abe: With potato chips?
Bea: They're not chips, they're crisps. Chips are hot. I've never tried brown sauce with crisps … Mmm, it's good. Try some.
Abe: Ah! That's the worst thing I've ever tasted! Ah! What's that?
Bea: Have you never tasted tea before?
Abe: I've never had tea like that. It's so strong!
Bea: I'll be ready in five minutes.

1 What is a full English breakfast? What is the typical breakfast in your country?

2 ▶ 14 ◀) 3.7 Watch or listen and answer the questions.
  1 What does Bea have for breakfast?
  2 What does Abe think of her breakfast?
  3 What do you think of it?

3 Study the Grammar box. Find more examples of the Present Perfect with *ever, never, just, already* and *yet* in the dialogue.

GRAMMAR | **Present Perfect with *ever, never, just, already* and *yet***

Have you ever tried beans on toast?
I've never heard of anyone eating beans for breakfast.
Bea's just got up.
I've already eaten.
She hasn't woken up yet.
Have you finished yet? Yes, I have./No, I haven't.

GRAMMAR TIME ▶ PAGE 128

---

4 Make sentences in the Present Perfect.
  1 Abe / just / eat / breakfast
  2 Bea / not have / her fried egg / yet
  3 Bea / already / eat / a plate of beans
  4 Bea / never / try / brown sauce with crisps
  5 brown sauce / the worst thing / Abe / ever / taste
  6 you / ever / taste / strong tea / ?
  7 you / have / your breakfast / yet / ?

5 ◀) 3.8 Complete the dialogue with the words in brackets. Use the Present Perfect form of the verbs. Listen and check.

Joe: I want to go out for my birthday on Friday, but I ¹_____ (not decide/where to go/yet).
Kim: ²_____ (you/try/that new Japanese restaurant/yet)?
Joe: No, I haven't. Have you?
Kim: Yes, I ³_____ (already/be) there twice. The noodles are great! ⁴_____ (you/ever/eat) sushi?
Joe: No, ⁵_____ (I/never/try) Japanese food.
Kim: You should. It's brilliant.
Joe: OK, that's it. ⁶_____ (I/just/book) a table for four for next Friday night.

VIDEO ▶ **WIDER WORLD**

6 ▶ 15 Watch four people talking about their favourite food and places to eat. Make notes about these things for each speaker.
  • place
  • when or how often they go/went there
  • food they like/have tried

7 In pairs, ask and answer questions about places to eat where you live.

Have you ever eaten at Big Burger Bar?

Unit 3 | I can use the Present Perfect to talk about experiences.

3.3 Reading and Vocabulary

Super healthy foods

1 Look at the foods in the photos. Which foods do you like the most/least?

2 🔊 3.9 Read the article quickly and choose the correct answer.
The article looks at five foods and describes how
a much they cost.   b healthy they are.
c to cook them.

3 Read the article again and complete the sentences with 1–3 words from the article.
1 Your memory can improve if you eat *chocolate regularly* .
2 Dark chocolate is better for you than _____ .
3 Salmon can stop you having _____ .
4 Pickles are good in burgers or on their own as a _____ .
5 You should eat pickles if you are _____ .
6 Eating raw pumpkin seeds is _____ .
7 You can add garlic to all sorts of _____ .

4 🔊 3.10 Complete the Vocabulary box with adjectives from the article. Listen and check.

VOCABULARY Word building: food

Noun	Adjective	Noun	Adjective
butter	*buttery*	health	5 ____
cream	1 ____	juice	6 ____
crisp	2 ____	salt	7 ____
crunch	3 ____	spice	8 ____
fat	4 ____	taste	9 ____

5 In pairs, ask and answer about foods using adjectives from Exercise 4.
A: Are raw carrots crunchy or juicy?
B: They're crunchy. Are peanuts creamy or salty?

6 🔊 3.11 **WORD FRIENDS** Complete the sentences with the phrases below. Listen and check. In pairs, say if the sentences are true for you.

| add to | ~~full of~~ | go well with | good/healthy for |
| protect from | | | |

1 I love sweet things that are *full of* sugar.
2 I think pickles _____ cheese.
3 I _____ too much salt _____ my food.
4 I never eat anything that isn't _____ me.
5 I try to eat foods that can _____ me _____ illnesses.

Five superfoods – they're tasty and healthy!

Eating chocolate regularly seems to improve your ability to multitask, to understand abstract ideas and to remember things like phone numbers. It's good for your skin and keeps your heart healthy, too! But it must be dark chocolate with 75–80 percent cocoa, not chocolate cake full of sugar!

Fresh or frozen, raw or cooked, salmon is a juicy fish with a rich, buttery flavour. It's also full of Omega-3 fatty acids. Studies have shown that Omega-3 can protect you from serious health problems such as heart disease, dementia and some kinds of cancer. It's also good for your eyesight and your hair. Salmon is the medicine your body needs.

We often eat pickles in a burger or sandwich. But have you ever thought of eating pickles as a crunchy snack instead of crisps or peanuts? You should because they're very good for you. Pickles also have a positive effect on the brain: they help shy and nervous people feel more relaxed.

If you've never tried pumpkin seeds, you should. These tasty little treats give you energy, make you feel happy and help you sleep better. Their slightly salty flavour goes well with all sorts of dishes, but it's healthier for you to eat them raw. Add them to salads, breakfast cereal or fruit and vegetable smoothies. Or just eat them as a healthy snack.

It's a medicine that keeps the common cold away, strengthens your bones and protects your heart. It can help you run faster and live longer. Its strong taste is great in recipes from spicy curries to creamy sauces. I fry it in olive oil until it's crispy and add it to salads. Have you guessed what it is yet? It's garlic!

YOUR WORLD

7 Make a list of the healthy and unhealthy food and drink you often consume. Then, in groups, compare your lists and say if you eat or drink too much/many or not enough of these things.
Healthy: carrots …   Unhealthy: crisps, …
I eat a lot of biscuits.
I don't eat any fresh fruit.

I can understand an article about superfoods.

3.4 Grammar

Present Perfect with *for* and *since* | Present Perfect and Past Simple

1 What's your favourite flavour for a fruit juice or smoothie?

2 🔊 3.12 Read the blog post. In pairs, answer the questions.
   1 What surprises Ashley about Rio?
   2 How many types of fruit are there in Brazil?
   3 What drink did Ashley try?

3 Study the Grammar box. Which set of words and phrases, a or b, do we use with *for*? Which do we use with *since*?
   a two o'clock, yesterday, Monday, last weekend, 1958
   b five minutes, a few hours, a long time, two weeks, three years

GRAMMAR — Present Perfect with *for* and *since* | Present Perfect and Past Simple

Present Perfect with *for* and *since*
I've lived in Rio *for* many years. (a period of time)
They've had this bar *since* 1970. (a point in time)

Present Perfect and Past Simple
We've been to São Paulo.
We went to São Paulo in 2012.
Have you ever drunk a mango smoothie?
Did you like it?

GRAMMAR TIME > PAGE 128

4 Find more examples of the Present Perfect and Past Simple in the blog post.

5 Make sentences in the Present Perfect. Use *for* or *since*.
   1 I / not have / a chocolate bar / a month
   2 my family / own / this café / 2010
   3 we / not eat / any food / breakfast time
   4 this cookery programme / be / on TV / a few months
   5 you / see / the cookery teacher / last lesson / ?
   6 they / be / at the juice bar / half an hour

6 🔊 3.13 Complete the dialogue with one word in each gap. Listen and check.

Mia: ¹*Have* you had any fruit juice yet today?
Leo: No, I ²_____ had any yet, but I'd like some now.
Mia: ³_____ you ever tried sugar apple juice?
Leo: Yes, I ⁴_____ some yesterday. Sugar apples look like pears! They're very good for you.
Mia: ⁵_____ you like it?
Leo: Yes, I ⁶_____ . Why don't you try some?
Mia: Yeah. I'd love to try it. Where ⁷_____ you buy it?
Leo: At the juice bar on the beach.

The best drink ever!

We've been in Rio since yesterday afternoon. I'm so excited! My parents are from Brazil, but we haven't visited the country many times – the plane tickets are very expensive. Anyway, I'm in Rio now and I love it here, especially the juice bars. They're on every street corner. I've never seen so much fruit!

The owner of one juice bar, Rodrigo, has lived in Rio for many years. His father opened Rio's first juice bar in 1958. Many other bars have opened since then. I found out that there are 300 different types of fruit in Brazil! Some of them are very unusual. Have you heard of cashew apple? It looks like a red apple, but the cashew nut grows at the top of the fruit. It makes delicious juice. I've just had some!

Ashley

YOUR WORLD

7 Write questions in the Present Perfect and Past Simple. Then ask and answer the questions in pairs.
   • Start with a general question with *ever* (Present Perfect).
     Have you ever eaten … ?
   • Then ask about details (Past Simple).
     When did you try it? Did you like it? What was it like?

I can use the Present Perfect and the Past Simple to talk about experiences.

3.5 Listening and Vocabulary
A dream cake

1 Is it important to have a special cake on your birthday? Compare your ideas with the class.

2 🔊 3.14 Study the Vocabulary box. Can you add more words?

> **VOCABULARY** | **Describing food**
>
> bitter   delicious   dry   hard   hot   rich   sour   spicy   sweet

3 🔊 3.15 Complete the sentences with words from the Vocabulary box. Listen and check.
1. I like chilli popcorn because it's so *sour / hot*.
2. This cupcake isn't *bitter / sweet* enough. Put some jam on it.
3. I love this fruit juice – it's really *dry / delicious*.
4. There's a lot of butter and cream in this cake, so it's very *rich / spicy*.
5. This milk has been in the sun too long – it tastes *fresh / sour*.
6. This bread is old – it's too *hard / hot* to eat.

4 🔊 3.16 Listen to Gianni talking about a very special cake and mark the sentences T (true) or F (false).
1. ☐ Gianni saw the cake in New York.
2. ☐ The cake took a week to make.
3. ☐ The baker didn't make the cake in his shop.
4. ☐ The cake weighed around seventy kilos.
5. ☐ Gianni didn't like the cake at all.

5 Read the advert. In pairs, decide what kind of information is missing from each gap: a word or a number?

6 🔊 3.17 Listen to information about how to enter the competition. Complete the text in Exercise 5.

VIDEO ▶   **WIDER WORLD**

7 ▶ 16 Watch four people talking about the best cake they have ever had. What flavour was each cake?

8 In pairs, describe the best cake you have ever had.

The best cake I've ever had was a chocolate cake I had for my last birthday.

Win your dream cake from Zany Cake Bakery!

Send us a photo or drawing of your ideal cake! We will make the best cake and send it to you.

- Email address: ¹orders@_____.com
- Usual cost: ²€_____
- Choose a flavour: chocolate, ³_____ or vanilla?
- Don't forget: tell us your ⁴_____ !
- Closing date of competition: Friday ⁵_____ January
- Other prizes for five runners-up: twelve ⁶_____

I can understand people describing food.

3.6 Speaking
Ordering food

VIDEO ▶ **ARE YOU READY TO ORDER?**

Abe: Hi, guys. Take a seat and I'll get you the menu. Here you are. Can I get you something to drink?
Bea: I'll have a large smoothie, please.
Mum: Just water for me, please.
Bea: Wow! That's a big smoothie!
Abe: It's good for you! Are you ready to order?
Mum: Could we share a starter? Nachos?
Abe: Sure thing. And for your main course?
Bea: I'd like a burger, please.
Mum: Sorry, I'm a vegetarian. Have you got any vegetable dishes?
Abe: Hold on! There's salad and pumpkin pie.
Mum: Pumpkin pie? That's a dessert, isn't it?
Abe: Yeah, it is … You can have more nachos if you prefer.
Mum: No, it's OK. I'll have salad and a slice of pumpkin pie. Can I have some cream with that?
Abe: Sure. Would you like fries with your meal?
Bea: Yes, please.
Mum: Not for me, thanks.

Later …
Abe: Would you like anything else?
Mum: You must be joking!

SOUNDS GOOD! • Sure thing. • Hold on! • You must be joking!

1 In pairs, list at least three typical American foods. Say which one you like the most. Then compare with the rest of the class.
pumpkin pie, …

2 ▶ 17 🔊 3.18 Watch or listen. What do Bea and Penny order?

3 Study the Speaking box. Find the phrases which are in the dialogue.

SPEAKING Ordering food

Customer
I'll have/I'd like a slice of …
Excuse me, can/could I/we have/share … ?
Just … for me, please.
Have you got any … ?
Not for me, thanks.

Waiter
Take a seat and I'll get you the menu.
What would you like to drink?
Are you ready to order?
Would you like anything else/to eat?
Can I get you something?
For the/your starter/main course/dessert?
Here you are.

4 Match questions 1–5 with answers a–e. Use the Speaking box to help you.
1 ☐ Are you ready to order?
2 ☐ Could we share a dessert?
3 ☐ Have you got any fresh fruit?
4 ☐ What can I get you to drink?
5 ☐ Would you like chips with that?

a Yes, we have pineapple or melon.
b A fresh orange juice, please.
c Yes, can I have a chicken curry?
d No, not for me, thanks.
e Yes, of course we can.

SET FOR LIFE

5 In groups of four, discuss how you could work together to do different tasks for an event. Use these ideas to help you.
• choose a leader
• make a list of tasks
• share the tasks

I'd like to organise a group to tidy up.
If you buy the snacks, I'll organise the music.

YOUR WORLD

6 In pairs or small groups, order food from the menu on page 142. Use the Speaking box to help you.

I can order food in a café or restaurant.

3.7 Writing

An email to a friend

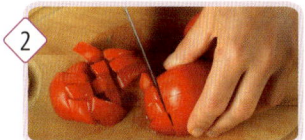

1 Work in pairs. What food do you usually have at a party with friends?

2 Match the verbs below with photos 1–4.

chop ☐ mix ☐ pour ☐ slice ☐

3 Read Elsie's email. Does it mention any of your ideas from Exercise 1?

Subject: Party time!

Hi Shannon,

① Thanks for getting in touch.

② It was great to hear about your school trip. The photos were awesome.

③ Liam and I have just finished our exams and we've decided to have a party tomorrow at his house to celebrate! He's bought lots of yummy food, including sausages and cheese. I'm thinking about making my famous chicken salad. Here's the recipe for you – it's really easy. First, boil some eggs and slice them. Then, chop a few tomatoes into small pieces. Next, add some roast chicken. After that, mix everything together. Finally, pour some olive oil on it. I can't tell you how good it is!

④ Anyway, I was wondering if you'd like to come. We're asking everybody to bring some fruit or some juice because we want to make lots of different flavoured smoothies.

⑤ Let me know if you can make it.

Elsie

---

4 Read the email again. Number the things below in the order Elsie does them in her email.
   a ☐ She talks about what's happening in her life now.
   b ☐ She invites her friend and asks her friend to do something.
   c ☐ She thanks her friend and comments on her friend's news.
   d ☐ She asks her friend to reply to the invitation.

5 Study the Language box. Find sentences with sequencers in the recipe in Elsie's email.

LANGUAGE Giving instructions

First, then, next, after that and *finally* are sequencers. We use them to explain the order in which we do things. We often use them with imperatives in recipes.

6 Study the Writing box. Find examples of the phrases in Elsie's email.

WRITING An email to a friend

1 Start your email
How are things?
Great to hear from you./Thanks for getting in touch.

2 Respond to news
It was great to hear about your school trip.
I can't wait to hear more about it.

3 Give your news
We have just finished our exams.
We've decided to have a party.
I'm making a cake for the party.

4 Explain why you're writing
Anyway/By the way, I was wondering if you'd like to come.
I'm writing to ask if you'd like to come to the party.

5 End your email
Let me know if you can make it.
See you soon./Bye for now.

WRITING TIME

7 Write an email inviting a friend to a party. Include a recipe for some food for the party.

1 Find ideas
• Where and when are you having the party?
• What are you celebrating?
• What food are you planning to make?

2 Plan
Organise your ideas into paragraphs. Use Elsie's email to help you.

3 Write and share
• Write a draft email. Use the Language box and the Writing box to help you.
• Share your email with another student for feedback.
• Use the feedback from your partner and write the final version of your email.

4 Check
• Check language: did you use sequencers and imperatives for your recipe?
• Check grammar: did you use the Present Perfect correctly?

I can write an email to a friend.

Vocabulary Activator

WORDLIST 🔊 3.19

Food
chillies (n)
garlic (n)
green pepper (n)
mushroom (n)
nuts (n)
oil (n)
olives (n)
onion (n)
peach (n)
pear (n)
pepper (n)
pineapple (n)
sausage (n)
seeds (n)
sweet potato (n)
tuna (n)
vinegar (n)

Cooking
boiled (adj)
cooked (adj)
flavour (n)
fresh (adj)
fried (adj)
frozen (adj)
ingredients (n)
raw (adj)
recipe (n)
roasted (adj)
sauce (n)

Flavours
chocolate (adj)
coconut (adj)
coffee (adj)
mango (adj)
melon (adj)
mint (adj)
strawberry (adj)
vanilla (adj)

Word building
(food)
butter – buttery
cream – creamy
crisp – crispy
crunch – crunchy
fat – fatty
health – healthy
juice – juicy
salt – salty
spice – spicy
taste – tasty

Word friends
(collocations about food)
add to (v)
full of (adj)
go well with
good/healthy for (adj)
protect from (v)

Describing food
bitter (adj)
delicious (adj)
dry (adj)
hard (adj)
hot (adj)
rich (adj)
sour (adj)
spicy (adj)
sweet (adj)

Extra words
bakery (n)
beef (n)
body (n)
bone (n)
carrot (n)
cereal (n)
chips (n)
chop (v)
cool (adj)
curry (n)
dairy (n)
dessert (n)
eyesight (n)
flour (n)
heart (n)
honey (n)
leaf/leaves (n)
meal (n)
meat (n)
medicine (n)
menu (n)
mix (v)
peanuts (n)
pickles (n)
pie (n)
plate (n)
pour (v)
salad (n)
salmon (n)
serious (adj)
skin (n)
slice (v, n)
smell (n)
snack (n)
strange (adj)
surprising (adj)
survey (n)
taste (v)
toast (n)
topping (n)
treats (n)
vegetarian (n)

1 Use the wordlist to find these things.
1 six foods which grow on plants above ground
2 three foods which grow under the ground in the soil
3 one food which grows on the ground
4 four things you can add at the table to make food tastier

2 Complete the menu for Tom's birthday meal with words from the wordlist. Then, in pairs, describe your ideal birthday meal.

- Pizza with a mushroom and pineapple topping
- Tomato, green ¹*pepper* and lettuce ²_____ with vinegar and olive ³_____
- Dessert: ice cream (choose from five different ⁴_____: vanilla, milk or dark ⁵_____, strawberry, mango)

3 In pairs, decide if the things below are healthy or unhealthy. Write them in two lists.

chillies chocolate mushrooms nuts oil pear
pineapple sausage sweet potato tuna

4 Read the information in the quiz and identify the food. Then, in pairs, write three clues about other foods from the wordlist. Give your clues to another pair.

What is it? — THE FOOD QUIZ
1
- It is white outside and inside.
- It grows under the ground.
- We use it to make food taste better.

2
- It is red and yellow, or orange outside, and yellow inside.
- It is soft, sweet, round and juicy.
- It has a big seed or 'stone' inside

5 🔊 3.20 **PRONUNCIATION** Listen to how we pronounce the underlined vowel in the words in the table. Write the words below in the correct column.

b<u>a</u>kery   m<u>u</u>shrooms   <u>o</u>lives   <u>o</u>nions
r<u>a</u>w   s<u>a</u>lty   s<u>au</u>sage   t<u>a</u>sty

1 h<u>o</u>t /ɒ/	2 n<u>u</u>ts /ʌ/	3 fl<u>a</u>vour /eɪ/	4 s<u>au</u>ce /ɔː/

6 🔊 3.21 **PRONUNCIATION** Listen, check and repeat.

Revision

Vocabulary

1 Choose the correct option.
1. What's your favourite ice cream *recipe / flavour*? Mine is *melon / olive*.
2. For lunch, I had a *boiled / roasted* egg on toast and a *vinegar / peach*.
3. *Chillies / Seeds* and green *pears / peppers* are vegetables.
4. I can't eat this cereal! It's too *hard / fresh* and the milk tastes *delicious / sour*.

2 Complete the advice with the words below.

add   frozen   ~~full~~   good   healthy
protect   raw   well

Eat right!

Fruit and vegetables are ¹*full* of good things like vitamins A, C and E.

Fresh vegetables taste better than ²_____ ones and are better for you.

Fruit and vegetables make your body strong and help to ³_____ you from illness.

Olives go ⁴_____ with lettuce and other salad vegetables, and they are ⁵_____ as well as tasty.

You can also ⁶_____ some sunflower seeds to your salad. They're really good for you!

Carrots are better for you ⁷_____ than cooked.

Don't put too much sugar on your breakfast cereal – it isn't ⁸_____ for you.

3 Complete the definitions with the correct words.
1. The different things you add when you are cooking are the i*ngredients* .
2. The instructions you follow when you are cooking are the r_____ .
3. S_____ food like chillies has a hot taste.
4. 'S_____' is the opposite of 'sweet'; it's the taste you get from lemons, for example.
5. 'D_____' means 'very tasty', 'great to eat'.

Grammar

4 Complete the dialogues with the words below.

already   ever   ~~just~~   never   yet

1. A: Oh dear! I've *just* broken a glass!
   B: Never mind.
2. A: Have you done your homework _____ ?
   B: I've _____ done Maths. I'm having a break now, before I do the rest.
3. A: Have you _____ been to Australia?
   B: No. I've _____ been outside Europe, actually, but I want to travel more in the future.

5 Complete the sentences with the Present Perfect form of the verbs in brackets and *for* or *since*.
1. I *have known* (know) my best friend _____ six years.
2. I _____ (not eat) anything _____ nine o'clock. I'm hungry!
3. The English teacher _____ (not give) us any homework _____ a few days.
4. The weather _____ (be) great here _____ last Friday.
5. I _____ (be) at this school _____ four years.
6. I _____ (have) my phone _____ March.

6 Rewrite the sentences in Exercise 5 to make them true for you.

7 In pairs, match words from A with words from B to make questions beginning *Have you ever … ?* Write one more question of your own. Then ask and answer the questions.

A   cook   drink   eat   read   visit

B   a cookbook   a meal   mint tea   Italy   sweet potato

Have you ever cooked a meal for your family?

Speaking

8 In pairs, follow the instructions to role play a dialogue at a restaurant. Then swap roles.
- Waiter (Student A): Show the customer a seat and give him/her a menu.
- Customer (Student B): Thank the waiter. Go to page 142, look at the menu and order.
- Waiter: Take the customer's order and ask if he/she would like something else/a drink.
- Customer: Finish your order and thank the waiter.

Dictation

9 🔊 3.22 Listen. Then listen again and write down what you hear.

Unit 3

BBC CULTURE — Fantastic food

POPULAR FOOD IN THE UK

Most people think that food in Britain is all about fish and chips or afternoon tea, but that's not the whole story. There are so many different cultures in the UK that you have a huge choice of flavours and cuisines to choose from.

1 Indian food has been the country's favourite for years. Almost every town has at least one Indian restaurant. A very popular dish is chicken tikka masala, a spicy curry usually served with rice or Indian bread called naan. It's delicious!

2 American food is everywhere. There's not only McDonald's now, but new gourmet burger restaurants like Five Guys. American food is popular because the recipes are very familiar to British people – hot dogs, pepperoni pizza, nachos and BBQ ribs are all big favourites.

3 People have a passion for fresh and healthy food these days, and that's why Japanese food is popular. It's also easy to eat as a takeaway meal. Young people now prefer to eat sushi at lunchtime to the traditional British sandwich, although some still have problems with using chopsticks!

Do you want to try more international food? Then check out the amazing Za Za Bazaar in Bristol! It opened in 2011 and quickly became one of the most popular places to eat in the city. It's also the biggest restaurant in the UK; they can serve over 1,000 people and have food from everywhere – Vietnam, Italy, China, Thailand, as well as Britain's three favourites, of course!

cuisine (n) style of cooking
gourmet (adj) (of food) high-quality

---

1 🔊 3.23 **VISIBLE THINKING** In pairs, follow these steps.

THINK
1 Look at the photo. What can you see? Where do you think you would see this?
2 What do people like eating in your country? What are your favourite dishes?

PUZZLE
3 Why do you think people enjoy eating food from other countries?
4 What do you think is the most popular international food?

EXPLORE
5 Read the article and find out more about international food in Britain. Answer the questions in the PUZZLE section.

2 Read the article again. What are these foods? Write *A* for American, *J* for Japanese or *I* for Indian.
1 curry ___
2 BBQ ribs ___
3 sushi ___
4 naan ___

3 In pairs, discuss the questions.
1 Pizza is an Italian food and nachos are Mexican. Why do you think American food includes pepperoni pizza and nachos?
2 What international food do you like? Is it easy to prepare?
3 What three national dishes from your country would you suggest to a British friend to try? Why?

BBC ▶ Indian food, Liverpool style

4 Look at the photo. What are the women doing?

5 ▶ 18 Watch Part 1 of the video and answer the questions.
1. Who are Anjum and Lynn?
2. What are they doing?
3. What three traditional dishes does Lynn learn how to cook?

6 In pairs, discuss the questions.
1. Do you go to food markets? Why?/Why not?
2. Would you buy food that you have never tasted before for charity? Why?/Why not?

7 ▶ 19 Watch Part 2 of the video. Does Anjum like Lynn's cooking?

8 ▶ 19 Watch the video again and tick (✓) the correct sentences.
1. ☐ Lynn always makes mistakes when cooking.
2. ☐ Lynn's daughter helps her.
3. ☐ Lynn also cooks at the market.
4. ☐ Everyone at the market buys food right from the start.
5. ☐ The food is a little spicy but delicious.

9 In pairs, discuss the questions.
1. Does cooking make people happy in your country?
2. Is it a good idea to cook food for charity?
3. What food would you like to learn to cook?

PROJECT TIME

10 In groups of three, prepare a digital poster of a menu for International Day Celebration at school. Follow these steps.

1 In groups, choose the country whose food will be in your menu. Decide who in your group can find information about the dishes in the menu: a starter, a main dish and a dessert. Find answers to these questions.
- Is the dish served cold or hot?
- Is it spicy, bitter or sweet?
- What ingredients does your dish contain?

2 Individually, prepare your part of the menu for the poster.
- Find information and write your text.
- Find photos to illustrate the information.

3 In your group, create your poster. You can use an online poster maker.
- Import everyone's text and photos.
- Decide on a layout.
- Think of a title for the poster.
- Check and edit the poster.

4 Share your poster with the class.
- Answer other students' questions.
- Look at other posters. Ask questions.

Progress Check Units 1–3

Vocabulary and Grammar

1 Choose the correct option.
1. Eat more fresh fruit. It's really good ___ you.
   a to   b for   c at
2. The weather is ___ boiling! Let's go for a swim.
   a absolutely   b quite   c very
3. You need to ___ a new password to keep your computer and social media safe.
   a do   b change   c set
4. Temperatures are often ___ in the mountains, so take warm clothing when you go there.
   a down   b small   c low
5. North Portugal has a ___ climate most of the year – it doesn't get too hot or cold.
   a weak   b mild   c medium
6. In our family we enjoy driving around the countryside ___ the weekend.
   a at   b in   c to

2 Complete the text with one word in each gap.

One sunny day last year ¹*on* a normal school day, we went outside the classroom for our Science lesson. The teacher took us to a local park full ²_____ trees and flowers. 'Use your eyes to look ³_____ unusual animals or plants and tell us what you find! And listen ⁴_____ the sounds of nature,' she said. While I ⁵_____ looking at an interesting flower, a bird started singing a beautiful song. The teacher told me the bird was called a 'blackcap'. Now the teacher ⁶_____ decided to have more 'nature walks'. We're going to go in spring, summer and autumn: three ⁷_____ a year. That's great!

3 Complete the second sentence with the word in bold so that it means the same as the first one. Use no more than three words.
1. This is the first time I have ever played hockey. **NEVER**
   I *'ve never played* hockey before.
2. I don't eat a lot of food between meals. **AVOID**
   I _____ a lot of food between meals.
3. We've been here since 9.15 and it is now 9.45. **THIRTY**
   We've been here _____ minutes.
4. It was lunchtime for the students when they heard the fire alarm. **HAVING**
   The students _____ lunch when they heard the fire alarm.
5. Nobody knew what to do when we saw a lost dog. **KNOW**
   We _____ what to do when we saw a lost dog.
6. Peter sent you an email a few seconds ago. **JUST**
   Peter _____ you an email.

Speaking

4 Match statements and questions 1–5 with responses a–f. There is one extra response.
1. ☐ I'm sorry I lost your pen.
2. ☐ Are you ready to order?
3. ☐ Why don't we phone and ask for help?
4. ☐ I have a problem with my computer.
5. ☐ Why did you do that?

a That's a good idea.
b Shall I help you?
c I didn't mean to. I'm sorry.
d You're welcome.
e Yes, I'll have a beef burger and chips please.
f Never mind.

5 In pairs, do the speaking task. Go to page 142.

Listening

6 What kind of lunch do you normally eat on school days? How would you change it? Discuss in pairs.

7 🔊 PC1–3.1 Listen to five students talking about lunchtime at their school. Match each speaker with what he/she says. There are two extra statements.
1. ☐ Ali
2. ☐ Sonya
3. ☐ Tim
4. ☐ Ian
5. ☐ Barbara

a sometimes eats meat for lunch.
b likes to eat outside.
c always eats lunch prepared by his/her parents.
d sometimes has simple snacks for lunch.
e gives some of his/her food to other students.
f has already read the menu before lunch.
g doesn't think it's important to eat healthily.

Reading

8 🔊 PC1–3.2 Read the article and choose the correct answer.

Enjoying the outdoors: to tech or not to tech?

We talked to three young people who visit the outdoors to find out what they do with their phones.

Carol

Do I take my phone and tablet? Of course I do! I don't believe that looking at screens is very bad; you can still enjoy nature. As well as looking at birds and flowers, I like doing exciting things. For example, on my last trip we built our own shelter and slept in it. I think friends and family like to see things like this too, so I take photos. I upload some of them and update my story so that people who follow me can see them.

Aron

I quite often go on camping trips with a group of friends who also enjoy the feeling of adventure. Adventure means leaving civilisation behind, including your phone! But enjoying the outdoors is about being safe too. So every time we go on a trip, one of us has to take their phone with a power bank. That way, if we need to phone family about something important, we can. They can message us too if they need to.

Ben

For us, the answer is simple: we switch on our phones when they're helpful. At other times we don't because we might look at the screen and miss seeing a wild animal. Last year we went for an interesting walk through the mountains. We thought we could remember how to get back to our campsite. We were wrong! But we had our phones and they helped us get there.

1. What does Carol say about taking a phone on outdoor trips?
   a It's fine if you don't look at the screen very often.
   b It doesn't stop you enjoying nature.
   c It can help with camping tasks like building shelters.
2. Why does Carol like to upload photos on social media?
   a She wants her friends to see some of the things she enjoyed doing.
   b She wants more people to follow her on social media.
   c She wants to remember how to do outdoor activities in the future.
3. Why do Aron and his friends take a phone with them on their trips?
   a One of Aron's friends does not like to be without his phone.
   b Their families want to connect with them once a day.
   c They can call someone if they need help.
4. What does Ben say about using phones on outdoor trips?
   a Phones can help them to see wildlife.
   b They use phones only when they need them.
   c They leave their phones at the place where they sleep.
5. What problem did a phone help with on one of Ben's trips?
   a They got lost on their way back to their camp.
   b They couldn't find an interesting walk to go on.
   c They didn't know the name of an animal they saw.

9 Read the article again and answer the questions. Use 1–3 words.
1. Where did Carol sleep on her last trip?
2. What other object do Aron and his friends take on their trips, with their phone?
3. How can the families of Aron and his friends contact them?
4. What would Ben and his friends not like to lose the chance of seeing?

Writing

10 Which of these outdoor activities sound interesting? Which one(s) have you tried?
- watching the sunset in the early evening
- cooking on an outdoor fire
- sleeping outside
- camping
- looking for interesting wildlife
- walking in the mountains or a forest
- making your own shelter

11 Write an email to a friend about a holiday when you visited some beautiful places in nature. Include information about:
- what the place was.
- what the weather was like.
- what you did there.
- what you ate there.

Entertain us!

4

VOCABULARY
Types of film | Word building: entertainment | Film and TV | Collocations: music | Compound nouns

GRAMMAR
Comparatives and superlatives, too/(not) enough, (not) as … as | Quantifiers

The *Raj Mandir* cinema, Jaipur, India

MMB MYRA'S MOVIE BLOG

Did you know India is the world's biggest film producer? Read on to find out more.

Indian directors make almost 2,000 films a year – about four times more than the USA. Bollywood, based in Mumbai, is the home of Hindi cinema, but Indians make films in over twenty languages for people that speak them in other regions of the country. Sometimes they make one film in several languages – the same dialogues and locations but different performers.

Indian audiences want entertainment so they love masala films, which are often musicals with spectacular dance scenes. Masala films mix different types, e.g. thriller and romance. A good example is the romantic comedy drama *Monsoon Wedding*, winner of the Golden Lion at the Venice Film Festival.

Indians produce cartoons too. Check out the 3-D animated film *Delhi Safari*! It's fun!

But the biggest hit in Indian film history is a biographical sports drama called *Dangal*. It won several awards including best actor for Aamir Khan and best director for Nitesh Tiwari.

Akshay Kumar, star of over 100 films, including the science fiction action film *2.0*, is one of the world's top five best-paid actors.

Have you seen any Indian films? Leave your comments below.

4.1 Vocabulary

Film and TV

1 What do you know about Bollywood films?

2 Read the blog post and check your ideas. Then, in pairs, answer the questions.
1 What language are Bollywood films made in?
2 How many films do Indian directors make each year?
3 What did *Monsoon Wedding* win?
4 What type of film is *Dangal*?

3 🔊 **4.1** Study Vocabulary box A and say which words are not mentioned in the blog.

VOCABULARY A	Types of film
action cartoon comedy documentary drama musical romance science fiction thriller	

4 What other types of films can you add to Vocabulary box A?

5 🔊 **4.2** Listen and identify the film types.
1 musical
2 _____
3 _____
4 _____
5 _____
6 _____

6 🔊 **4.3** Study Vocabulary box B. Then complete the review below with the correct form of words from the box. The first letter of each word is given. Listen and check.

VOCABULARY B	Word building: entertainment	
Verb	**Noun**	**Person**
act	acting	actor
entertain	entertainment	entertainer
perform	performance	performer
produce	production	producer
review	review	reviewer

Tanhaji: The Unsung Warrior

⭐⭐⭐⭐⭐

An Indian version of *Braveheart*

Based on the true story of a seventeenth-century soldier, *Tanhaji* is an exciting action film that is one of Indian cinema's most successful ¹p<u>roductions</u>. ²R_____ of this film agree that Om Raut knows how to tell a historical story and ³e_____ an audience at the same time. He gets his actors to ⁴p_____ at their very best. Although the ⁵a_____ in general is fantastic, I must mention an absolutely wonderful ⁶p_____ by lead ⁷a_____ Ajay Devgn. The ⁸p_____ and everyone else involved in this film should be proud. It's great ⁹e_____ .

Ajay Devgn

7 🔊 **4.4** Study Vocabulary box C. Choose the correct option to complete the text below. Listen and check.

VOCABULARY C	Film and TV
audience channel character episode hit series special effects TV show viewer	

How TV has changed

In the UK, ¹*viewers / characters* are watching less TV a day than ten years ago, but does this mean they are not watching TV at all? While many Brits still like to watch traditional TV ²*episodes / channels*, the younger ³*audience / viewer* prefers to watch on-demand TV like Netflix or Amazon. The ⁴*hit / series* show Cobra Kai for example, became one of the most watched ⁵*series / episode* on Netflix. The first ⁶*TV show / episode* of the comedy drama, which has no ⁷*hits / special effects* but some great action scenes, was watched by over 48 million households. Not only are people finding different places to watch their favourite ⁸*TV shows / special effects*, but many are watching on different screens too – laptops, tablets and smartphones.

8 In pairs, ask and answer the questions.
1 What kind of TV shows do you prefer?
2 Which TV channels have the best shows?
3 Who is your favourite character from a TV series?
4 What happened in the last episode of your favourite series?
5 Would you like to go on a TV show? Why?/Why not?

VIDEO ▶ **WIDER WORLD**

9 ▶ **20** Watch two people talking about TV series they like. Write down what kind of series it is and why the speakers like it.

10 In pairs, talk about your favourite film or TV series. Use these phrases to help you.
- My favourite film/show is … It's a comedy.
- What's it about? It's about a group of friends.
- Who's in it? … is/are the main actor(s).
- What's it like? It's dramatic/exciting/funny/scary/strange.

My favourite TV series is Anne With an E. It's about a teenage girl with no parents. It's dramatic and exciting and sometimes it's quite funny.

I can talk about films and television.

4.2 Grammar

Comparatives and superlatives, too/(not) enough, (not) as … as

1 Do you prefer watching films at home or at the cinema? Why?

2 🔊 4.5 Read the article quickly and choose the correct option.
   1 Adam, Jessica and Alice watched a film in *3-D / 4-D*.
   2 They watched the film *at home / at the cinema*.

4-D experience

Your seat moves, you feel water on your face and you can smell something. It's the latest 4-D cinema experience. The screens are bigger and the seats are in the most comfortable position for your eyes and neck. But is it fun? 'It's more exciting than 3-D,' said fifteen-year-old Adam, 'because it's brighter and louder.' His friend Jessica agrees. 'The most exciting scene was in the car. I felt like I was driving, but my car wasn't fast enough.' For others, the experience isn't as good as 3-D and you can feel sick.

'The moving seats were worse than the sound!' said Alice. 'I was too uncomfortable.' Some special effects are also scarier in 4-D. Of course, the tickets are also more expensive, but it seems some people are happy to pay for 'the best feeling in the world'!

3 Study the Grammar box. Find more examples of comparatives and superlatives in the text.

GRAMMAR — Comparatives and superlatives, too/(not) enough, (not) as … as

Comparatives
The screens are bigger.   It's more exciting than 3-D.

Superlatives
It's the latest 4-D experience.
The most exciting scene was in the car.
It's the best feeling in the world.

too/(not) enough
I was too uncomfortable.   My car wasn't fast enough.

(not) as … as
The experience isn't as good as 3-D.

GRAMMAR TIME > PAGE 129

4 Complete the sentences with the correct form of the words in brackets.
   1 They filmed the *best* (good) *Doctor Who* episodes in Wales.
   2 It's _____ (cheap) to watch films at home than at the cinema and it's _____ (relaxing).
   3 *Top Gear* is the _____ (funny) show on TV.
   4 The book is often _____ (interesting) than the film.
   5 The _____ (expensive) cinema ticket I bought cost £20.
   6 It can be noisy in the cinema. The _____ (bad) thing is when people keep talking.

5 Complete the second sentence so that it means the same as the first one.
   1 The adults aren't as good as the children in that film.
     The children are *better than* the adults in that film.
   2 Our town isn't big enough for a theatre.
     Our town is _____ for a theatre.
   3 The film is funnier than the book.
     The book isn't _____ the film.
   4 The main character in the film is too boring.
     The main character in the film isn't _____ .
   5 The French thriller isn't as scary as the Danish thriller.
     The Danish thriller is _____ the French thriller.

VIDEO — **WIDER WORLD**

6 ▶ 21 Watch six people talking about entertainment. Make notes about each person's opinion.

7 What's your opinion? Write two sentences for each comparison. Use the adjectives in brackets or your own ideas.
   1 the theatre/the cinema (cheap/exciting)
   2 comedies/documentaries (funny/interesting)
   3 books/films (good/relaxing)

   The cinema is cheaper than the theatre.
   The theatre isn't as exciting as the cinema.

Unit 4 | 52 | I can use the comparative and superlative of adjectives to describe things.

4.3 Reading and Vocabulary
How do you listen to music?

1 How do you get and listen to music? In pairs, make a list.

2 Read the post on a music blog. Which ideas from Exercise 1 does it mention?

What's the best way to listen to music?

The way we listen to music has changed since the days of CDs. Downloading playlists and streaming lip-synch music videos have ¹____ very popular ways to enjoy your favourite music, but there are lots of other options too. I asked friends from my music college for their opinions.

Damon
Damon, a guitarist, doesn't like streaming music playlists or watching ²____ . Instead, he prefers going to live performances. 'Live performances are more exciting than videos and they're very important for musicians. We can ³____ our music with the audience and see their reaction.'

André
André is a singer and he thinks online streaming services are fantastic. 'I'd rather ⁴____ to music on my headphones and sing along to the songs. It's a fun way to practise!' He also says that musicians can find a new audience through the playlists on streaming services. That's a big help when you're starting in the music business.

Carmela
Finally, I find someone who agrees with me that music videos are the best. Carmela is a singer and guitarist, and she explains her reasons. 'I've learned a lot of great lyrics from lip-synching to music videos because you can often see them on your screen.' She says, 'I write my own song lyrics and streaming music videos is a good ⁵____ to study other people's lyrics and learn what works. Most of all, I love making music videos and livestreaming my own songs.'

After I've spoken to everyone, I feel lucky that we have so many different ways to enjoy music. Are music videos the best? Send me your comments.

Next week: What's the best way to get a part in a musical?

3 🔊 4.6 Choose the correct answer to complete the blog post. Listen and check.
1. a grown b become c happened
2. a music videos b songs c radios
3. a make b share c take
4. a sound b hear c listen
5. a idea b time c way

4 Read the blog post again and write D (Damon), A (André) or C (Carmela).
1. ☐ Who thinks you reach different people on streaming services?
2. ☐ Who has similar views to the blogger?
3. ☐ Who plays and instrument and also sings?
4. ☐ Who likes going to concerts?
5. ☐ Who makes his/her own music?

5 🔊 4.7 **WORD FRIENDS** Complete the sentences with the correct form of the verbs from the phrases below. Listen and check.

> download a playlist   go to a live performance
> lip-synch to music videos   livestream an event
> record a track   sing along to songs   stream music
> write lyrics

1. When there's nobody else around, my mum _____ along to songs.
2. The organisers of the popular annual event are _____ it on the internet too.
3. I love music videos, but I also enjoy _____ to live performances.
4. We've booked a studio so we can _____ some new tracks.
5. Yesterday evening I _____ a new playlist.
6. She's always written poems and she sometimes _____ lyrics for singers.
7. I love that app that you can use to _____ to your favourite music videos.
8. I often stream lots of different kinds of _____ that I wouldn't usually listen to.

YOUR WORLD

6 In pairs, tell your partner about some music you listened to this week. What was it? How did you listen to it? Did you like it?

I can understand a post on a music blog.

4.4 Grammar

Quantifiers: *some, any, much, many, (a) few, (a) little, a lot of, lots of*

VIDEO ▶ THE SHORT VIDEO CHALLENGE

Abe: Look, I've got more information about the video challenge. First, it can't be more than three minutes long. Second, there aren't many actors.

Eren: How many actors are there?

Abe: Three. And there are some things we need to include: a song, a postcard and an interview. What do you think, Bea?

Bea: I've got lots of ideas, but I like this one the best: this girl wants to be a star. She's got a lot of style, but she hasn't got any talent. She can't act or sing or …

Abe: Great idea!

Carla: I love it! There are very few people who sing as badly as I do. But I haven't got any clothes for this part. How much money have we got? Can we get a nice dress, for example?

Abe: We haven't got any money, so we can't buy any costumes.

Carla: Oh, and I only have a little make-up. Can I buy some more?

All: No!!!

TAKE 3 VIDEO CHALLENGE

Rules:
1. No more than 3 actors,
2. No more than 3 minutes long,
3. You must include 3 things:
   • a song,
   • a postcard,
   • an interview.

1 Read the poster. What is it about?

2 ▶ 22 ◀)) 4.8 Watch or listen and answer the questions.
1. What are the rules for the film challenge?
2. What kind of person is the character in Bea's idea for the video challenge?
3. What do Abe and Carla think of Bea's idea?
4. Would you like to make a short video? Why?/Why not?

3 Study the Grammar box. Find the sentences in the dialogue. Who says each sentence?

GRAMMAR Quantifiers

Countable nouns	Uncountable nouns
I've got a lot of/lots of ideas. How many actors are there? There aren't many actors.	She's got a lot of/lots of style. How much money have we got? We haven't got much money.
There are some things we need to include. I haven't got any clothes. Have you got any ideas?	I've got some information. She hasn't got any make-up. Have you got any make-up?
I've written down a few things. There are very few people.	I only have a little make-up. We've got very little time.

GRAMMAR TIME ▶ PAGE 129

4 ◀)) 4.9 Read about making a film. Choose the correct option. Listen and check.

You don't need ¹*much / few* money to make a short film. In fact, you probably have ²*any / some* of the things you need at home! With your smartphone and a ³*few / little* imagination you can create a short film in a ⁴*little / few* hours. Ask your friends to be stars – there aren't ⁵*little / many* people who haven't got ⁶*any / many* acting talent. Finally, think about how ⁷*many / much* things around your house you can use – costumes, make-up … and get filming!

5 Complete the sentences with one word in each gap.
1. How *much* time do you think it takes to make a short video?
2. Have you got _____ funny videos on your phone?
3. How _____ films have you seen in the last month?
4. I don't spend _____ time on my phone. Do you?
5. There are only a _____ actors I really like. What about you? Who are they?
6. There's _____ music from films or TV series that everyone knows. Do you agree? Can you think of _____ examples?

YOUR WORLD

6 In pairs, ask and answer the questions in Exercise 5.

Unit 4 54 I can talk about quantities.

4.5 Listening and Vocabulary
The June Festival

1 What's your favourite festival?

2 🔊 4.10 Listen to the first part of an interview with Bruno. Where are his parents from?
   a the USA
   b Portugal
   c Brazil

3 🔊 4.11 Listen to the second part of the interview and choose the correct answer.
   1 Why is the festival special for Bruno?
      a He doesn't have to go to school.
      b He enjoys the winter in Brazil.
      c He likes being with his family.
   2 How are the costumes different now?
      a Girls often wear the same type of clothes as boys.
      b Many boys don't wear checked shirts any more.
      c They don't paint their faces now.
   3 What happens in one funny race?
      a People in the race get a secret message.
      b Runners hold a spoon with an egg in it.
      c The winner gets some fish.
   4 What does the music celebrate?
      a old and young people
      b country life
      c carnival tradition
   5 What is Bruno's favourite food at the festival?
      a corn cake
      b popcorn
      c corn pudding

4 🔊 4.12 Study the Vocabulary box. Make compound nouns from the words below. Listen and check.

cake   clothes   dance   dress   hat   holiday   music   party

VOCABULARY — Compound nouns

Noun	+	noun
family		*holiday, party*
summer		*party*
country		_____
straw		_____
party		_____
carnival		_____
square		_____

5 Write a few sentences to describe a festival or an event. Use the compound nouns from Exercise 4.
Last summer we had a big family party.

YOUR WORLD

6 In pairs, discuss what makes a good festival for you. How important are the things below? Compare your ideas with the class.

☐ carnival music   ☐ cheap tickets
☐ friendly people   ☐ fun games
☐ good entertainment
☐ sunny weather   ☐ tasty food

✗ not important   ✓✓ important
✓ quite important   ✓✓✓ very important

We think fun games are very important for all the family.
We don't think sunny weather is important.

I can understand an interview about a festival.

4.6 Speaking
Talking about preferences

VIDEO ▶ **I'D RATHER NOT DANCE**

Abe: And … action!
Carla: Hello, I'm Gloria and I want to be a star!
Bea: Sit down, Gloria. You're in the right place.
Eren: I'm Van Dixon, agent to the stars. The most successful agent in the UK. Now, do you want to be a theatre actor?
Carla: No, I'd rather not perform on the stage.
Eren: Would you rather work in film or TV?
Carla: No, I'm too shy to be an actor. I'd rather work in the music business.
Eren: Fantastic! What instrument do you play?
Carla: Well, I played the triangle in the school orchestra.
Eren: Hmm, there aren't many big stars who play the triangle. Can you sing? Why don't you sing this song for me?
Carla: I'd prefer to sing a different song if that's all right.
Eren: Which song would you prefer to sing?
Carla: *All By Myself*. It suits my voice much better.
Eren: OK, please sing the song.
Carla: 'All by myself in the morning … '
Eren: I don't think singing is your special talent. Wouldn't you rather do something else? Perhaps dancing?
Carla: I'd rather not dance, but I can show you a trick.
Eren: Sure. Show me a trick that's better than your singing and you can have the job!

Carla: Great! Well, I can read your mind. I know the next word you're going to say. Do you know what word is on this card?
Eren: No, I don't know. Ha ha, well done!
Abe: Cut!

SOUNDS GOOD! You're in the right place. • I can read your mind.

1 What do you like doing with your friends? Choose two of the things below and say which one is better.

> doing dance classes   eating out   listening to music
> performing on stage together   playing games

I think eating out is better than doing dance classes.

2 ▶ 23 ◀) 4.13 Look at the photo. What can you guess about Eren and Carla's characters? Watch or listen and check.

3 Is Carla's character clear about her career plans? How does Eren's character help her?

SET FOR LIFE

4 Have you thought about your future career? Discuss in pairs. Think about:
- your dreams
- your skills, interests and hobbies
- how you can learn about your strong and weak points

5 Study the Speaking box. Find examples of the phrases in the dialogue. What reasons does Carla give for her preferences?

SPEAKING Talking about preferences

Asking about preferences
(What) would you rather + verb?
(What) would you prefer to + verb?

Expressing preferences
I'd rather (not) + verb   I'd prefer (not) to + verb

Giving reasons
It sounds funny/great/boring.
It looks good.   It's healthier.

YOUR WORLD

6 Make questions from the prompts below. Then, in pairs, ask and answer the questions.
1 you / rather / do / tonight / ? (stay in/go out)
A: *What would you rather do tonight?*
B: *I'd rather stay in.*
2 you / prefer / watch / ? (a film/a sports programme)
3 you / rather / be / ? (an actor/a director)
4 you prefer / go / after school / ? (home/to a festival)
5 you rather / learn / ? (singing/a musical instrument)

Unit 4   56   I can talk about preferences.

4.7 Writing

A review on a blog

TRENT'S THEATRE BLOG

MY LATEST REVIEW

BACK TO THE FUTURE THE MUSICAL
the Manchester Opera House

1. I've just seen a wonderful new musical that took me back to the past. It's *Back to the Future*.

2. The musical is based on the well-known 1985 Hollywood movie. It tells the story of a teenager (Marty McFly) who travels back in time to the 1950s with a crazy scientist, Doc Brown. In order to save his life, he has to work fast to make his parents fall in love before he can go back to the future.

3. The special effects with the time-travelling car are amazing, the dance routines are fantastic, the musicians play their instruments really well and the songs are incredibly catchy. Lots of people in the audience were singing along happily. All the actors perform brilliantly, but Olly Dobson as Marty is particularly good.

4. I love the film, but the musical is even better. Time flies in *Back to the Future* – it's over before you know it. Go and see it; it's the best show in town.

5. What's the best play you've seen recently? Write about it below.

---

1 Have you ever seen a play or musical at the theatre? What was it like?

2 Read the review quickly and answer the questions.
1 What is the play about?
2 Does the reviewer tell us the whole story?
3 How good are the performers?

3 Study the Writing box. Find examples of the phrases in the review.

WRITING ▶ A review on a blog

1 **Start your review**
Today I'm going to tell you about …   You must see …
I've just seen a wonderful new musical.
It's the latest new film/play/book …

2 **Describe the story**
The play is based on a movie/book …
It tells the story of a teenager who …
The story is about a girl who …

3 **Describe the performance**
The special effects are amazing.
All the actors perform brilliantly.
A few people were crying quietly.

4 **End your review**
I really love the film, but the musical is even better.
I highly recommend this show.
It's the best show in town.

5 **End your blog post**
What's the best play you've seen recently? Write about it below.

---

4 Which other phrases from the review could you add to part 3 of the Writing box?

5 Study the Language box. Find examples of adverbs in the review. Then use adverbs to talk or write about films or live performances you have seen.

LANGUAGE ▶ Adverbs

Adverbs come **after** a verb or subject
All the actors performed brilliantly.

or **before** an adjective or adverb.
She sang really well.

WRITING TIME

6 Write an online review of a film or a live performance.

1 **Find ideas**
Make notes for a review.
• Where and when did you see it?
• What was it about?
• What's your opinion about the performance/performers?

2 **Plan**
Organise your ideas into paragraphs. Use the review in Exercise 2 to help you.

3 **Write and share**
• Write a draft review. Use the Language box and the Writing box to help you.
• Share your review with another student for feedback.
• Use the feedback from your partner and write the final version of your review.

4 **Check**
• Check language: don't forget to use adjectives and adverbs.
• Check grammar: did you use comparatives, superlatives and quantifiers correctly?

I can write a review on a blog.

Vocabulary Activator

WORDLIST 🔊 4.14

Types of film
action (n)
cartoon (n)
comedy (n)
documentary (n)
drama (n)
musical (n)
romance (n)
science fiction (n)
thriller (n)

Word building (entertainment)
act (v)
acting (n)
actor (n)
entertain (v)
entertainer (n)
entertainment (n)
perform (v)
performance (n)
performer (n)
produce (v)
producer (n)
production (n)
review (v, n)
reviewer (n)

Film and TV
audience (n)
channel (n)
character (n)
episode (n)
hit (n)
series (n)
special effects (n)
TV show (n)
viewer (n)

Word friends (music)
download a playlist
go to a live performance
lip-synch to music videos
livestream an event
record a track
sing along to songs
stream music
write lyrics

Compound nouns
carnival dress (n)
country music (n)
family holiday (n)
family party (n)
party dress (n)
square dance (n)
straw hat (n)
summer holiday (n)

Extra words
4-D experience (n)
album (n)
animated film (n)
based on (adj)
biographical (adj)
carnival (n)
celebrate (v)
challenge (n)
check out (v)
collect (v)
costume (n)
dialogue (n)
dramatic (adj)
drummer (n)
exciting (adj)
fantastic (adj)
film festival (n)
get a part
guitarist (n)
headphones (n)
interview (n)
location (n)
main character (n)
make-up (n)
musician (n)
old-fashioned (adj)
personal (adj)
programme (n)
proud (adj)
radio station (n)
reaction (n)
record player (n)
romantic comedy (n)
scary (adj)
scene (n)
seat (n)
spectacular (adj)
stage (n)
star (n)
style (n)
successful (adj)
talent (n)
theatre (n)
voice (n)
wonderful (adj)

1 Use the wordlist to find these things.
  1 six words for people that end in *-er*
  2 five verbs about things you do when you work in film
  3 two types of film that can make you laugh

2 Choose the correct option. Then tick (✓) the sentences that are true for you. In pairs, compare your answers.
  1 ☐ I like going to live *performers / performances*.
  2 ☐ I read *reviews / reviewers* of films.
  3 ☐ I watch a lot of *special effects / series*.
  4 ☐ I sing along *at / to* songs.
  5 ☐ I'd like to take part in a TV *channel / show*.

3 In what type of film might you hear each of these lines?

  I love you. I've always loved you. Marry me!
  1 _____

  Put your hands up and lie face down!
  2 _____

  This is a rare animal that you can only see in this part of Africa.
  3 _____

  There is life here, but not the kind we know on Earth.
  4 _____

4 In pairs, talk about the types of film you prefer.

5 Choose the odd one out.
  1 episode   viewer   channel   audience
  2 voice   lyrics   actor   song
  3 musician   producer   thriller   entertainer
  4 musical   drama   romance   viewer

6 🔊 4.15 **PRONUNCIATION** Listen to the words below and write them in the correct column according to the word stress.

~~audience~~   character   comedy   performance   producer   production   reviewer   theatre

1 Ooo	2 oOo
audience	

7 🔊 4.16 **PRONUNCIATION** Listen to the first word from Exercise 6 again. The underlined sound is a weak sound (/ə/). Listen to the rest of the words again and underline all the weak /ə/ sounds.
  aud<u>ie</u>nce

Revision

Vocabulary

1 Complete the sentences with words formed from the words in brackets.

WHAT MAKES A GOOD FILM?

1. ☐ The director knows how to get the best _performance_ (perform) from the film stars.
2. ☐ The _____ (act) is good.
3. ☐ The _____ (act) are famous.
4. ☐ The _____ (produce) spends a lot of money on the film.
5. ☐ The film gets good _____ (review) from most _____ (review).

2 Put the sentences in exercise 1 in order of importance for you (1 = most important). Then, in pairs, compare your answers.

3 Complete the compound nouns in the sentences with the words below.

> country   dress   family   holiday   ~~party~~
> square   straw

1. We need to help Gina choose a _party_ dress for her 18th birthday party.
2. The summer _____ begins in a few weeks when the spring school term ends.
3. We have a _____ party every Saturday when I see my grandparents, uncles and aunts.
4. In a _____ dance, dancing partners stand on four sides looking to the middle.
5. The carnival _____ that people are wearing often tells you about what they are celebrating.
6. I like _____ music: I like the sound of banjos and guitars.
7. Wear a _____ hat because it will keep your head cool and go with your clothes!

4 Write the correct word for each definition.
1. A type of film that has a lot of songs in it. _musical_
2. A selection of songs for a particular purpose, or that you most enjoy listening to. _____
3. The people who watch or listen to a film, play, concert, etc. _____
4. You change this on your TV to watch a different programme. _____
5. Play video or sound on your computer directly from the internet. _____

Grammar

5 Complete the sentences with one word in each gap. Then, in pairs, say if you agree or disagree.
1. Some films just aren't funny _enough_ to be called comedies – they should be called something else.
2. Musicals are better _____ science fiction films.
3. Animated films are _____ best kind of film.
4. The seats in the back of the cinema aren't _____ good as the ones at the front.
5. One-hour TV documentaries are _____ long for me to watch – I get bored at the end.
6. Action films are _____ exciting than comedies.

6 Complete the sentences to show your opinion. Use the superlative form of the adjectives in brackets.
1. _Salads are the healthiest_ (healthy) kind of food.
2. _____ (good) kind of TV show.
3. _____ (easy) musical instrument to learn.
4. Documentaries about _____ (interesting) ones.
5. _____ (difficult) job in film-making.

7 Complete the dialogue with the words below.

> any   few   little   lot   ~~lots~~   many   much (x2)   some

Jo: Come on! Let's go and see this film tonight. It had ¹_lots_ of good reviews.
Ian: When does it start? We need a ²_____ time to get ready.
Jo: 8 p.m. We've got a ³_____ of time. How ⁴_____ tickets do we need?
Ian: Four. Can you get them at the front?
Jo: No, there aren't ⁵_____ seats left at the front.
Ian: How ⁶_____ money do we need, with drinks and maybe a ⁷_____ snacks?
Jo: Not ⁸_____. I think ten pounds each should be enough for everything.
Ian: Hmm… I'll need to ask my mum for ⁹_____ money, then. I've only got six pounds!

Speaking

8 In pairs, follow the instructions to role play a dialogue. Then swap roles.

You want to watch a film together. Decide what to watch.
- Student A: Ask Student B about his/her preference.
- Student B: Express your preference.
- Student A: Ask why.
- Student B: Give reasons for your preference.

Dictation

9 🔊 4.17 Listen. Then listen again and write down what you hear.

SET FOR LIFE

Team up!

SCHOOL CHARITY EVENT

We need volunteers!

Do you want to help us to raise money for charity?

- We're planning this year's school charity event and we need your help.
- If you're interested, please write and tell us about your personality, skills and interests.

Layla, Connor, Tessie and Ed
Charity Team Leaders

✉

Dear Charity Team Leaders,

Well done for your posters. I hope you've got lots of volunteers now.

How is your other planning going? Have you chosen the type of event yet? Remember, you can hold it either on the sports field or in the school hall. And you'll need to start thinking about the jobs that you want your volunteers to do. You are leading the team!

Please let me know your plans.

Yours,

Mr Hussein

Head Teacher

---

charity video games competition

charity concert    charity cake sale

charity fashion show

1 Work in pairs. Have you ever been to the types of event in the photos? Would you like to go to one? Why?/Why not?

2 Read the advert and email. What does the charity team have to do?

3 In pairs, answer the questions about the events in the photos.
  1 How can these events raise money for charity?
  2 What are the advantages and disadvantages of each type of event?

4 🔊 4.18 Listen to the first part of the charity team meeting. Which event do they choose? Do they mention any of your ideas from Exercise 3?

5 🔊 4.19 Listen to another part of the meeting. Answer the questions with the names below.

Connor and Stanley   David   Ed and Lucy   Tessie

  1 Who will print and sell the tickets?
  2 Who will invite the bands?
  3 Who will design tickets and prepare the sports field?
  4 Who will move the tables and equipment?

6 Why do they think these are the right people for the jobs?

Units 3–4   60   I can lead a team of people.

7 🔊 4.19 Study the Useful Phrases box. Listen again and tick (✓) the expressions you hear in the second part of the meeting.

8 You are organising a charity fashion show. In pairs, discuss which job is the most suitable for each volunteer.

I think that's a good job for … because …

JOBS LIST

Before the event
1. encourage local shops to lend clothes for the show
2. advertise the event
3. design and sell tickets
4. move furniture to prepare the hall

During the event
5. announce each clothes design to the audience
6. help the models change clothes and do hair and make-up – at least two people

After the event

LIST OF VOLUNTEERS

Mia: 'I'm confident, polite and organised. I want to have my own business one day.'

Adi: 'I'm very friendly and confident. I love to make people laugh. I'm good at Maths.'

Alfie: 'I'm very kind and helpful. I'm good at swimming and I love video games.'

Sairi: 'I'm friendly and I'm good at making people feel more confident. I'm good at doing make-up, and arts and crafts too.'

Rachel: 'I'm creative and good with technology, but I'm quite shy. I can design websites.'

Will: 'I write a blog about everything from fashion to food. I like to be a leader, but I can be a bit bossy sometimes!'

9 Read the Useful Tips. In pairs, discuss the questions.
1. Do you think it's easy to be a good leader? Why?/Why not?
2. Would you like to be the leader of a team or group? Why?/Why not?
3. Why do you think it is a good idea to vote on decisions?

SET FOR LIFE

10 In small groups, plan a charity event. Follow these steps.

1. Vote on which charity event to organise and who or what to raise money for.
2. Decide on a jobs list with tasks to do before, during and after the event.
3. Match volunteers with the tasks. Remember to consider their skills, strengths and interests.
4. Present your plan for the charity event to the class.

Lead a team

USEFUL TIPS

When you are leading a team of people, it's important to think carefully about how you work together.

- Vote to make team decisions.
- Remember that you can't do everything yourself.
- Spread the jobs fairly between the people in the team.
- Explain clearly what you want people to do.
- Encourage people and thank them for their ideas.

USEFUL PHRASES

Choosing an event
- ☐ I love the idea of a …
- ☐ … is probably (not) the best way to make a lot of money for charity.
- ☐ Let's vote. Who votes for a … ?

Giving the right job to the right person
- ☐ People who … are usually good at …-ing.
- ☐ I think creative/shy/funny people enjoy that kind of job.
- ☐ We need creative/strong/confident people to …
- ☐ Can … print … ?
- ☐ Who can we ask to … ?
- ☐ Let's ask … to …

To the limit

5

VOCABULARY
Sports equipment | Sporting events | Sports collocations | Fitness and training | Word building: sport

GRAMMAR
Future forms: *will, be going to*, Present Continuous and Present Simple | First Conditional with *if* and *unless*

Four amazing sporting records

1 Surfing
Standing on a surfboard is difficult enough normally, but in 2013 American Bernie Boehm surfed for thirty-three seconds while spinning a basketball on one finger!

2 Athletics
In 2008 German Christopher Irmscher ran 100 metres along a running track and jumped over ten hurdles. It took him 14.82 seconds. That's not fast. That's because he was wearing flippers on his feet instead of trainers, and a mask and snorkel on his head! How strange!

3 Cycling
In 2013 another German, Jens Stotzner went cycling ... underwater! He rode his bike around the bottom of a swimming pool seventy-eight times – a distance of 6.708 kilometres! I wonder if he was wearing a helmet!

4 Ice hockey
In 2008, the Slovakian women's ice hockey team beat Bulgaria. They won the match very easily, scoring a goal every forty-four seconds! On the electronic scoreboard, the final score was 82–0!

5.1 Vocabulary

Sport

1 I KNOW! Add as many sports as you can to these groups.
1 indoor sports: *table tennis, …*
2 outdoor sports: *running, …*
3 team sports: *football, …*
4 individual sports: *jogging, …*
5 water sports: *swimming, …*
6 winter sports: *skiing, …*

2 🔊 5.1 Study Vocabulary box A. Which of the things in the box can you see in photos A–C?

VOCABULARY A Sports equipment

basketball bat flippers football kit helmet
life jacket mask mat net racket skateboard
skates skis snorkel snowboard surfboard

3 Answer the quiz questions with words from Vocabulary box A. What sports do you do? What equipment do you use? In pairs, compare your answers and discuss the questions.

Test your sports knowledge

1. What do you hit a baseball or a cricket ball with?
2. What do you wear on your head to protect you when you go cycling?
3. What do you wear when you go kayaking or sailing to keep you safe?
4. What equipment do you need to do snorkeling?
5. What can you put on the floor to make yoga exercises more comfortable?
6. What two things do you need to play badminton or tennis?
7. What can you use to ride the waves on the sea?

4 Read the article quickly. Find all the items of sports equipment it mentions.

5 Read the article again and answer the questions. In pairs, compare your answers.
1. Which record do you think is the most amazing?
2. Which is your favourite? Why?
3. What other sporting records do you know?

6 5.2 Listen to a radio interview. According to Sandi, which two sports are NOT Olympic sports?

7 5.3 Study Vocabulary box B. Complete the blog post below with words from the box in the correct form. Listen and check.

VOCABULARY B — Sporting events

changing room   court   fan   opponent   pitch
scoreboard   stadium   tournament   track

8 5.4 **WORD FRIENDS** Complete the phrases with the words below. Listen and check.

beat   goal   medal   record   take part
take up   team   ~~volunteer~~

1. *volunteer* at a sports event/club
2. _____ in a race/competition
3. _____ a sport
4. win a _____/game/match
5. break/hold a _____
6. score a _____
7. support a _____
8. _____ a team/an opponent

YOUR WORLD

9 In pairs, ask and answer the questions.
1. Do you prefer team sports or individual sports? Why?
2. What is your favourite sporting event to watch on TV?
3. What sport would you like to take up in the future?

My greatest sporting success

My greatest sporting success didn't take place on a running ¹*track* in a big ²_____ . It was on the tennis ³_____ behind my school last June. It was the first game in a tennis ⁴_____ . I didn't feel nervous as I took my kit out of my bag in the ⁵_____ rooms. Nobody expected me to win, not even me. (I'm not very good at tennis.) But that day I played brilliantly. My racket felt like part of my arm. Almost every ball I hit went flying over the net. My ⁶_____ didn't know what to do. I won the match easily. The final score was 6–1, 6–2. I've never played so well since then!

I can talk about sports equipment and sporting events.

5.2 Grammar

Future forms: *will*, *be going to*, Present Continuous, Present Simple

VIDEO ▶ **THE FITNESS CLASS**

Bea: You're wet.
Abe: It's raining. I'm doing the 5K Fun Run next month, so I need to train or I won't be able to finish. But they say it's going to rain all week.
Bea: Are you really going to run five kilometres? It's hard. Carla's coming round to do our fitness class. It starts in ten minutes. Do you want to do it with us?
Abe: Fitness class? Will that help me run 5K?
Bea: Yes, it will. Come on, you'll enjoy it!
Abe: OK, I'll do it.
Later …
Bea: Right, this is going to be fun. First, skipping.
Abe: I can't do it!
Bea: I'll show you.
Carla: Maybe you'll do better with this.
Abe: I'll fall off.

Carla: No, you won't. Oh!
Bea: OK, I'm sure you'll manage this.
Abe: This is tough. This is going to kill me!
Bea: Abe! What are you doing?
Abe: I'm going home. And you know what? I'm never going to complain about running in the rain again!

1 In groups, ask and answer the questions.
1 What do you do to keep fit?
2 Is it better to go to a gym to keep fit or to exercise at home? Why?

2 ▶ 24 ◀)) 5.5 Watch or listen and answer the questions.
1 Why is Abe unhappy?
2 What's Bea's suggestion?
3 How easy does Abe find the class?

3 Study the Grammar box. Find all the examples of future forms in the dialogue.

GRAMMAR ▶ **Future forms**

Predictions or decisions made at the moment of speaking
I'll do it!
I won't be able to finish.
Will that help me run 5K? Yes, it will.

Plans and predictions based on things we know now
It's going to rain all week.
Are you really going to run five kilometres?

Arrangements
I'm doing the 5K Fun Run next month.

Timetables
It starts in ten minutes.

GRAMMAR TIME ▶ PAGE 130

4 Complete the sentences with the correct form of the verbs in brackets. Use the future form in bold.
1 Over 200 people *are going to take* (take) part in the 5K charity run. **be going to**
2 The run _____ (start) at 10 a.m. tomorrow. **Present Simple**
3 I'm sure I _____ (not win) the race. **will**
4 What _____ (we/do) after the run? **be going to**
5 We _____ (have) a picnic in the park. **Present Continuous**
6 I _____ (bring) some crisps and juice. **will**

5 ◀)) 5.6 Choose the best option. Listen and check.
A: What ¹*are you doing / do you do* tomorrow morning?
B: I don't know. ²*I / I'll* probably just stay in. Why?
A: I've decided ³*I'll / I'm going to* get fit this summer, so ⁴*I'll take / I'm taking* part in a new fitness class in the park. It's ⁵*being / going to be* great. Why don't you come?
B: What time ⁶*does it / is it going to* start?
A: ⁷*It's starting / It starts* at 8 o'clock, but ⁸*I'll / I'm going to* try to get there ten minutes early.
B: OK, ⁹*I'll try / I'm trying* it.
A: Great! ¹⁰*I / I'll* see you there!

YOUR WORLD

6 Complete the sentences to make them true for you.
1 I think I'll … this evening.
2 When I'm fifty, I won't …
3 Next weekend I'm going to …
4 My best friend is never going to …
5 My football team is playing …
6 This year the school holidays begin …

Unit 5 — I can talk about plans, predictions, arrangements and timetables.

5.3 Reading and Vocabulary
Sports and hobbies

Competitive sport or just a hobby?

We talked to three teenagers about how they train and how seriously they take their sports.

Carrie, 14 – rhythmic gymnastics

I go to the gym twice a week. My coach says it's really important to warm up, so we do lots of exercises before the class: we stretch and jump and jog. Then we practise the different techniques. I prefer working with the ribbon. Afterwards, we warm down to some relaxing music. I love rhythmic gymnastics, but I don't think I'll ever take part in any serious competitions. I just do it for fun and to keep fit. But I'm going to volunteer at the next big competition.

Ryan, 16 – ice hockey

You have to be fit to play ice hockey, so I work out at a local gym most days to build up strength in my legs and body. Being fit and strong helps you keep your balance when you're on the ice. I watch a lot of games on my computer to learn new skills and I practise with my team at the ice rink three times a week. My dad's our coach. He's a volunteer, not a professional, but he's really good. I'm never going to take up ice hockey professionally, but it's a great hobby.

Suzy, 15 – triathlon

In a youth triathlon competition, you have to swim 750 metres, cycle 20 kilometres and run 5 kilometres. So, you have to train very seriously. I'm going to follow a new training programme from next week. My mum's a doctor. She says that at my age, you shouldn't train more than twenty hours a week, so I'm going to swim two kilometres three times a week, go running on Tuesdays, Thursdays and Saturdays, and cycle every Sunday for three hours. That's eighteen hours. Maybe one day I'll be good enough to compete in the Olympics. I hope so!

1 In which sports do athletes train the hardest, in your opinion?

2 🔊 5.7 Work in pairs. Look at the photos and read the article quickly. Have you tried any of these sports? If not, which would you like to try?

3 Read the article again, and write C (Carrie), R (Ryan) or S (Suzy).
1. ☐ Who follows his/her sport online to get better?
2. ☐ Who mentions a favourite piece of equipment?
3. ☐ Who trains with a family member?
4. ☐ Who would like to get involved in competitive sport?
5. ☐ Who mentions how training starts and finishes?
6. ☐ Whose coach warns younger people not to train too much?

4 🔊 5.8 Study the Vocabulary box and find the words in the article. Then complete the sentences below with the correct form of words from the box. Listen and check.

VOCABULARY — Fitness and training

balance   coach   exercise   practise   skill
strength   stretch   training programme
warm up/down   work out

1. I find it easy to learn new *skills*.
2. I'm good at keeping my _____ .
3. I get bored if I have to _____ a sport a lot.
4. I've never had a personal fitness _____ or followed a _____ .
5. I think it's important to _____ up before you jog or do _____ .
6. I think I'll start going to a gym so I can _____ out and build up my _____ .

5 In pairs, say if the sentences in Exercise 5 are true for you.

VIDEO — WIDER WORLD

6 ▶ 25 Watch four people talking about volunteering at a sports event. What reason(s) does each speaker give for wanting to be a volunteer?

7 In pairs, say what sports event you would like to volunteer at and why.

I would like to volunteer at a rhythmic gymnastics event because I love watching it and I'd like to get free tickets.

I can understand an article about fitness and training.

5.4 Grammar

First Conditional with *if* and *unless*

SLACKLINING CLUB

Have you ever thought of slacklining? If you like gymnastics, you'll love this modern sport! The only equipment you need is a simple rope, or 'line', about five centimetres wide. You start with a very low line, about fifty centimetres above the ground. If you fall, you won't hurt yourself and if you improve, you will soon try some new tricks. You can do slacklining anywhere, but you need a tree or something strong to fix each end of the line.

Are you a climber, a surfer or a skateboarder? Slacklining can help your balance. Also, if you don't enjoy team sports, this will be a good choice for you. So, if you want to try something different, come along.

Our club is free!

Will you be a champion slackliner? You won't know unless you try!

WHERE? Baxter's Park   **WHEN?** Saturdays, 10 a.m.

---

1 Look at the photo in the advert. What is the girl doing? Use the words below to help you. Do you think you can do this activity? Why?/Why not?

> balance   fall   jump   rope   walk

2 🔊 5.9 Read the advert. What is a slackline?

3 Study the Grammar box. Find more examples of the First Conditional in the advert.

> **GRAMMAR** — **First Conditional with *if* and *unless***
>
> You won't know **if** you **don't try**!
> You won't know **unless** you **try**!
>
> Time clauses with *when* follow a similar pattern.
> **When** I'm back home, I'll watch some slacklining videos.

GRAMMAR TIME > PAGE 130

4 Match the sentence halves.
1. ☐ If you do slacklining,
2. ☐ You won't do any special tricks
3. ☐ I won't go to the slacklining club
4. ☐ You'll see people slacklining

a unless you're very good.
b if you go to the park on Saturday.
c you will improve your balance.
d unless a friend comes too.

5 🔊 5.10 Read the information and complete the sentences below with the correct form of the verbs in brackets. Listen and check.

> **Goodbye to the sports centre!**
> The old Riverside Sports Centre is closing next week. The new sports centre, with a large pool, tennis courts and a modern gym, won't be ready until next year.

1. If they *close* (close) the sports centre, we _____ (not be) able to play handball for ages.
2. I _____ (not stop) playing badminton if they _____ (close) it.
3. We _____ (not have) karate lessons unless the teacher _____ (find) a new classroom.
4. I _____ (go) swimming every week if they _____ (build) a pool at the new centre.
5. If there _____ (be) tennis courts, I _____ (take up) tennis.
6. We _____ (join) the new gym if it _____ (not be) too expensive.

VIDEO **WIDER WORLD**

6 ▶ 26 Watch four people talking about different situations. How do they complete the sentences below?
1. If there's a new sports centre in town, …
2. If my friends are free this evening, …
3. If I get some money for my birthday, …

7 Finish the sentences in Exercise 6 to make them true for you. In pairs, discuss your ideas.

Unit 5   I can use the First Conditional to talk about possible situations in the future.

5.5 Listening and Vocabulary
A fascinating footballer

1. Who is your favourite sportsperson? Why?

2. Read the fact file and mark the sentences T (true) or F (false).
   1. ☐ The Sports Personality Award is over sixty years old.
   2. ☐ You must be British to win the award.
   3. ☐ Nobody has won the award more than once.

FACT BOX

The BBC Sports Personality of the Year Award

Every December since 1954 the British public have chosen their sports personality of the year. He or she is the sportsperson that has achieved the most in that year. The winner must be British or live and play sport in the UK. Tennis player Andy Murray is the only person who has won the award three times.

3. What do you think sportspeople have to do to get a nomination for Sports Personality of the Year Award?

4. 🔊 5.11 You will hear two friends talking about the Sports Personality of the Year Award. Listen and choose the correct answer for each question.
   1. Callum thinks Marcus Rashford is
      a. the best sportsperson in the UK.
      b. the best English football player.
      c. not as good as another player.
   2. When Marcus Rashford plays for Manchester United, he wears the number
      a. seven.   b. ten.   c. eleven.
   3. Megan thinks the winner of the BBC award should be
      a. the best athlete.   b. the top goalscorer.
      c. the best person.
   4. How many free meals did Marcus Rashford's charity pay for?
      a. 20 million   b. 3 million   c. 400,000
   5. Marcus Rashford
      a. can understand sign language.
      b. studies at university.
      c. writes for a magazine.

5. 🔊 5.12 Study the Vocabulary box. Then look at the sentences below and decide if each underlined word is a verb, a noun for an action or a noun for a person.

VOCABULARY   Word building: sport

Verb	Noun (action)	Noun (person)
attack	attack	attacker
support	support	supporter
score	score	scorer
defend	defence	defender
manage	management	manager
train	training	trainer
coach	coaching	coach
practise	practice	–

1. He scored two goals in his first match.
2. The supporters want their team to attack more.
3. There's no football practice today because of the snow.
4. Our new coach makes us train very hard.
5. They lost 5-0 so their manager wasn't happy with the defence.

6. Complete the table.

Verb	Noun (action)	Noun (person)
kick	1_____	–
play	–	2_____
present	–	3_____
race	4_____	–
win	5_____	6_____

7. 🔊 5.13 Complete the text with the correct form of words from Exercises 5 and 6. The first letter of each word is given. Listen and check.

5–0! That's a great ¹w__in__, isn't it? I'm not surprised our ²s_____ are singing. I'm delighted with the ³p_____ . I always tell them that ⁴p_____ makes perfect and I've got to say they've been great in ⁵t_____ all week. Our ⁶d_____ didn't have much to do today because our ⁷a_____ were so good. They ⁸s_____ some great goals. I'm so lucky to be their ⁹m_____ !

YOUR WORLD

8. Imagine you are going to vote for a Sports Personality of the Year. In groups of four, decide on three people. Share your ideas with the class, defending your choices. Then vote to decide.

I can understand a conversation about sports personalities.

5.6 Speaking
Talking about plans

VIDEO ▶ **WHAT ARE YOU UP TO TODAY?**

Eren: Guys, what are you doing next Saturday?
Abe: Nothing special. I don't have any plans.
Eren: Have you got any plans, Bea?
Bea: I don't think so.
Eren: What about you, Carla? What are your plans?
Carla: I don't know yet. Why?
Eren: I'm playing an important tennis match at 3 p.m. If you guys don't come, I won't have any fans. Can you make it?
All: Sure!/Yeah!/ Maybe.

Later …
Carla: I'm sorry, Eren, but I won't be able to come on Saturday. We're visiting my grandma …

Bea: Look, I'm so sorry. I'm going to help a friend paint her room on Saturday. And then we're going to the cinema.

Abe: Hey, Eren. What are you up to today?
Eren: I'm training for the tennis match.
Abe: Oh yeah, about that … I won't be able to make it. I'm going to a soccer match with my dad.

On Saturday …
Eren: What are you guys doing here?
Abe: We changed our plans!

SOUNDS GOOD! • Nothing special. • Can you make it?

1 In pairs, describe the photo. Why do you think the kids are at the tennis court? How does Eren feel?

2 ▶ 27 🔊 5.14 Watch or listen and check your answers to Exercise 1. Then match the people (1–4) with the plans they had (a–d).
1 ☐ Abe 2 ☐ Bea 3 ☐ Carla 4 ☐ Eren
a hang out with a friend
b play a sports match
c spend time with his/her family
d watch a sport event

SET FOR LIFE

3 In pairs, talk about a time in your life when you changed your plans for someone or when they changed their plans for you. Then decide on good reasons for changing your plans.

4 Study the Speaking box and read the dialogue again. Who says each sentence in the box?

SPEAKING Talking about plans

Asking
What are you up to today/at the weekend?
Have you got any plans for this evening/tomorrow?
What are you doing on Sunday/next Saturday?

Answering and following up
I'm/We're visiting my grandma/going to the cinema.
First I'm going to a soccer match …
I'm going to help …
Then …   After that …   Later …
I don't have any plans.   I don't know yet.
What about you?   And you?   What are your plans?

5 🔊 5.15 Put the dialogue in the correct order. Use the Speaking box to help you. Listen and check.
a ☐ Sam: Yes, that's a great idea.
b ☐ 1 Sam: What are you up to this weekend?
c ☐ Tara: Sunday? Well, I'm definitely going to have a lie-in. Then I'll probably do some homework. Have you got any plans?
d ☐ Tara: Well, first I'm visiting my aunt on Saturday morning. Then we're going to an ice hockey match. It starts at 3 p.m.
e ☐ Sam: Sounds good. What are you doing on Sunday?
f ☐ Tara: Do you want to go cycling?
g ☐ Sam: I don't know yet. Nothing special.

YOUR WORLD

6 In pairs, ask and answer questions about your plans for the weekend. Use these ideas to help you.
• sports and activities   • shopping
• family and friends   • relaxation
• homework   • entertainment
• trips   • special events

7 Tell the class about your partner's plans.

Unit 5 68 I can ask and talk about plans.

5.7 Writing
Short messages

1 How do you and your friends usually send messages to each other? How long does it usually take you to reply?

2 Read the messages. What event did Dev, Alison, Callum and Mo take part in? Who won?

3 Read the messages again and answer the questions.
  1 What does Dev thank the volunteers for? Why does he congratulate them? What request does he make?
  2 What does Alison thank her friends for? What request does she make?
  3 Why does Mo congratulate his friend? What request does he make?

4 Study the Writing box. Find examples of the phrases in the messages in Exercise 2.

Hi everyone,
Just a quick note to thank you all for volunteering at the parkrun on Saturday. And congratulations on making it such a success! Did anyone take photos of the event? If so, could you please send them to me so I can post them on the parkrun blog?
Best wishes,
Dev

← Alison

Hey guys,
Thanks for your help during the parkrun. I was ready to stop after running up that first hill, but then you stayed with me and encouraged me. Thanks so much! I'm already looking forward to taking part in next month's race. Would it be possible to train together this weekend? Let me know if that's OK.
Cheers,
Alison

Hi Callum,
Well done on winning the race! You're a fantastic runner! By the way, I forgot my trainers in your dad's car. 😦 If it's OK with you, I'll pick them up before going to school on Monday. Would you mind cleaning them for me? (Just joking!)
See you later,
Mo

WRITING — Short messages: thanking, congratulating and making requests

1 **Greeting**
Hi …   Hi there …   Hiya …   Hey …

2 **Thank someone**
Thanks (so much) for your help/note/message/present …
Just a quick note to thank you for …

3 **Congratulate someone**
Congratulations on making/doing/organising …
Well done on winning/helping to …

4 **Make a request**
Could you (please) … ?   Would you mind … ?
If it's OK with you, I'll … ?
Would it be possible to … ?   Let me know if that's OK.

5 **End your message**
Bye,   Cheers,   All the best,   Best wishes,
See you later,

---

5 Study the Language box. Find similar sentences in the messages in Exercise 2. Then, in pairs, finish the sentences using your own ideas.

LANGUAGE — Prepositions + -*ing* form

Thanks **for** help**ing** me.
I felt nervous **before** start**ing** the race.
I was tired **after** runn**ing** so far.
I'm looking forward **to** see**ing** you again.
I'd like to congratulate you **on** winn**ing** the race.

WRITING TIME

6 You participated in a sports event. Write three short messages to people involved in the event.

1 **Find ideas**
Make notes for your messages.
• Who do you want to write to?
• What do you want to thank them for, or to congratulate them on?
• What would you like them to do for you?

2 **Plan**
Organise your ideas into three short messages. Use the messages in Exercise 2 to help you.

3 **Write and share**
• Write your draft messages. Use the Language box and the Writing box to help you.
• Share your messages with another student for feedback.
• Use the feedback from your partner and write the final version of your messages.

4 **Check**
• Check language: did you use the -*ing* form after prepositions?
• Check grammar: did you use future forms correctly?

I can write a short message to thank, congratulate and make a request.

Vocabulary Activator

WORDLIST 🔊 5.16

Sports equipment
basketball (n)
bat (n)
flippers (n)
football kit (n)
helmet (n)
life jacket (n)
mask (n)
mat (n)
net (n)
racket (n)
skateboard (n)
skates (n)
skis (n)
snorkel (n)
snowboard (n)
surfboard (n)

Sporting events
changing room (n)
court (n)
fan (n)
opponent (n)
pitch (n)
scoreboard (n)
stadium (n)
tournament (n)
track (n)

Word friends (sports)
beat a team
beat an opponent
break a record
hold a record
score a goal
support a team
take part in a competition
take part in a race
take up a sport
volunteer at a club
volunteer at a sports event
win a game
win a match
win a medal

Fitness and training
balance (n)
coach (n)
exercise (n)
practise (v)
skill (n)
strength (n)
stretch (v)
training programme (n)
warm down (v)
warm up (v)
work out (v)

Word building (sport)
attack (v, n)
attacker (n)
coach (v, n)
coaching (n)
defence (n)
defend (v)
defender (n)
manage (v)
management (n)
manager (n)
practice (n)
practise (v)
score (v, n)
scorer (n)
support (v, n)
supporter (n)
train (v)
trainer (n)
training (n)

Extra words
award (n)
badminton (n)
baseball (n)
champion (n)
charity (n)
compete (v)
competition (n)
competitive (adj)
Congratulations!
cricket (n)
encourage (v)
event (n)
fitness (n)
follow (v)
ice hockey (n)
kayaking (n)
keep fit
professional (n)
race (n)
rink (n)
rope (n)
rugby (n)
sailing (n)
skipping (n)
spin (v)
sports personality (n)
sports centre (n)
success (n)
trick (n)
yoga (n)

1 Use the words from the wordlist to find these things.
1. three things you can wear on your feet
2. five pieces of equipment for water sports
3. two things you need to play tennis
4. three kinds of board you use for sports
5. four places where you can do sport

2 Choose the odd one out.
1. flippers   coach   mat   mask
2. track   pitch   fan   court
3. fan   opponent   exercise   coach
4. stretch   volunteer   work out   warm up
5. mask   skill   helmet   kit

3 Answer the questions with words from the wordlist.
1. What do you hit the ball with in tennis? *racket*
2. What can help you breathe if you are swimming underwater?
3. Where can you put on your sport clothes before you play a sport?
4. What object shows how many points the players or teams have?
5. What can you lie on to make some sport activities more comfortable?

4 Complete the questions with words from the wordlist in the correct form. Then, in pairs, ask and answer the questions.
1. Which football team do you *support*?
2. Have you ever taken _____ in a race?
3. Have you ever _____ a medal?
4. Would you like to volunteer at a sports _____?
5. Which sport would you like to _____ up?

5 Write the correct word for each definition.
1. The person you play against in a game. o*pponent*
2. You wear this to stay safe in water sports. l_____
3. A competition with planned games to find a winner. t_____
4. To win against a player or team. b_____

6 🔊 5.17 **PRONUNCIATION** Listen to how we pronounce the underlined sound in each group of words. Write the words below in the correct group.

c<u>oa</u>ch   c<u>ou</u>rt   opp<u>o</u>nent   r<u>a</u>cket   sk<u>a</u>tes
snowb<u>oa</u>rd   st<u>a</u>dium   tr<u>a</u>ck

1. /əʊ/: g<u>oa</u>l, pr<u>o</u>gramme, _____ , _____
2. /eɪ/: t<u>a</u>ke up, tr<u>a</u>in, _____ , _____
3. /ɔː/: sp<u>o</u>rt, sc<u>o</u>re, _____ , _____
4. /æ/: f<u>a</u>n, m<u>a</u>tch _____ , _____

Revision

Vocabulary

1 Choose the correct option. Then, in pairs, say which sentences are true for you.
1. I like to wear a football *net / kit* with my favourite team's colours.
2. My school has a full-sized football *pitch / mat*.
3. We *won / beat* the other school 1–0 at football and I scored the goal.
4. After training hard I always *warm down / work out* for a few minutes to help feel relaxed.
5. I'm good at sports where I have to stay on my feet and not fall because I have good *skill / balance*.

2 Complete the text with the words below. There are two extra words.

> attack   hold   manage   score   ~~support~~
> take part   take up   train   volunteer

I'm football crazy and I ¹<u>support</u> a famous team. They ² _____ in both national international competitions. They ³ _____ the record in one of those competitions for winning the most times. My friend Josh thinks I should ⁴ _____ football as well as just watching it. I think it's a good idea. I haven't played in a team before, but when I play with friends, I always ⁵ _____ the most goals. Josh says that if I ⁶ _____ hard, I'll be a great player one day. As well as playing, I'll I'm also going to ⁷ _____ at my school football club – I'd like to help in any way I can.

3 Complete the second sentence so that it means the same as the first one. Use the correct form of the underlined word.
1. I've <u>supported</u> this football club since I was a child.
   I've been a _____ of this football club since I was a child.
2. We need to <u>defend</u> better – we're losing!
   We need a better _____ – we're losing!
3. You need a lot of <u>practice</u> to be good at karate.
   You need to _____ a lot to be good at karate.
4. Who <u>manages</u> the team?
   Who is responsible for the team's _____ ?
5. You can play many sports if you're <u>strong</u>.
   There are many sports where _____ helps you play well.

Grammar

4 Complete the dialogues with the correct form of *will* or *be going to* and the verbs in brackets.
1. A: Who do you think <u>will win</u> (win) the world cup this summer?
   B: I'm not sure yet, but I _____ (read) about the teams in my football magazine.
2. A: Hi, Sally. Change of plan: we _____ (not practise) outdoors today. It's too cold.
   B: Oh. So where _____ (we/practise)?
   A: In the school sports hall. I haven't told Sharon yet.
   B: No problem. I _____ (tell) her.
3. A: Why are you carrying a football?
   B: I _____ (play) football in the park with some friends. Do you want to play?
   A: Sure! I _____ (be) there there in a minute.

5 Make a plan for next week. Use the ideas below or your own ideas.

> compete in a school quiz   go to the gym
> meet friends after school   train with my team
> watch a match on TV

1. Monday: <u>I'm competing in a school quiz.</u>
2. Tuesday: _____
3. Wednesday: _____
4. Thursday: _____
5. Friday: _____

6 Choose the correct option.
1. What time *will we meet / are we meeting* tomorrow?
2. I'm sure we'll win our next basketball game, *if / unless* we do something silly!
3. *We'll have / We have* a chance to try snowboarding if we go to Austria this winter.
4. Welcome to our club! Training *starts / is going to start* at 7 p.m. every Tuesday evening.
5. Please give me a call when *you get / you'll get* home from the match.

Speaking

7 In pairs, talk about your plans for this evening, tomorrow and next Saturday. Student A, go to page 137. Student B, go to page 143. Follow the instructions.

Dictation

8 🔊 5.18 Listen. Then listen again and write down what you hear.

Unit 5

BBC CULTURE

Sporting tradition

AUSSIE RULES

If you think the most popular sport in Australia is rugby or cricket, think again. It's a sport that you have probably never heard of, called Australian Rules Football. Commonly known as 'Aussie Rules', big matches attract huge crowds, especially in the large stadiums of Sydney or Melbourne.

So what is Aussie Rules? Well, it's very different from the football that you and I know. Two teams of eighteen players take part in each match, and the field is oval-shaped. Though called football, it is more similar to rugby. For example, the ball is oval and you score points by kicking it between two goalposts, just like in rugby. However, players can be anywhere on the field and they can use any part of their bodies to move the ball. Running with the ball is fine, but you have to bounce it or touch it on the ground at the same time. Throwing the ball is not allowed. Aussie Rules includes a lot of physical contact and can be dangerous. Players can tackle each other with their hands or even their whole body!

The sport was invented in the 1850s in Melbourne, but amazingly, a national competition didn't take place until the 1980s. It is equally popular among men and women, and children learn to play it at school. Because it is purely Australian, it is rich in cultural history and references. Australians are very proud to have a sport that they can call their own. It is only really played in Australia, but it has fans worldwide. Who knows? Perhaps one day it will become very popular in the UK too!

bounce (v) (of a ball) hit the ground then go back up
league (n) a group of sports teams or players who compete against each other
tackle (v) try to take the ball from another player

1 🔊 5.19 **VISIBLE THINKING** In pairs, follow these steps.
   CONNECT
   1 Look at the photo. Would you like to play Aussie Rules football? Do you think this sport is dangerous? Why?/Why not?
   EXTEND
   2 What is the national sport of your country?
   3 Why is it important in your country?
   CHALLENGE
   4 Read the article and answer the questions.
      a In what ways is Aussie Rules culturally important for Australians?
      b Do you think many sports have this cultural role? Why?/Why not?

2 Read the article again and mark the sentences T (true) or F (false).
   1 ☐ Aussie Rules is played only in Sydney and Melbourne.
   2 ☐ Aussie Rules and football are two different sports.
   3 ☐ You can bounce, touch and throw the ball.
   4 ☐ Players use their bodies to stop another player.
   5 ☐ It plays a big role in Australian culture and history.
   6 ☐ People all over the world enjoy Aussie Rules.

3 In pairs, discuss the questions.
   1 What are the most popular sports in your country?
   2 Are they traditional or international sports?

BBC ▶ The Highland Games

4 Look at the photo. Where are the girls? What do you think they are doing and why?

5 ▶ 28 Watch Part 1 of the video. Put the activities below in the order you see them (1–4).

☐ playing bagpipes ☐ running a race
☐ throwing wood ☐ traditional dancing

6 ▶ 28 Watch the video again and complete the sentences with the words below.

disappeared   families   strength   tradition

1 The Highland Games are a very old _____.
2 They aim to bring together Scotland's historical _____.
3 They include symbols of a culture that almost _____.
4 They are a meeting place of _____, speed and celebration.

7 ▶ 29 Watch Part 2 of the video. Which is the most important sport?

8 ▶ 29 Watch the video again and choose the correct option.
1 The Games usually include athletics and *sometimes / always* heavy events.
2 The wooden pole used in the caber toss event weighs *fifteen / fifty-five* kilos.
3 There are more Highland Games celebrated *in / outside* Scotland.
4 The Games are about competing and making time for old *events / friends*.

9 In pairs, discuss the questions.
1 Would you like to go to the Highland Games? Why?/Why not?
2 Which traditional sport would you like to try? Why?

PROJECT TIME

10 In groups of three, prepare a video podcast about a traditional sport. Follow these steps.

1 In groups, choose a traditional sport. Decide who can find the answers to these questions.
- When did it start? Why is it culturally important? Who plays and watches it?
- Is it a dangerous sport? What equipment do you need?
- What are the rules of the sport?

2 Individually, create your part of the video podcast.
- Find the information and write the script for your section.
- Find photos, music or videos for each piece of information.

3 In your group, create your video podcast. You can use a video app.
- Review your research and decide what to include.
- Decide the order, who will say what and when.
- Record the script and add photos or videos.
- Make and edit your video podcast.

4 Show your video podcast to the class.
- Answer other students' questions.
- Watch the other video podcasts. Ask questions.

# Explore more 6

VOCABULARY
Types of holidays | Going on holiday | Holiday equipment and accommodation | Traffic and transport | Travel: confusing words

GRAMMAR
Modal verbs: *must, have to, ought to, should* | Modal verbs: *must, could, may/might, can't*

6.1 Vocabulary
Holidays and travel

TRENT'S TOP TRAVEL TIPS

How to have a great holiday without spending too much

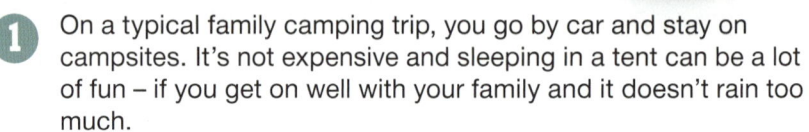

1. On a typical family camping trip, you go by car and stay on campsites. It's not expensive and sleeping in a tent can be a lot of fun – if you get on well with your family and it doesn't rain too much.

2. Activity camps are fun and everything is included, so you know how much you're going to spend before you go. It's the same with ocean cruises, but it costs a lot more to go on a cruise!

3. For a family, there's nothing better than a relaxing beach holiday in the sun. Is it expensive? It depends where and when you go. It can be cheaper to get on a plane and go abroad than to travel by train in your own country. Crazy, right?

4. Why not have a short city break instead of a long holiday? You'll spend less money, especially if you rent a holiday flat and eat in instead of booking a hotel room and eating out all the time. Go with friends and you'll save even more.

5. Sightseeing holidays needn't be expensive. A backpacking holiday where you travel around Europe by rail and stay in youth hostels can be surprisingly cheap.

Unit 6 74

1 🔊 6.1 Study Vocabulary box A. Which of the types of holidays can you see in the photos?

VOCABULARY A — Types of holidays
activity camp   backpacking holiday   beach holiday
camping trip   city break   ocean cruise   sightseeing holiday

2 Read the blog post. What is your favourite type of holiday. Discuss in pairs.

3 🔊 6.2 **WORD FRIENDS** Find the phrases below in the blog post. Then choose the correct option in sentences 1–7 below. Listen and check.

book a hotel
eat in/out
get on/off a bus/coach/plane/train
go abroad
go/travel around Europe/the world
go/travel by car/road; train/rail; plane/air; boat/sea
go on a cruise
have a city break
rent a holiday flat/a car/a bicycle
stay on a campsite

1 I've *booked / gone on* a hotel for next weekend.
2 I'd love to go *around / by* the world one day.
3 Last year we went *on / around* a trip to France.
4 It's cheaper to *eat / travel* by coach.
5 Are you old enough to *go / rent* a motorbike?
6 We're going to *rent / stay* in a youth hostel.
7 Don't *get / have* off the bus until it stops.

WATCH OUT!
We say **by** sea/road/rail/air and **by** boat/car/bus/train/plane but **on** foot.

4 🔊 6.3 Study Vocabulary box B. In pairs, take turns to describe a word from the box for your partner to guess.

A: *This has your personal information and a photograph, and you need it when you go abroad.*
B: *Is it a passport?*

VOCABULARY B — Holiday equipment
☐ guidebook ☐ map ☐ passport
☐ rucksack/backpack ☐ sleeping bag ☐ suitcase
☐ sun cream ☐ sunglasses ☐ swimsuit ☐ tent
☐ torch

5 🔊 6.4 Listen and match the words in Vocabulary box B with dialogues 1-4.

6 🔊 6.5 Study Vocabulary box C. Complete the messages below with words from the box in the correct form. Listen and check.

VOCABULARY C — Holiday accommodation
check in/out   double room   facilities   floor   guest
pool   reception   reservation   single room   view

Where did you stay on your last holiday? What was it like?

Bskybloo 11.24
The campsite has fantastic sports ^{1}*facilities* : two tennis courts, a football pitch and a large outdoor ^{2}_____ .

DcCd 11.06
When we tried to ^{3}_____ at the hotel, the guy at the ^{4}_____ said there was a problem with our ^{5}_____ . They had too many ^{6}_____ , so we shared a tiny ^{7}_____ .

emmmeee 11.01
The flat's lovely. It's on the top ^{8}_____ , with a brilliant ^{9}_____ of the city. We slept in a large ^{10}_____ with a big bed. At the end of our stay, we didn't want to ^{11}_____ .

VIDEO ▶ **WIDER WORLD**

7 ▶ 30 Watch four people talking about what to take on holidays 1–3. What things do they mention?
1 a backpacking holiday with friends
2 a city break in Ireland
3 a cruise around the Mediterranean

8 In pairs, talk about the last time you travelled. Use these questions to help you.
1 Where did you go?
2 What did you take with you?
3 How did you get there?
4 Where did you stay?
5 What facilities were there?

I went to Austria with the school. We went by coach and we stayed in a big hotel. We had a view of the mountains, but we didn't have a pool.

I can talk about holidays and travel.

6.2 Grammar

Modal verbs: must, have to, ought to, should

VIDEO ▶ A WEEKEND BREAK

Bea: I'm so excited about this boat trip.
Abe: Do we have to sleep on the boat?
Bea: Yes. Oh! That reminds me – we have to get something from upstairs.

A few minutes later …

Abe: What's in this box?
Bea: Wait and see … We should take sleeping bags. It can get cold at night. And you ought to take these to help you swim. Seriously, you shouldn't forget your swimsuit, but you must have a shower after swimming in the canal. The water can be dirty.
Abe: Do we have to wear life jackets?
Bea: No, if you're fourteen or older, you don't have to wear a life jacket, but you must be careful. And you mustn't do anything silly.
Abe: Is there anything else I ought to know?
Bea: You should bring a torch and mosquito spray.
Abe: Seriously? Mosquitoes?
Bea: We have to clean the boat three times a day. And there must always be one person awake at night so we'll have to take turns. Two hours each.
Abe: Please tell me we don't have to do that. Oh, you're joking!

1 Look at the photo. What kind of trip do you think Abe is getting ready for?

2 ▶ 31 ◀)) 6.6 Watch or listen and check your ideas from Exercise 1. What things does Abe need for the trip?

3 Study the Grammar box. Find more examples of these modal verbs in the dialogue.

GRAMMAR — Modal verbs: must, have to, ought to, should

Obligation and prohibition
You **must** be careful.
Do we **have to** sleep on the boat?
You **mustn't** do anything silly.

Advice
You **ought to** take these to help you swim.
You **shouldn't** forget your swimsuit.

Lack of obligation
You **don't have to** wear a life jacket.

GRAMMAR TIME > PAGE 131

4 Choose the correct option.

How to rent a canal boat
¹*Do you have to / Ought you* have a licence to drive a canal boat? You ²*mustn't / don't have to* have a licence for small groups, but you ³*must / should* have one if there are more than twelve passengers. You ⁴*don't have to / ought to* take care when getting on or off. You ⁵*should / shouldn't* keep the boat neat and tidy. You ⁶*should / shouldn't* run or play silly games on board. You ⁷*mustn't / ought to* forget to take a torch. It can be very dark at night.

5 ◀)) 6.7 Complete the advert with the words below. Listen and check.

| don't have to | have to | must | mustn't | ~~ought~~ | should |

Are you looking for adventure this summer? Then you ¹*ought* to try our sailing holiday in the Mediterranean. You ²_____ bring any special equipment because we provide everything. You ³_____ be between thirteen and seventeen years old and have your parents' permission. All you ⁴_____ bring are suitable clothes for a week of sailing and, of course, you ⁵_____ forget your swimsuit! You ⁶_____ bring something warm too. It can get cold at night on board!

VIDEO ▶ WIDER WORLD

6 ▶ 32 Watch two people completing sentences 1–3. What do they say?
1 When you're on a beach holiday, you should …
2 When I am on holiday with my family, I …
3 On an activity camp, you …

7 Finish the sentences in Exercise 6 to make them true for you. In pairs, compare your ideas.

Unit 6 — I can talk about obligation, prohibition and advice.

6.3 Reading and Vocabulary

Getting around Venice

1 Look at the photo and title of the text. What can you see in the photo? What do you know about Venice? Would you like to go there? Why?/Why not?

2 🔊 6.8 Read the text quickly. What kind of text is it?
   a   a leaflet for a water bus company
   b   an advert for a travel agent
   c   an article in a travel guide

3 Read the text again. Answer the questions.
   1   Why can't water buses take you to some places?
   2   What kind of trips are gondolas best for?
   3   What transport can you take to cross the Grand Canal if there's no bridge?
   4   What two problems might you have if you rent a boat?
   5   Why should you take a map when getting around Venice on foot?

4 🔊 6.9 Study the Vocabulary box. Find the words in the text. Then complete the sentences below with words from the box in the correct form.

> **VOCABULARY** Traffic and transport
>
> pedestrian   route   return ticket   single ticket
> traffic jam   travel card

   1   I've got a *travel card* so I don't have to worry about buying a _____ every time I travel.
   2   It's not easy to walk around my home town. In fact, it's quite dangerous for _____ .
   3   My house is on the bus _____ , so it's really easy to get into the city centre quickly.
   4   When I'm in a _____ and can't move on, I close my eyes and listen to music.

5 In pairs, change the sentences in Exercise 4 so they are true for you.

I haven't got a travel card, so I just buy a single or return ticket when I take the bus.

6 In pairs, think about a city you visited and ask and answer the questions.
   1   How did you get around the city?
   2   Did you need a travel card or did you buy single tickets?
   3   What was the city like for pedestrians and cyclists?
   4   Was there a lot of traffic?

Getting around Venice

118 islands, 400 bridges, 177 canals … and no cars. It's the perfect place for pedestrians, and Europe's largest car-free city. But how do people get around Venice?

By boat, obviously. You can catch water buses called vaporetti at bus stops all around the city. They're fast and convenient. But they're not cheap. A single ticket costs €7.50 and a one-day travel card, which lets you get on and off as often as you like, is €20 for tourists. Another problem is that the water buses are too wide to take you everywhere. So, to get to some places, you have to take a water taxi.

Venice is famous for its gondolas, but gondolas aren't taxis. They won't go everywhere; they follow fixed routes. A gondola trip is like a sightseeing tour – it's not for getting from A to B.

To get a cheap ride, take a traghetto. These are special boats that cross the Grand Canal in places without bridges. It takes no more than a minute or two, but you can't complain. It only costs €2!

Jet skis, kayaks and other small boats are banned from the canals. However, you can rent a motor boat – you don't even need a licence. But you shouldn't be surprised if you get stuck in traffic. With all the water buses, gondolas, rowing boats and speedboats, there are lots of traffic jams. You ought to drive carefully. There are accidents on canals just as there are on roads.

Venice isn't very big, so the best and safest way to get around the city isn't on the water, but on foot. Walk through the narrow streets and discover beautiful canals and bridges. But don't forget to take a map. Venice is a lovely place, but it's easy to get lost there.

YOUR WORLD

7 How do you and the people in your family get around when you are in a big city? Discuss in pairs.

We usually buy travel cards and use public transport. It's quick, and easy to get around on the tram or bus and it's fun too.

I can understand an article about traffic and transport.   **77**   Unit 6

6.4 Grammar

Modal verbs: *must, could, may/might, can't* (speculation)

In the wild

Hi guys,
Welcome to my camping blog – the best place for all the latest camping news. This month I've discovered these amazing tree tents. It might be difficult to find them in the shops at the moment, but I think they're going to be popular. They're warm, comfortable and great fun. I slept in one last weekend in the middle of a forest and it was awesome! Have a look and let me know what you think.

Jo123 — They don't look very big. It can't be easy to stand up in them if you're tall. *6.30 p.m.*

TimABC — They're cool! But they must be expensive because I haven't seen many of them. *8.00 p.m.*

TentFan — It might be fun to sleep up in the air, but it must be difficult to go to the loo in the middle of the night! *7.10 p.m.*

Camper — They may look cool, but I think they could be really uncomfortable because they move around with the wind. *8.30 p.m.*

1 Look at the photo in the blog post. Is this a fun place to sleep? Why?/Why not?

2 🔊 6.10 Read the blog post and comments. What are the advantages and disadvantages of tree tents?

3 Study the Grammar box. Find more examples of modal verbs for speculation in the blog post and comments.

GRAMMAR — Modal verbs: *must, could, may/might, can't*

Speculation
It **must** be cold outside. People are in jackets.
It **may/might/could** be difficult to travel with the suitcase because it's very big.
That **can't** be our tent. It's the wrong colour.

GRAMMAR TIME > PAGE 132

---

4 Choose the correct option.

A: That's a strange tent. It looks like a balloon.
B: Oh, that ¹*must / can't* be the new tree tent. I've seen them on the internet.
A: I'd love to get one. Are they expensive?
B: They ²*can't / could* be expensive because my uncle's got one and he hasn't got much money.
A: Is there a campsite near here?
B: I'm not sure. There ³*might / must* be one near the lake. I've seen people there in summer. Why?
A: I'd love to try a tree tent. Can we ask your uncle if we can borrow it?
B: OK but today ⁴*could / can't* be a bad time. He's going on holiday with it!

5 Complete the second sentence with a modal verb for speculation. Sometimes more than one answer is possible.

1 I'm sure this is Ellie's tent. That's her rucksack.
   This <u>must</u> be Ellie's tent. That's her rucksack.
2 They're very quiet. Perhaps they're sleeping.
   They're very quiet. They _____ be sleeping.
3 I'm sure this isn't the same campsite.
   This _____ be the same campsite.
4 Dad thinks this is your ticket, but your ticket is in your hand.
   This _____ be your ticket because your ticket is in your hand.
5 I'm sure the map is on the table. I put it there.
   The map _____ be on the table. I put it there.
6 Here's a guidebook but perhaps it's the wrong one.
   Here's a guidebook but it _____ be the wrong one.

YOUR WORLD

6 What do you think of these ideas for unusual holiday accommodation? In pairs, share your ideas using modal verbs for speculation.
- a tree house in a forest
- a canal boat in Holland
- an ice hotel in Sweden
- a castle on an island

It could be noisy in a tree house in a forest because of all the animals.

Unit 6 — I can speculate about the present.

6.5 Listening and Vocabulary

Jess lives the dream!

1 In pairs, describe the photo. What do you think is happening?

They're on a boat.
It might be a sailing holiday.

2 🔊 6.11 Listen to the first part of an interview. What does Mike do?

3 🔊 6.12 Listen to the second part of the interview and mark the sentences T (true) or F (false).
  1. ☐ Mike was working in South America when he met a girl who couldn't see.
  2. ☐ The girl was on holiday with her family.
  3. ☐ Special bikes are popular with kids who don't usually cycle.
  4. ☐ Mike thinks the journey is less important than the holiday.
  5. ☐ Hotel staff don't always realise how difficult it is for blind guests.
  6. ☐ The winter holidays are the most popular.

4 🔊 6.12 Listen again and write down the following. Then compare your answers in groups of three.
  1. four activities mentioned in the interview
  2. three kinds of holidays
  3. three problems that blind people might have

5 🔊 6.13 Listen and compete the information form about Jess with one or two words in each gap.

Activity camp information form

Name: ¹*Jess*
Age: ²_____
Where from: ³_____
Disability: Jess is ⁴_____
Likes: ⁵_____
Recent holidays: went to a ⁶_____ last year
Activity camp achievement: climbed a ⁷_____

6 In pairs, discuss why this sort of holiday is important for people like Jess. Compare your ideas with the class.

It's an adventure.
It might help them to meet people.

7 🔊 6.14 Study the Vocabulary box and check you understand the words. Then choose the correct option in the sentences below. Listen and check.

VOCABULARY ▸ Travel: confusing words

excursion journey travel (n) travel (v) trip voyage

  1. It was a three-hour car *journey / excursion* to the beach.
  2. The *trip / voyage* across the Atlantic took two months and the cabins were comfortable.
  3. Air *travel / journey* is very expensive at the moment.
  4. The school is organising a two-day *travel / trip* to London.
  5. Let's get tickets for the afternoon *journey / excursion* to the castle.
  6. I'd love to *travel / trip* to the North Pole one day.

YOUR WORLD

8 Imagine your school has invited some students from another country. In pairs, discuss the best trips and excursions in your area. Compare your ideas with the class.

They could go on an excursion to the water park.
They could visit the capital city but it's a long journey.

I can understand a radio interview about travelling.

6.6 Speaking

Understanding a conversation

VIDEO ▶ **CAN YOU SAY THAT AGAIN?**

Bea: Hi, Carla. You know I'm staying in London with my gran? Well, there's an exhibition on Hyperloop at the Transport Museum and …
Carla: Sorry, I didn't catch that. Hyper what?
Bea: Hyperloop! It's like a train but cooler. I just wanted to ask if you'd like to come and see it tomorrow.
Carla: That might be fun. Yeah!

The next day …

Carla: Hi, I'm at the station. How do I get there? Should I take a bus?
Bea: No, you shouldn't take a bus. The tube's better.
Carla: Sorry, what was that?
Bea: I was just saying you can take the underground. It's the Piccadilly line.
Carla: Can you say that again? I didn't get the last part.
Bea: I said you have to take the Piccadilly line.
Carla: Sorry, but could you speak more loudly? It's really noisy here. I can't hear a thing.
Bea: Take the Piccadilly line to Covent Garden. It's the third stop. You can walk from there.
Carla: OK, thanks. See you soon.

Later …

Bea: You made it!
Carla: Thanks to your directions. Sorry, I couldn't hear you before.
Bea: Oh, never mind. You're here now. Let's go!

SOUNDS GOOD! I can't hear a thing. • You made it! • Never mind.

1 Have you ever had problems finding your way around a city? What did you do? Discuss in pairs.

2 ▶ 33 🔊 6.15 Watch or listen and answer the questions.
 1 Why does Bea call Carla at the start of the dialogue?
 2 Why does Carla find it hard to understand Bea?
 3 How does Carla get from the station to the museum?

3 Did Bea's instructions help Carla find the way? Why/why not? Discuss in pairs.

SET FOR LIFE

4 What can you do to make sure you understand the information someone is giving you? Discuss in pairs. Use the ideas below to help you.
 • listen carefully
 • ask for clarification if you don't understand
 • ask for more information
 • repeat the information with your own words

5 Study the Speaking box. Find examples of the phrases in the dialogue.

SPEAKING Understanding a conversation

Asking for clarification
Sorry, I didn't catch that.   What was that?
Can you say that again?
Sorry, I didn't get the first/last part.
Could you speak more loudly/more slowly?

Clarifying
What I said/asked was …   I said (that) …
I was just saying …   I just wanted to ask (you) if/about …

6 Complete the dialogue with phrases from the Speaking box. Sometimes more than one answer is possible. In pairs, practise the dialogue.

A: We're going to Italy on holiday this summer.
B: Sorry, ¹_____ .
A: What ²_____ we're going to Italy this summer. I just ³_____ if you wanted to go with us.
B: Great, thanks! I'll have to get a passport.
A: ⁴_____ ?
B: I was ⁵_____ I need to get a passport.
A: Could ⁶_____ ? I couldn't hear you.
B: ⁷_____ I need a passport.

YOUR WORLD

7 In pairs, go to page 137 and role play the situations.

Unit 6   80   I can clarify what I have said and ask for clarification.

6.7 Writing

An email about travel arrangements

1 If you could travel by train across Europe, where would you like to go?

2 Read the emails and answer the questions.
1 What does Jill need to buy before the trip?
2 Who else is going on the trip?
3 Which places might they visit?

Hi Jo,

I'm so looking forward to our rail trip across Europe. Let me know what the plan is. I'll write more later.

Bye for now,
Jill

PS I must buy a rucksack for the trip!

Hey Jill,

1 I just wanted to check the plan with you.

2 We're meeting at the station at 8 p.m. Mum and I have got the tickets, so I'll give you your ticket when you arrive. We'll have something to eat at the station before we catch the train.

3 We still need to decide on the route. I don't think we should stop in Geneva overnight. It might be better to spend a day in Geneva and do a walking tour of the city. Then we could travel overnight to Turin. Or we could catch a train to Lyon. We should decide before we leave. Let me know what you think.

4 Let's talk later.

5 Love,
Jo

---

3 Study the Writing box. Find examples of the phrases in Jo's email.

WRITING   An email about travel arrangements

Say why you are writing
1 Here's a quick note to tell you about the plan.
I just wanted to check the plan with you.

Explaining arrangements
2 We're meeting at the station at 8 p.m.
Jane's mum will drive us to terminal 1.

Make suggestions about the route
3 I don't think we should stop in Geneva overnight.
It might be better to spend a day in Geneva.
We could catch a train to Lyon.

Before you finish
4 Let's talk later.
Let me know what you think.

Ending your email
Bye for now,
5 Love,
See you soon,
Speak soon,

4 Study the Language box. Find three sentences with future time clauses in Jo's email.

LANGUAGE   Future time clauses

We use the Present Simple in future time clauses with *when, after, before, until* and *as soon as*.

We'll decide our route **before** we **leave**.
When the time clause comes first, we use a comma.
As soon as they arrive, I'll call you.

5 Write sentences about yourself. Use future time clauses with *when, after, before, until* and *as soon as*.

WRITING TIME

6 You are going on a trip with a friend. Write an email about the travel arrangements.

1 Find ideas
Make notes about:
• the type of trip and means of transport.
• the time and place to meet.
• what to take with you.
• the route to take.

2 Plan
Organise your ideas into paragraphs. Use Jo's email to help you.

3 Write and share
• Write your draft email. Use the Language box and the Writing box to help you.
• Share your email with another student for feedback.
• Use the feedback from your partner and write the final version of your email.

4 Check
• Check language: did you use future time clauses correctly?
• Check grammar: did you use modal verbs correctly?

I can write an email about travel arrangements.

Vocabulary Activator

WORDLIST 🔊 6.16

Types of holidays
activity camp (n)
backpacking holiday (n)
beach holiday (n)
camping trip (n)
city break (n)
ocean cruise (n)
sightseeing holiday (n)

Word friends (going on holiday)
book a hotel
eat in/out (v)
get on/off a bus
get on/off a coach
get on/off a plane
get on/off a train
go abroad
go/travel around Europe
go/travel around the world
go/travel by boat/sea
go/travel by car/road
go/travel by plane/air
go/travel by train/rail
go on a cruise
have a city break
rent a holiday flat
rent a bicycle

rent a car
stay on a campsite
stay in a hostel

Holiday equipment
guidebook (n)
map (n)
passport (n)
rucksack/backpack (n)
sleeping bag (n)
suitcase (n)
sun cream (n)
sunglasses (n)
swimsuit (n)
tent (n)
torch (n)

Holiday accommodation
check in/out (v)
double room (n)
facilities (n)
floor (n)
guest (n)
pool (n)
reception (n)
reservation (n)
single room (n)
view (n)

Traffic and transport
pedestrian (n)
return ticket (n)
route (n)
single ticket (n)
traffic jam (n)
travel card (n)

Travel: confusing words
excursion (n)
journey (n)
travel (v, n)
trip (n)
voyage (n)

Extra words
abroad (adv)
airport (n)
banned (adj)
bridge (n)
brilliant (adj)
bring (v)
campsite (n)
canal (n)
complain (v)
convenient (adj)
country (n)
dark (adj)

dirty (adj)
get stuck
gondola (n)
island (n)
jet ski (n)
lovely (adj)
Mediterranean (n)
mosquito spray (n)
narrow (adj)
on board
on foot
permission (n)
provide (v)
rail trip (n)
reserve (v)
resident (n)
ride (n)
rowing boat (n)
sailing holiday (n)
station (n)
stay (n)
suitable (adj)
super-friendly (adj)
take turns
tour (n)
travel agent (n)
youth hostel (n)

---

1 Use the words from the wordlist to find these things.
1 three things you can pack for a beach holiday
2 three things you can pack for a camping holiday
3 two things you can do to prepare for a holiday before you go

2 Read what the people say and recommend a type of holiday for each one. In pairs, recommend a holiday for each other.

Louise, 21
I want to visit interesting places and take photos of them.

1 *sightseeing holiday*

Derek, 47
We have one day and night to eat in a nice restaurant and visit museums.

2 _____

Peter, 15
I want to hear the sounds of nature as I fall asleep.

3 _____

Helen, 66
We want to just look at the sea and have everything we need close by.

4 _____

Julia, 13
My friends don't want to be bored! We need things to do.

5 _____

Tim, 23
I love to lie on the sand and enjoy the sun.

6 _____

3 Answer the quiz questions with words from the wordlist. Then write one more question. In pairs, answer each other's questions.

TRAVEL QUIZ

1 What kind of ticket do you need if you plan to come back the same way? *return ticket*
2 What kind of book can tell you about interesting places to visit?
3 What will help you find walking routes and not get lost?
4 What's it called when a lot of cars are moving slowly?
5 What can you get to save money if you plan to use local transport a lot?
6 What kind of hotel room is for two people?

4 🔊 6.17 **PRONUNCIATION** Listen to the chant and underline two stressed syllables in each line.
I packed my suitcase
And made my reservation.
Then I travelled to the airport
But I forgot my passport.

5 **PRONUNCIATION** Practise saying the chant in Exercise 4 in a rhythmic way. Stress the correct syllables.

Revision

Vocabulary

1 Choose the correct option.
1 We checked *in / out of* our hotel at noon and arrived back home at 6 p.m.
2 In our family, we go *on / to* holiday every year.
3 We want to include *a voyage / an excursion* to a castle on one day of our holiday.
4 Cars can't enter this area. It's for *residents / pedestrians*.
5 They won't let you get on the plane without your *passport / guidebook*.
6 Let's all take a *trip / travel* to Africa next year!

2 Complete the advert with the words below.

> ~~facilities~~   guest   pool   reception
> reservation   shower   single   view

Stay at our backpacking hostel!

If you want great accommodation at the right price, our backpacking hostel is for you! We have all the ¹*facilities* of a hotel, for people who need to save money. Every ² _____ and double room has its own ³ _____ and a fantastic ⁴ _____ : the sea on one side and the mountains on the other. The beach is near the hotel, but we also have a small ⁵ _____ . You can make a ⁶ _____ online or simply arrive and ask for a room at ⁷ _____ . We do our best to help each ⁸ _____ to enjoy their stay.

3 Complete the email with the words below. There is one extra word.

> break   floor   guidebook   passport
> pool   sightseeing   ~~traffic~~

Hi Jan,

We've arrived at the hotel safely, but a bit late because there was a ¹*traffic* jam! But we're relaxing now. Ella and I are in our room, and Mum and Dad are swimming in the ² _____ . We're on the highest ³ _____ and we have a great view of the city. It looks beautiful, so I'm happy we're taking a city ⁴ _____ here before we visit the rest of the country. It's a ⁵ _____ holiday, so we have our cameras ready to take photos of the interesting places. We also have an excellent ⁶ _____ with all the information we need.

I'll write again soon. Bye for now!
Gordon

Grammar

4 Choose the correct option to complete the information about visiting a new country.
1 You *should / must* talk to local people to learn something interesting about the culture.
2 You *must / should* show your passport when you enter the country.
3 You *don't have to / mustn't* learn the language because a lot of people speak English.
4 You *ought / should* to be polite and show respect for their way of life.
5 You *ought to / must* learn something about the country first, to make your trip more interesting.
6 You *don't have to / mustn't* take photos of people without their permission.

5 Make questions you can ask about visiting wild areas like mountains or jungle. Then, in pairs, choose a wild area and discuss the questions.
1 should / check / the weather before we go / ?
2 should / tell / someone where we plan to go / ?
3 have / get / permission to visit / ?
4 might / see / any wild animals / ?
5 should / take / our own food and water / ?
6 what clothes / should / wear / ?

6 Complete the dialogue with *must*, *might* or *can't*.
A: Look at this poster of a river. There's information and prices, so it ¹*must* be an advert for a river trip. Do you like the idea?
B: I thought rivers were kind of boring, but it ² _____ be interesting if there's an organised trip.
A: It says, 'You need a camera,' so there ³ _____ be some cool things to see.
B: Yes, but what? There ⁴ _____ be any museums or historical buildings. There aren't any cities.
A: No, but the boat ⁵ _____ go near some places with wild animals to see. I hope so.
B: Why? Are you interested in going?
A: Well it ⁶ _____ hurt to find out more! I'm going to phone them.

Speaking

7 In pairs, turn to page 137 and follow the instructions to role play a dialogue. Then swap roles and role play a different situation where you ask for and give clarification.

Dictation

8 🔊 6.18 Listen. Then listen again and write down what you hear.

SET FOR LIFE

Eco-friendly travel

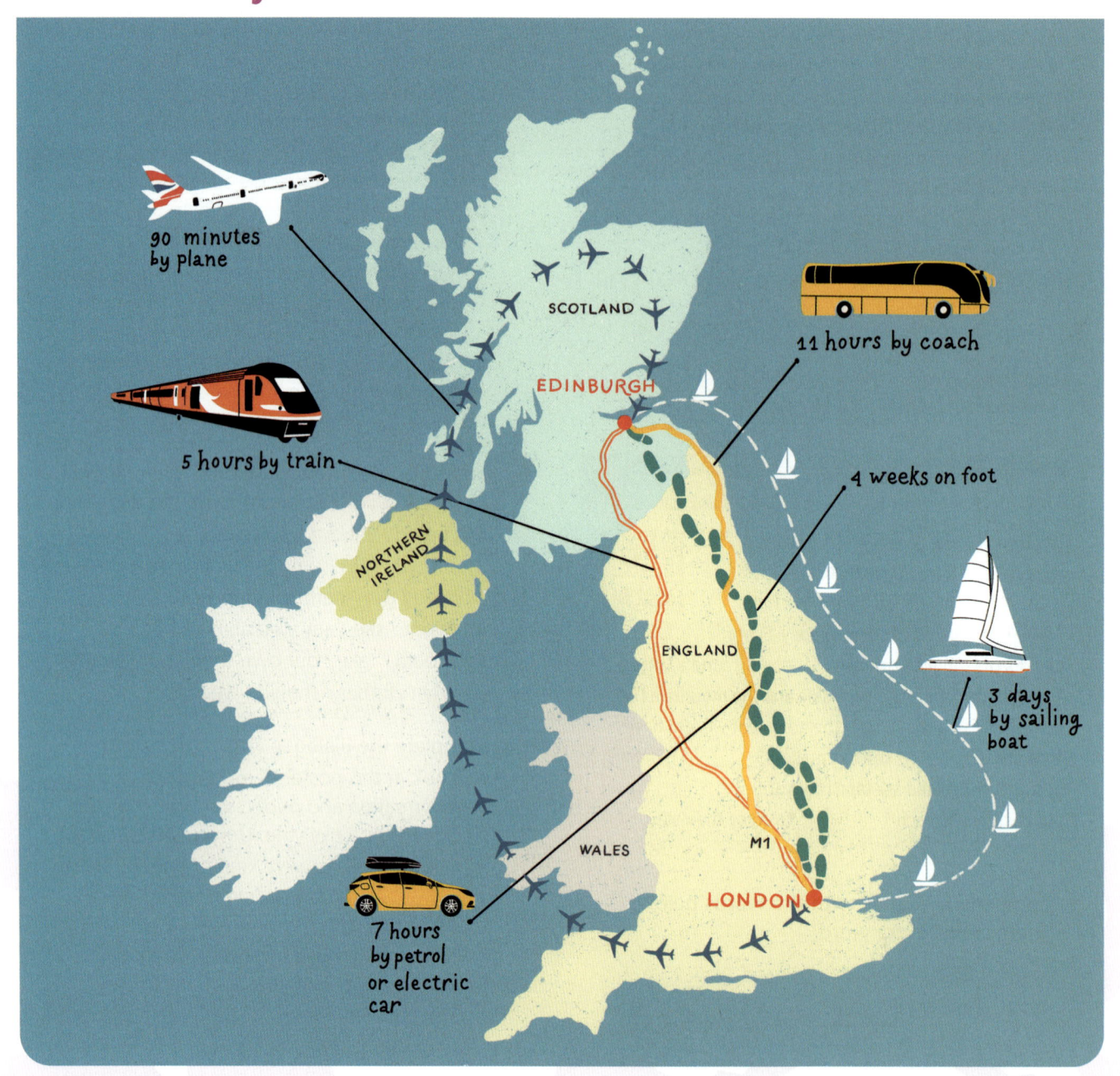

90 minutes by plane

SCOTLAND

11 hours by coach

EDINBURGH

5 hours by train

4 weeks on foot

NORTHERN IRELAND

3 days by sailing boat

ENGLAND

WALES

M1

LONDON

7 hours by petrol or electric car

1 In pairs, look at the map. How would you prefer to travel from London in England to Edinburgh in Scotland? Why?

I'd prefer to travel by … because it's the … -est way to get there.

2 🔊 6.19 Listen to a dialogue. Which two types of transport is Charlie using for his holiday? Why?

3 In pairs, do the quiz. Use types of transport from the map to help you.

The eco-friendly transport QUIZ

1 What has the advantages of a petrol car, but produces much less air pollution?
2 Which types of public transport aren't as fast as flying, but produce less greenhouse gas?
3 By which type of transport can a three-hour journey produce as much greenhouse gas as someone in Uganda produces in a whole year?
4 Which types of transport don't produce any greenhouse gas?

Units 5–6 | 84 | I can plan an eco-friendly holiday.

4 🔊 **6.19** Listen to the dialogue from Exercise 2 again and check your answers to Exercise 3.

5 In pairs, imagine you are going on a weekend trip together. Choose a destination and discuss which means of transport you can use to get there. (Think about the cost, ecology and time). Use expressions from the Useful phrases box.

A: Why don't we go by train? It's an eco-friendly choice.
B: True, but it'll be slow. It takes only two hours by car.

6 Do the questionnaire. In pairs, compare your answers.

What are your travel habits?

1 **How do you usually get to school?**
  a on foot or by bike b by public transport
  c by car

2 **How far do you travel by car in a typical week?**
  a less than 5 km b 5–20 km
  c more than 20 km

3 **If you go away from home for a holiday, how do you usually travel there?**
  a by train or coach b by car
  c by plane

4 **How do you usually travel when you are at your holiday destination?**
  a on foot or by bike b by public transport
  c by car

7 Read the Useful Tips. In pairs, discuss how you can become more eco-friendly travellers.

SET FOR LIFE

8 In small groups, plan an eco-friendly holiday. Follow these steps.

1 Decide where you are going to go.

2 Plan how to travel to your holiday destination. Use expressions from the Useful Phrases box.

3 Plan how to travel around when you are at your destination.

4 Present your plan for the eco-friendly holiday to the class.

Be an eco-friendly traveller

USEFUL TIPS

When you choose transport, it's important to make eco-friendly choices when you can. Transport can have a big effect on the environment.

- Avoid vehicles with engines. Use vehicles without engines and travel on foot.

- Avoid planes and petrol cars. Share transport, or use coaches, trains and electric cars.

- Avoid longer journeys.

USEFUL PHRASES

Why don't we … ?
Maybe we could …
… is an eco-friendly choice.
… is better for the environment than …
… (don't) produce a lot of greenhouse gas.
It'll be fun/interesting/cheaper.
It'll be slow/boring/more expensive.

Progress Check Units 1-6

Vocabulary and Grammar

1 Choose the correct answer.
1. We have a ___ time before the other players get here; let's practise!
   a some   b little   c few
2. I've only watched two ___ , but this looks like a very interesting series.
   a episodes   b channels   c productions
3. We don't ___ take food on the trip because the teachers are going to give us a packed lunch.
   a must   b ought to   c have to
4. The runners are on the ___ in their starting positions. The race will start any moment.
   a court   b race   c track
5. Please check in at the hotel ___ and you will get a key card to your room.
   a reception   b facilities   c reservation
6. Horse-riding is ___ than swimming.
   a the most exciting
   b most exciting   c more exciting

2 Complete the second sentence with the word in bold so that it means the same as the first one. Use no more than four words.
1. In my opinion, an ocean cruise is better than a beach holiday for relaxing. **GOOD**
   In my opinion, a beach holiday isn't _as good as_ an ocean cruise for relaxing.
2. I don't know what Rome is like because I haven't seen it yet. **BEEN**
   I don't know what Rome is like because I've _____ there.
3. I'm sure Jeff is already in the swimming pool – his bike is next to the building. **BE**
   Jeff _____ in the swimming pool already – his bike is next to the building.
4. Is learning Spanish part of your travel plans to Argentina? **GOING**
   Are _____ Spanish when you travel to Argentina?
5. Try to hit the ball hard when you train for tennis. **PRACTISE**
   You should _____ the ball hard when you train for tennis.
6. We have many different kinds of sports on our camp. **LOTS**
   There _____ different kinds of sports on our camp.

3 Complete the text with the correct form of the words in brackets.

A lot of ¹_reviewers_ (REVIEW) these days are writing about *On the Pitch*, Giles Holmes' new film about a young footballer. For this film, Holmes found that he needed people with ²_____ (ACT) and football skills. He used real ³_____ (ACT) for most of the players on the pitch. They played all the ⁴_____ (DEFEND). However, he decided to get a real footballer to play an ⁵_____ (ATTACK). She gave a good ⁶_____ (PERFORM) both on and off the pitch. This film is a great ⁷_____ (PRODUCT) and everyone should go and see it!

Speaking

4 Complete the dialogue with the words below. There is one extra word.

> meeting   plans   prefer   rather   sounds   ~~up~~   yet

A: Hi! What are you ¹_up_ to on Saturday?
B: I don't know ²_____ . What are you going to do?
A: I'm ³_____ a few friends in the afternoon. Do you want to join us?
B: Thanks. Maybe I will. What are your ⁴_____ ?
A: Maybe we'll watch a film or check out the new shopping centre. Which do you think is better?
B: I'd ⁵_____ watch a film. There's a really good new science fiction film at the cinema.
A: That ⁶_____ good! I'll ask the others.

5 In pairs, follow the instructions to role play two dialogues.

1 Plan a fun afternoon.
Student A
- Ask Student B what his/her plans are for Saturday afternoon.
- Suggest doing something together and ask what he/she prefers to do: visit the park or the shops? walk or cycle? something else?

Student B
- Respond to what Student A says. Decide together what you're going to do.

2 Plan another fun afternoon.
Student B
- Ask Student A what his/her plans are for this afternoon.
- Suggest doing something together and ask what he/she prefers to do: café or cinema? pizza or ice cream? something else?

Student A
- Respond to what Student A says. Decide together what you're going to do.

Listening

6 🔊 PC1–6.1 Listen to part of a podcast and complete the sentences. Use 1–3 words in each gap.

1. Melanie trains _____ a week and at weekends.
2. She has to do _____ as well as play tennis.
3. Tomorrow she has a meeting with _____ .
4. She's going to try to improve her tennis skills by finding out and practising _____ parts of her game.
5. She says that if players fall over during a game, they usually _____ .
6. Melanie took up playing tennis when she saw _____ on a bus journey.
7. She admires Serena Williams because she always tries _____ .

7 🔊 PC1–6.2 Listen. Then listen again and write down what you hear.

Reading

8 🔊 PC1–6.3 Read the article quickly. In pairs, say which album you would like to listen to.

9 Read the article and answer the questions.

Which album (A–C):
1. is a recording of a live music event? ☐
2. has songs about real people? ☐
3. has a song which is the best song because of a musical instrument? ☐
4. was made by two people working together? ☐
5. was recorded partly outdoors? ☐
6. used technology later to improve the sound? ☐
7. has music for TV programmes? ☐

Writing

10 Think about a film or a documentary where people live in or travel to another place. Answer the questions. Then, in pairs, take turns to tell your partner about the film/documentary. Would they like to see it?
1. What was it about?
2. What places did you see in it?
3. What was one thing you learned about the place(s)?
4. What two things did you like about the film/documentary? (e.g. photography, music, presenter/actor)

11 Write a review of the film or documentary about a place (100–150 words). In your review:
- say the name and at least one more fact about the film/documentary.
- describe the story and say why the place is important.
- say why you liked/didn't like the film/documentary.

Top albums this year

Which albums have we all enjoyed this year? There have already been a few really good ones and here are three of them.

A *Stage Style* – Banana Bread

It isn't often that a recording of a concert performance makes it to a short list of the best albums of the year. But *Stage Style* certainly does. The album has many Banana Bread favourites, but also a few surprises we've never heard, including the wonderful *Know Me Better*. Why is the sound so clean? It's because further production after the concert used computers to take out the audience noise.

B *The Dried and the Roasted* – The Fine Fellows

If you're a fan of the soap *Pretty Players*, then you probably enjoy the great music at the start of each episode. This album has it, but there are a lot of other great tracks too. The Fellows – duo Sally Oddy and Mark Freeman – recorded some songs for the screen and others not. But the best song, *Darkness Calls*, appeared in the film of the same name. Why is it the best? It's the drum parts which create the excitement the director really wanted in that key scene. No spoilers!

C *Painted Creatures* – Lisa Scott

Some people want to be successful in the music business and others just want to tell their own story! The lyrics on *Painted Creatures* are so interesting that you want to stop lip-synching and just read and think about them.
If you do that, you'll learn a lot about Lisa and those closest to her. Another thing that makes this album special is the way the sounds of weather and wildlife are mixed in! 'We took the microphones into the open air for those tracks,' Lisa explains in a recent music documentary.

People power

7

VOCABULARY
Word building: family | Phrasal verbs | Collocations: relationships | Relations | Collocations with *get*

GRAMMAR
Second Conditional | Relative clauses

Family Maths

It doesn't matter if your family is big or small; some numbers are the same for all of us. For every person on the planet there are ¹_____ people who are their biological parents. That means you have four biological grandparents and ²_____ great-grandparents.

16
8
4
2

The diagram shows one person's parents and their parents' parents over ³_____ generations. You can see that one person has ⁴_____ great-great grandparents.

It's interesting to think of all their different experiences. How did they meet? Did they all grow up in the same place or did some of them move away?

This diagram doesn't tell the whole story. There might be many brothers and sisters in each family, or even step-parents and half-brothers and half-sisters. Also, you can't see all the aunts, uncles and cousins on this diagram. Most people have many first, second and third cousins. Even if you're in a city with ⁵_____ of people, it's possible that you have relations there. So be kind to those loud neighbours of yours – they might be your cousins!

7.1 Vocabulary

Family and friends

1 How many people are there in your family, including all of your relations? How often do you see them?

2 🔊 7.1 Look at the diagram and complete the text with the words below. Listen and check.

| eight | four | sixteen | thousands | two |

Unit 7 88

3 🔊 **7.2** Study Vocabulary box A. Complete the explanations with the prefixes in bold in the box.

> **VOCABULARY A** — **Word building: family**
>
> **great**-grandmother   **great**-grandfather
> **great**-grandparent
> **half**-brother   **half**-sister
> **step**mother   **step**father   **step**son   **step**daughter
> **step**brother   **step**sister

1 The prefix _____ - describes a family relative who is three generations away from you. Add an extra _____ - for each extra generation.
2 The prefix _____ - describes a brother, sister or parent who is related to you by marriage but not by blood.
3 The prefix _____ - describes a brother or sister who is related to you through one shared biological parent.

4 🔊 **7.3** Study Vocabulary box B. Then complete the quiz. Listen and check.

> **VOCABULARY B** — **Phrasal verbs**
>
> deal with (a problem)   grow up
> get on with/get along with   hang out (with)
> get together   move away
> go out (with)

Have you got great people skills?

Give yourself a score between 1 and 5 for each statement.
1 = strongly disagree 2 = disagree 3 = it depends
4 = agree 5 = strongly agree

a ☐ My cousins and I always helped each other when we were growing _____ .
b ☐ I get _____ well with my cousins, aunts, uncles and grandparents.
c ☐ When I get _____ with my friends, I always include everyone.
d ☐ I enjoy going _____ with a group of my friends.
e ☐ I'm not sure how to deal _____ friendship problems.
f ☐ My friends and I like to hang _____ at one another's homes.
g ☐ I would hate to move _____ from my home town.

5 Do the quiz in Exercise 4. In pairs, compare your answers. Are you similar or different?
Both of us like/dislike …
I think I'm quite similar to/different from …

6 🔊 **7.4** **WORD FRIENDS** Check you understand the phrases below. Then complete the texts with them. Listen and check. Who do you agree with? Stefan or Nadia?

get to know someone
have an argument
have something in common
have the same sense of humour
see each other after school
share an interest in something
spend time with someone

Friends: similar or different?

Stefan: I think it's good to be similar. I ¹*got* to know Adam after I moved away from my home town last year. Adam and I ² _____ a lot in common. We both like volleyball and comedy films. We ³ _____ the same sense of humour too. We ⁴ _____ loads of interests and we're like brothers or cousins.

Nadia: I'm completely different from my friend Marta, but we get on well. Marta hates to ⁵ _____ arguments, but I think it's good to disagree. Marta loves to ⁶ _____ time on her own, but I like to go out. We don't ⁷ _____ each other often, but when we meet, we get on well.

7 **YOUR WORLD** Is it important for friends to have similar interests? In pairs, discuss your opinions.

I can talk about relationships with my family and friends.

7.2 Grammar
Second Conditional

VIDEO ▶ **A DILEMMA**

Abe: Yay, a party invite! Oh no!
Bea: Hi, Abe!
Abe: Hiya. I can't go to the end-of-term party on Saturday.
Bea: Why not?
Abe: Because if I went to the party, I wouldn't be able to meet my mum at the airport. My dad wouldn't be very happy with me if I did that.
Bea: Oh! That's true. And I think you'd feel bad if you didn't meet her.
Abe: I guess you're right. I do miss her. What would you do if you were me?
Bea: If I were you, I'd try to go to both. What time does your mum arrive?
Abe: She arrives at 9.00. The party starts at 8.00.
Bea: Yeah, it's complicated.
Abe: It's impossible!
Bea: How would your mum react if you told her about the party?
Abe: She'd tell me to go to the party, of course.

On Saturday …
Dad: The airport, then?
Abe: The airport!
Dad: Are you sure? Mum would understand if you chose to go to that party.
Abe: I know, but I never listen to my parents, remember?

1 Look at the photo of Abe looking at an end-of-term party invitation. How do you think he feels? Why?

2 ▶ 34 ◀) 7.5 Watch or listen and check your ideas from Exercise 1. What does Abe decide to do?

3 Study the Grammar box. Find more examples of the Second Conditional in the dialogue.

> **GRAMMAR** ▶ **Second Conditional**
>
> **If** her flight **arrived** earlier, **I'd be** able to go to the airport.
> What **would** you **do if** you **were** me?

4 ◀) 7.6 Complete the Second Conditional sentences with the correct form of the verbs in brackets. Listen and check.
1 If I *had* (have) enough time, I _____ (help).
2 If you _____ (listen) carefully, you _____ (understand).
3 _____ (you/go) to the beach if you _____ (be) free today?
4 He _____ (not come) here if he _____ (not want) to.
5 What _____ (you/do) if you _____ (earn) a lot of money?
6 I _____ (phone) your dad if I _____ (be) you.

5 What would you do if you were Abe? Why? Discuss in pairs.

VIDEO ▶ **WIDER WORLD**

6 ▶ 35 Watch four people talking about different situations. How do they complete the sentences below?
1 If my friend phoned when I was busy, …
2 If there was a big wedding in our family, …
3 If I was late for a family meal, my parents …
4 I'd be very worried if …
5 It would be a nightmare for me if …

7 Finish the sentences in Exercise 6 to make them true for you. In pairs, compare your ideas.

If my friend phoned when I was busy, I'd probably talk to her. What about you?

GRAMMAR TIME ▶ PAGE 132

I can use the Second Conditional to talk about unreal or imaginary situations.

7.3 Reading and Vocabulary

Making friends

1 Is it important to make new friends? Why?/Why not?

2 🔊 7.7 Read the article quickly and match headings a–e with steps 1–5.
- a ☐ Understand each other's identity
- b ☐ Chat about a few different things
- c ☐ Make a friendly comment
- d ☐ Spend time talking or being together
- e ☐ Show interest by listening

3 Read the article again and complete the sentences with 1–3 words in each gap.
1. The article tells us that there are five steps to _____ .
2. For the first step, you may share information about things you like or _____ .
3. When you've shared information, it's easier to have _____ .
4. If both friends often listen and support each other, they have reached step _____ .
5. A friend who supports your social identity acts like _____ .
6. If you and your friend are in different places, you can call or _____ .

4 🔊 7.8 Study the Vocabulary box. Find the words in the article. Check you understand them.

VOCABULARY ▶ Relations

People
best friend   classmate   mate   stranger   teammate

Phrases with friend(s)
be friends   have a friend   keep friends   make friends

---

5 🔊 7.9 Complete the sentences with words from the Vocabulary box. Listen and check.
1. I've made friends with a few of my _____ from volleyball.
2. Sara was nervous about the new school, but it was easy to _____ .
3. When we moved here, I felt like a _____ as nobody knew me.
4. I've got lots of friends, but Ben is my _____ because he understands me.
5. Sam changed secondary school, but his new _____ are friendly.

Five steps to friendship

If you wanted a new friend, what would you do? It's not as simple as you might think. We usually find friends in the places where we live, study, work or relax. So our classmates and teammates can easily become friends, but how?

1 The first step normally happens when one person shares some information. This could be anything from a comment about a funny TV show to food that you can't stand. Or you could tell someone about your likes and dislikes, for example.

2 That's a great start. You aren't strangers, but you aren't best friends yet. Next, we need the other person to reply with similar thoughts about that TV show or another horrible food. From here, it's easier to have more conversations about other things. When two people have talked about their thoughts and opinions, they're starting to make friends.

3 The third step involves being a good friend. To take this step, you need to listen to your friend and help them. Over time, you can share problems and talk about lots of things. You know the other person is always ready to listen and support you. That's a really good friendship.

4 The fourth step is about looking for friends who support our social identity. What does that mean? If dancing or basketball is really important in your life, then you will probably want friends who see you as a good dancer or a basketball player. That's why we choose friends who are like a mirror. They show us a picture of how we want to be.

5 Finally, remember to stay in touch with your friends. A good way to do this is to make time to see your friends or to phone them and send messages when you're not in the same place. It's important to remember that friendship needs work!

6 Work in pairs. What else is important for making and keeping friends?

YOUR WORLD

I can understand an article about friendship.

7.4 Grammar
Relative clauses

1. What are two things that you always carry with you? Are they your favourite objects?

2. 🔊 7.10 Read the quiz questions below (1–10). Match them with Hannah's answers (a–j). Listen and check.
   a. The guy next door, Ben, is a friend who always listens.
   b. *We Will Rock You*, which is my dad's favourite, is in my head.
   c. The evening is best for me to work.
   d. Iceland, where there are loads of volcanoes, is a place I'd love to visit.
   e. My uncle Joe is the funniest person I know.
   f. Mr Ketling, who was my first teacher, was the most helpful.
   g. One thing which I'd rescue is my handheld console.
   h. One place where I like to relax is our youth club.
   i. A teddy bear, which my grandmother gave me, used to be my favourite.
   j. I eat olives any time I feel hungry.

What makes you YOU?

Name:
1. one thing which you would rescue in a flood
2. one person who you always have fun with
3. a place where you like to relax
4. one food that you often eat as a snack
5. the primary school teacher who helped you the most
6. a place where you want to go in the future
7. a friend who always listens
8. a toy that you loved when you were small
9. a song which you can't stop singing
10. the time of day when you work best

3. Do the quiz in Exercise 2. In pairs, compare your answers.

4. Study the Grammar box. Find more examples of defining and non-defining relative clauses in the quiz and in Hannah's answers in Exercise 2.

> **GRAMMAR** — Relative clauses
>
> **Defining relative clauses (essential information)**
> Ben is a friend **who/that always listens**.
> One thing **which/that I'd rescue** is my handheld console.
> Our youth club is one place **where I like to relax**.
>
> **Non-defining relative clauses (extra information)**
> Mr Kipling, **who was my first teacher**, was the most helpful.
> *We Will Rock You*, **which is my dad's favourite**, is in my head.
> Iceland, **where there are loads of volcanoes**, is a place I'd love to visit.
>
> GRAMMAR TIME > PAGE 133

⚠️ **WATCH OUT!**
The woman who/that lives next door is my great-aunt. (defining relative clause)
Mrs Baker, who/~~that~~ lives next door, is my great-aunt. (non-defining relative clause)

5. Rewrite the sentences using defining relative clauses.
   1. Holly has a good friend. She lives next door.
      Holly has a good friend who lives next door.
   2. In Gran's house there's a picture. It's 100 years old.
   3. This is the camera. My dad uses it on holiday.
   4. There's a park. The children play in it.

6. Write sentences using non-relative clauses. Add commas where necessary.
   1. Mrs Morris is sixty-seven. (who / be / Lucy's grandmother)
      Mrs Morris, who is Lucy's grandmother, is sixty-seven.
   2. Paddy uses his bike every day. (which / be / new)
   3. Number 24 is an old house. (where / Molly / live)
   4. They live in Park Street. (which / be / near the town centre)
   5. Mr Jones often leaves the house early. (who / work / at the hospital)
   6. Our school is very big. (which / be / two kilometres away)

YOUR WORLD

7. Make one true and one false sentence about your favourite place, music, object or food. Use relative clauses. In pairs, guess which of your partner's sentences is true and which is false.

I can use defining and non-defining relative clauses to describe people, things and places.

7.5 Listening and Vocabulary
A helpful friend

Finn and Nala

Tilly and Prince

1 Can animals be your friend or part of your family? Why?/Why not?

2 Can dogs help people? How? Look at the photos. How can the dogs help the people?

3 Read the questions. What do you think Finn's sister will talk about?
  1 What did Finn think of his morning routine?
     a It was boring. b It was sad. c It was stressful.
  2 How old was Finn when he got Nala?
     a a baby b a child c a teenager
  3 What does Nala do to help with Finn's everyday routine?
     a She brings his shoes. b She washes his feet.
     c She puts his shoes on.
  4 Based on what Finn's sister's says, which adjective best describes Nala?
     a busy b funny c clever

4 🔊 7.11 Listen and choose the correct answer in Exercise 3.

5 Read the questions and answers. What does each question ask about? Match the questions with the types of information below.

   detailed meaning of a word or phrase   feelings
   general topic   specific information

  1 A puppy trainer
     a looks after old dogs.
     b teaches young dogs special skills.
     c finds new homes for unwanted dogs.
  2 When the dogs left, Tilly felt
     a sad. b bored. c happy for them.
  3 Who trained Prince?
     a Tilly on her own. b Tilly's step-mum.
     c Tilly and her step-mum together.
  4 What is the main thing we learn about assistance dogs from Tilly's account?
     a They often go to different owners.
     b They take a long time to learn things.
     c They can help with a wide range of needs.

6 🔊 7.12 Listen and choose the correct answer in Exercise 5.

7 🔊 7.13 **WORD FRIENDS** Match the different meanings of *get* with the verbs below. Listen and check.

   arrive   become   bring/fetch   buy   find   receive

   The verb *get* can have several meanings:
   1 **get** a pet = _____
   2 **get** a job = _____
   3 **get** home = _____
   4 **get** a letter/a phone call/an email = _____
   5 **get** a hot drink drink (for someone) = _____
   6 **get** better/worse; **get** dressed; **get** old(er); **get** ready; **get** bored/excited/upset = _____

8 Choose the correct option.
   1 My brother wants to get *a job / ready* in the police force.
   2 I've just got *dressed / a text* from my gran!
   3 Shall I get *a glass of water / better* for you?
   4 The train was late so we didn't get *home / a pet* until midnight.

VIDEO ▶ **WIDER WORLD**

9 ▶ 36 Watch Corinne talking about a situation. What was her pet? How did Corinne feel? Why?

10 In pairs, tell your partner about one of these situations. Describe how you felt and why.
   • a time when you got a pet
   • a time when you got the results of an important exam
   • a time when you got an important letter/email/phone call

I can understand a conversation about helping people in need.

7.6 Speaking

Identifying people in a group

VIDEO ▶ **WHO'S THAT GIRL ON THE RIGHT?**

Eren: What a day! Oh hey, Grandad. What are you up to?
Grandad: I'm watching this programme about music in the 1970s.
Eren: Oh, right. Well, that's, er … interesting.
Grandad: I used to go to lots of live performances like this when I was young.
Eren: No way! Really?
Grandad: Hey! That's me!
Eren: Where? Which guy do you mean?
Grandad: The good-looking one, right there. Pause the programme.
Eren: I can't recognise you. Let's rewind.
Grandad: I'm the one on the left, in the flowery shirt.
Eren: This one?
Grandad: No, rewind it some more. There. The guy with the brown hair.
Eren: Look at your clothes. They're so funny!
Grandad: Oh, and that's my friend, Harry, in the background. The tall one with curly hair.
Eren: And who's this girl on the right? Is that Grandma?
Grandad: Yes, it is. She was my girlfriend then.
Eren: Aww! How romantic!
Grandad: Yes, she was a lovely girl. We got married soon after that.

SOUNDS GOOD!
- What are you up to?
- How romantic!

1 Describe the man in the photo. What is he doing?

2 ▶ 37 🔊 7.14 Watch or listen and answer the questions.
  1 Why is Eren's grandad surprised?
  2 How does Eren help his grandad?
  3 Which three people do they see on TV?

SET FOR LIFE

3 How can you show interest during a conversation? Discuss in pairs. Use these ideas and add you own tips.
  - ask open questions
  - observe the person's body language
  - don't interrupt when someone is talking

4 Study the Speaking box. Find examples of the phrases in the dialogue.

SPEAKING ▶ **Identifying people in a group**

Talking about people in a group
He's/She's standing/sitting/talking to/playing with …
He's/She's wearing …
He's/She's in front of/behind/next to/near …
He's/She's on the left/on the right/in the middle.
He's/She's at the front/at the back/in the foreground/in the background.

Asking
Who's this/that boy/girl on the left/who is wearing … ?
Which one/girl/boy/man/woman/guy?
Which one do you mean?

Explaining
The one with/who is …
The tall/good-looking one.

5 Work in pairs. Student A, go to page 137. Student B, go to page 143.

YOUR WORLD

6 In pairs, take it in turns to ask and answer questions about someone in the photo on page 89. Use phrases from the Speaking box. Describe the people and talk about their personality. Use the ideas below to help you.

  seems calm   has a great sense of humour
  is confident/shy/cheerful

He's/She's the kind of person who …

Unit 7 94 I can explain who I am talking about.

7.7 Writing

A short story

1 What makes a friend a true friend?

2 Read the text. What do we find out about each friend in Flavia's story? Who are your real friends?

> ① Last week I learned an interesting lesson about true friends. I was feeling stressed about my Science homework. I didn't understand it and I needed someone to explain it.
>
> ② First, I asked my best friend Sienna to help. 'I'd explain it if I was free, but I'm quite busy.' Sienna and I get on well, and she's good at Science, so I was disappointed.
>
> ③ Next, I went to another friend who is also my neighbour. 'If I understood the homework, I'd help you,' said Harry, 'but it's too difficult.' Then I felt really stressed!
>
> ④ Just then a new classmate heard us. Lara is popular, but we don't speak often because she's quite loud and I'm a bit shy. I was surprised by her next words. 'I can help,' she offered.
>
> ⑤ Lara explained the Science homework to me carefully. Afterwards, we sat and chatted. We discovered we have a lot in common and the same sense of humour. It's been a great way to make a new friend!

3 Read Flavia's story again. Match the descriptions (1–5) with the events from the story (a–e).
1. ☐ setting the scene
2. ☐ the first event
3. ☐ the second event
4. ☐ the main event – the climax
5. ☐ the solution or outcome

a Flavia's neighbour can't help her.
b Lara and Flavia become friends.
c Flavia's friend who is good at science can't help her.
d Flavia has a problem.
e Flavia has a surprise offer of help.

4 Study the Writing box. Find examples of the phrases in Flavia's story.

WRITING — A short story

① Starting your story and setting the scene
Last week I learned an interesting lesson about true friends.
Have you ever had a really unusual day?

② Introduce your characters
My friend Sienna …   A new classmate …

③ Use direct speech
'I'd explain it if I was free, but I'm quite busy.'
'I'm sorry I can't help,' said Harry.

④ Main event – the climax (e.g. a surprise)
You'll never guess what happened next.   Then I had a real surprise.

⑤ End your story
All's well that ends well.   I never want to do that again!

5 Study the Language box. Write a few sentences about something strange/surprising that happened to you last week. Use the sequencers from the box.

LANGUAGE — Sequencers

We use sequencers to show the order of events in a story.
First, …
Next, …
Just then, …
Afterwards, …

I had a busy week. First, …

WRITING TIME

6 Write a story with the title *A friend in need*. It can be true or fictional.

1 Find ideas
Make notes about:
- the scene, the characters and the events.
- examples of direct speech.
- the ending.

2 Plan
Organise your ideas into paragraphs. Use Flavia's story to help you.

3 Write and share
- Write a draft story. Use the Language box and the Writing box to help you.
- Share your story with another student for feedback.
- Use the feedback from your partner and write the final version of your story.

4 Check
- Check language: did you use sequencers correctly?
- Check grammar: did you mostly use the Past Simple and some conditionals? Did you use relative clauses correctly?

I can write a short story.

Vocabulary Activator

WORDLIST 🔊 7.15

Word building (family)
great-grandfather (n)
great-grandmother (n)
great-grandparent (n)
half-brother (n)
half-sister (n)
stepbrother (n)
stepdaughter (n)
stepfather (n)
stepmother (n)
stepsister (n)
stepson (n)

Phrasal verbs
deal with (a problem) (v)
get along with (v)
get on with (v)
get together (v)
go out (with) (v)
grow up (v)
hang out with (v)
move away (v)

Word friends (relationships)
get to know someone
have an argument
have something in common
have the same sense of humour
see each other after school
share an interest in something
spend time with someone

Relations
(people)
best friend (n)
classmate (n)
mate (n)
stranger (n)
teammate (n)
(phrases with *friend*(*s*))
be friends
have a friend
keep friends
make friends

Word friends
(phrases with *get*)
get a hot drink (for someone)
get a job
get a letter/a phone call/an email
get a pet
get better/worse
get bored/excited/upset
get dressed
get home
get old(er)
get ready

Extra words
arrive (v)
aunt (n)
biological (adj)
character (n)
complicated (adj)
cousin (n)
dilemma (n)
disagree (v)
disappointed (adj)
end-of-term party (n)
family meal (n)
fetch (v)
flight (n)
friendly (adj)
friendship (n)
generation (n)
hand-held console (n)
home town (n)
invitation (n)
likes and dislikes
long-lost (adj)
loud (adj)
marriage (n)
miss somebody (v)
neighbour (n)
nightmare (n)

opinion (n)
parent (n)
positive (adj)
recognise (v)
related by blood
relation (n)
relative (n)
reply (v)
rescue (v)
researcher (n)
rewind (v)
shared (adj)
similar (adj)
social identity (n)
step (n)
tell the whole story
thought (n)
uncle (n)
volunteer (v)
wedding (n)

1 Complete the sentences with words from the wordlist. Then, in pairs, say if the sentences are true for you.
 1 I want to *get* to know my classmates better.
 2 I _____ a lot of interests in common with my parents.
 3 I like to spend time _____ other people.
 4 I _____ upset when people forget my birthday.
 5 I prefer to keep old friends than to _____ new ones.
 6 My family _____ together every weekend.
 7 I sometimes _____ arguments with classmates when they want different things.

2 Choose three phrases with *get* from the wordlist. Then, in pairs, share your phrases and make a short story with them.

3 Choose the correct option.
 1 No, I don't know that man. He's a complete *mate / stranger* to me.
 2 He doesn't live with his parents anymore – he moved *away / over* last year.
 3 She always gets his jokes – they have the *common / same* sense of humour.
 4 My grandmother grew *up / off* in this village.
 5 We need to talk about how to deal *off / with* this problem.

4 Complete the sentences with words from the wordlist. Then write a similar sentence. In pairs, complete each other's sentences.
 1 The opposite of 'friend' is *stranger*.
 2 A sister who has one parent different from you is your _____ .
 3 Someone who is on the same side as you in a game of football is your _____ .
 4 My grandmother's dad is my _____ .
 5 When a man marries a woman who has a son, the boy is the man's _____ .

5 🔊 7.16 **PRONUNCIATION** Listen to what happens when we say words together in speech.
 1 get together
 2 go out with someone
 3 grow up
 4 share an interest
 5 get dressed

6 🔊 7.17 **PRONUNCIATION** Listen again and repeat. Then, in pairs, practise saying the phrases.

Revision

Vocabulary

1 Match phrases 1–6 with phrases a–f with a similar meaning.

1. ☐ get dressed
2. ☐ move away
3. ☐ grow up
4. ☐ go out with
5. ☐ get along with
6. ☐ hang out with

a communicate and spend time well together
b visit a fun place with friends
c spend time together
d go to live in a different place
e put your clothes on
f go from child to adult

2 Complete the text with the words below.

> common   ~~great-grandfather~~   humour   interest
> stepdaughter   stranger   time

We had a big family meal at my house last weekend. My mum's grandfather was there – my ¹*great-grandfather*. He was with a girl about my age. He said, 'This is my son's ²_____ from his second wife. Have you met her? Her name's Lara.' I said no. She was a ³_____ to me. But we started talking and found that we had a lot in ⁴_____ . We also shared a(n) ⁵_____ in comedy films, and we had the same sense of ⁶_____ ! We spent a long ⁷_____ talking, which was fun.

3 Write the correct word for each definition.

1. A brother you share one parent with. h*alf-brother*
2. Someone who is in the same team as you. t_____
3. An informal word for 'friend'. m_____
4. When you solve a problem, you d_____ with it.
5. A person you share lessons with. c_____
6. When you spend time with a friend, you h_____ o_____ with him/her.

Grammar

4 Complete the Second Conditional questions with the correct form of the verbs in brackets. Then, in pairs, ask and answer the questions.

1. If your computer *stopped* (stop) working, how _____ (you/deal) with the problem?
2. If your parents _____ (want) to get a new family pet, what animal _____ (you/choose)?
3. If a new student _____ (join) the class, how _____ (you/make) him or her feel welcome?
4. How _____ (you/help) a grandparent to get started if he or she _____ (want) to use social media for the first time?
5. What _____ (you/do) if a dog _____ (try) to follow you home?

5 Complete the sentences with relative pronouns.

1. My favourite school subject, *which* is on Friday morning, is Art.
2. It's good to have a friend _____ can stay positive in difficult situations.
3. A place _____ I sometimes do my homework is on the sofa.
4. I came first in a singing competition, _____ was a surprise for everyone.
5. We have to find a TV show _____ everyone wants to watch.
6. My great-grandfather, _____ is ninety-five years old, always beats me at chess.

6 Choose the correct relative pronoun. Then complete the sentences to make them true for you. In pairs, compare your sentences.

1. I like shops *where / who*
   *I like shops where*_____ .
2. I like playing games *which / who*
   _____ .
3. A good friend is a person *where / who*
   _____ .
4. A place *which / where* I like to hang out with friends _____ .
5. The thing *that / where* helps me study best is _____ .
6. I enjoy family meals *who / which*
   _____ .

Speaking

7 In pairs, imagine you are looking at a family photo. Student A, go to page 137. Student B, go to page 143. Follow the instructions for Student A's 'family photo'. Then swap roles.

Student A: Talk about one person in the photo and say what they are doing.
Student B: Comment on that person. Then ask about another person in the photo.
Student A: Answer Student B's question. Then talk about and comment on another person.

Dictation

8 🔊 7.18 Listen. Then listen again and write down what you hear.

Unit 7

BBC CULTURE

From generation to generation

Lessons from Grandad

Have you ever thought about what you get and learn from your elders? Take food, for example. Where does your food really come from? For example, think about modern milk production. Milk goes from a farm to a milk factory, where it is processed and put in milk bottles or cartons. Then someone buys it for you from a supermarket or a local shop. That's a lot of steps!

Mark Holland, from Surrey, didn't like the large number of steps involved in producing food. 'It seemed that the food was not as fresh as we thought. So, I decided to go to a farmer's market one day. My grandfather sells food from his farm there. The food is a little more expensive, but it is organic. This means it is more nutritious and there are no added chemicals in the food. It is much more delicious too. I spend a lot of time on my grandfather's farm. He shows me traditional methods of farming and cooking. Next year I want to study farming. I think with my grandfather's help and my studies, I can become a very successful farmer.'

Sarah became interested in organic food a few years ago. She enjoys hanging out with Grandad. 'One year he taught me how to make a vegetable salad. All the vegetables were from his garden. The salad was delicious – very different from the ones from supermarkets. This made me think about where our food comes from and how fresh it is. Now I'm a teenager I still visit Grandad and he teaches me so many things about food, like how to cook it and where it comes from. When I finish school, I want to become a chef and cook with food straight from my own market garden.'

nutritious (adj) healthy and good for you to eat
organic (adj) (of food) that has no added chemicals

---

1 **VISIBLE THINKING** In pairs, follow these steps.
   CONCEPT
   1 Look at the photo. What is the boy learning from his grandad?
   2 Where do you get your food from? How fresh is it?
   CHALLENGE
   3 Is there a problem with food that comes from supermarkets?
   4 Can farmer's markets be a better choice than supermarkets?
   CHANGE
   5 Do you think you will choose to buy only organic food?

2 🔊 7.19 Read the article. Do you think people like Mark and Sarah can change how we buy food in the future?

3 Read the article again and mark the sentences true (T) or false (F).
   1 ☐ Food in supermarkets usually comes straight from a farm.
   2 ☐ Mark's grandfather sells his produce at a farmer's market.
   3 ☐ Organic food is usually a little cheaper.
   4 ☐ Mark gets to know traditional methods of farming.
   5 ☐ Sarah learns about where food comes from with her grandad.
   6 ☐ Sarah wants to cook with her own fresh food in the future.

4 In pairs, discuss the questions.
   1 Where do people in your country buy fresh food?
   2 Do you think modern and traditional methods can work together to produce healthy food?

BBC ▶ Arctic life

5 ▶ 38 Look at the photo. What do you think the woman is teaching her granddaughter? Do you think they get on well? Watch Part 1 of the video and check your ideas.

6 ▶ 38 Watch Part 1 of the video again and complete the sentences with the words below.

> collect food   generations   hard life   sea

1 The _____ freezes for half of the year in the Arctic.
2 Minnie doesn't think it is a _____ in her village.
3 Eva learns how to _____ from her grandmother.
4 The women in Minnie's family have collected food for _____.

7 In pairs, discuss the questions.
1 Do you think you would find life in this village good? Why?/Why not?
2 Do you think the methods they use to find food are easy or difficult? Why?

8 ▶ 39 Watch Part 2 of the video and tick (✓) the correct sentences.
1 ☐ They make sure there is no sea water in the sea cave.
2 ☐ They have more than half an hour to work.
3 ☐ They find the food they are looking for.
4 ☐ When they hear the sea, they leave quickly.
5 ☐ The sea closes the ice hole.
6 ☐ Eva learns a traditional skill she can use.

9 In pairs or groups, discuss the questions.
1 What problems do you think the people in this village have?
2 How do you think the older generation help in this village?
3 What skills can older people teach us?

PROJECT TIME

10 In groups of three, prepare a presentation about how people in remote places collect food. Follow these steps.

1 In groups, choose a remote place to focus on. Decide who can find the answers to these questions.
- Where is the place and what is it like?
- How do they find food? Is it a dangerous/traditional method?
- How do younger generations learn about traditional methods of collecting food?

2 Individually, create your part of the presentation.
- Find information and photos for your slides.
- For each slide, write a short text and add the photos.

3 In your group, create your presentation.
- Put all the slides together and think of a title for your presentation.
- Check and edit your presentation.
- Practise giving the presentation as a group.

4 Share your presentation with the class.
- Answer other students' questions.
- Listen to the other presentations. Ask questions.

Just justice

8

VOCABULARY
Crimes and criminals | Solving crimes | The law | Word building: negative adjectives | Investigating crimes

GRAMMAR
Present and Past Simple passive | have/get something done

SAFE NEIGHBOURHOODS

Let's stand up to crime

Hopefully, you haven't been unlucky and been the victim of a crime. But if you have, we have some tips and advice to help you. First, let's look at the type of crime some of you have experienced. Then click on the link to find out how you can stop the crime happening in the first place.

1 Rhea, Newcastle
I was a witness to a bank robbery. Two robbers ran into the bank and stole a lot of money. After robbing the bank, they got away on a motorbike. I spoke to the detective who's trying to solve the crime.

2 Mhairi, Glasgow
There have been a lot of burglaries in our area recently. Last month some burglars broke into our neighbour's house. The thieves stole her purse and some jewellery. She was really upset.

3 Jason, Bristol
Pickpocketing is a big problem in the city. Last night I was on a busy train when I felt someone's hand in my back pocket. I turned around quickly, but the pickpocket wasn't there. And neither was my wallet!

4 Humza, Coventry
I work in a small shop with a big problem: theft, or shoplifting, to be specific. The shoplifters steal all sorts of things. We're going to install security cameras to try to stop them.

5 Emma, Leeds
Some vandals ran through our neighbourhood last night. They damaged the swings in the children's park, broke a street light and threw a stone at a shop window. Why do people commit such stupid crimes? I don't understand vandalism.

Tips and advice **Read more**

8.1 Vocabulary

Crime

1 Read crime stories 1–5 and match them with photos A–E.
1 ☐   2 ☐   3 ☐   4 ☐   5 ☐

2 Read the stories again. Who do you think had the most unpleasant experience? In pairs, discuss your ideas.

3 🔊 8.1 Study Vocabulary box A. Find the words in the stories in Exercise 1 and check you understand them.

VOCABULARY A   Criminals
burglar   pickpocket   robber   shoplifter   thief   vandal

Unit 8   100

4 🔊 8.2 **WORD FRIENDS** Complete the sentences with the correct form of the verbs below. Use one of the verbs twice. Listen and check.

> break   break into   ~~commit~~   damage
> rob   solve   steal

1. A criminal is someone who *commits* a crime and _____ the law.
2. A shoplifter is someone who _____ things from a shop.
3. A bank robber is someone who _____ a bank.
4. A burglar is someone who _____ homes.
5. A vandal is someone who _____ buildings and other things.
6. A detective is someone who _____ crimes.
7. A thief is someone who _____ things from people.

5 🔊 8.3 Study Vocabulary box B. Find the crimes in the stories in Exercise 1 and complete the table. Listen and check.

VOCABULARY B — Word building: crimes

Person	Crime
(bank) robber	*(bank) robbery*
burglar	_____
pickpocket	_____
shoplifter	_____
thief	_____
vandal	_____

6 🔊 8.4 Look at Vocabulary box B again and listen to a boy talking about crime. Write the examples of crimes and criminals you hear. What crimes have you heard or read about where you live? Discuss in pairs.

7 🔊 8.5 Study Vocabulary box C and complete the story below with the correct form of words from the box. Listen and check.

VOCABULARY C — Solving crimes

> case   clue   detective   fingerprint   security camera
> suspect   witness

8 🔊 8.6 Study Vocabulary box D and choose the correct option in the newspaper headlines below. Listen and check.

VOCABULARY D — The law

> court   fine   judge   lawyer   prison   punishment
> reward   sentence

1. £500 *punishment / reward* for information on local vandals
2. Ten-year prison *judge / sentence* for bank robbers
3. *Judge / Lawyer* decides shoplifter should work for the community
4. Train pickpocket gets a *fine / reward* of £250
5. Ex-burglar goes back to school to become a *lawyer / court*!
6. Vandals should go to *fine / prison*, says politician

YOUR WORLD

9 In pairs, discuss the questions.
1. What punishments would you give the criminals in the crime stories in Exercise 1?
2. Would you like to be a police officer/detective/lawyer/judge? Why?/Why not?

I'm the lead ¹*detective* investigating the recent bank robbery. It wasn't a difficult ²_____. We interviewed several ³_____ and from their descriptions, I immediately thought of two possible ⁴_____, so we brought them in for questioning. They said they had nothing to do with it, but I knew they were lying. We had two ⁵_____ that helped us solve the crime. First, the recording from the ⁶_____ showed their faces. Secondly, their ⁷_____ were all over the bank. I arrested them. Then some police officers searched their flat and found the money from the robbery.

I can talk about crime and criminals.

8.2 Grammar

Present and Past Simple passive

1 What do you know about Sherlock Holmes? In pairs, make a list.

2 🔊 8.7 In pairs, do the quiz. Listen and check.

The Sherlock Holmes QUIZ

1. The *Sherlock Holmes* detective stories were written 100 years ago by
   a Arthur Conan Doyle.
   b Agatha Christie.
2. Holmes had a famous assistant. What was his name?
   a Doctor Who
   b Doctor Watson
3. The stories were first published
   a in a book.
   b in a magazine.
4. Sherlock's flat is located at number 221B of a famous London street. It is
   a Sherlock Street.
   b Baker Street.
5. Which famous Sherlock Holmes quote is never really used by Sherlock Holmes?
   a 'Elementary, my dear Watson.'
   b 'My mind is like a racing engine.'

3 Study the Grammar box. Find more examples of the Present and Past Simple passive in the quiz.

> **GRAMMAR** › **The passive**
>
> **Present Simple passive**
> The quote **is** never really **used** by Sherlock Holmes.
>
> **Past Simple passive**
> The detective stories **were written** by a British author.

GRAMMAR TIME › PAGE 133

> ⚠️ **WATCH OUT!**
> Use *by* + name/person to say who did the action.
> The detective stories were written by a British author.

4 Write the Past Simple and past participle forms of the verbs below. Underline the verbs which are the same in the Past Simple and Past Participle. Use the irregular verbs list on page 136 to help you.

| ask | build | catch | chase | hide |
| make | see | use | watch | write |

ask – asked – asked

5 Complete the sentences with the past participle form of the verbs in brackets.
1. Security cameras are *used* (use) to find clues about many crimes.
2. The thief escaped but was _____ (catch) when she fell.
3. Yesterday evening two car thieves were _____ (chase) by police in fast cars.
4. Sometimes a recording from security cameras is _____ (watch) by special detectives.
5. Last night the witnesses were _____ (ask) questions by police officers.
6. This security camera is _____ (hide) so that shoplifters don't see it.

6 Complete the text with the Present or Past Simple passive form of the verbs in brackets. Add *by* where necessary.

> The *Nancy Drew* stories are among the most famous detective stories ever. The first stories about Nancy Drew [1] *were published* (publish) in the 1930s. Other, newer stories have appeared since then. The books [2] _____ (create) for teenagers. The *Nancy Drew* detective stories [3] _____ (write) several different authors. The name Carolyn Keene [4] _____ (use) by all the authors, but Nancy's name [5] _____ (change) in some countries. It may be surprising, but this old series [6] _____ (read) thousands of young people even today, and each year lots and lots of copies [7] _____ (sell).

YOUR WORLD

7 Tell the class about a detective story or film that you know.

Unit 8 — 102 — I can use the Present and Past Simple passive.

8.3 Reading and Vocabulary

The right punishment?

1 Look at the photos and title of the article. Describe the photos. What do you think the article is about?

2 🔊 8.8 Read the article and check your answers to Exercise 1. What kind of court did Lisa and Ian choose? What countries have such courts?

3 Read the article again and choose the correct answer.
  1 What did the police officer do that was surprising?
    a He arrested Lisa and Ian for stealing.
    b He sent Lisa and Ian to a youth court.
    c He asked Lisa and Ian to choose where to go.
    d He gave Lisa and Ian something from the shop.
  2 Why did Lisa and Ian choose to go to a youth court?
    a They thought it was difficult to understand adults.
    b They believed their actions were legal.
    c They wanted to make their own choices.
    d They wanted to be heard by people of their own age.
  3 Which of these statements is true about youth courts?
    a You listen to stories about all kinds of crimes.
    b You are heard by people who are a similar age.
    c You can choose a punishment that works for you.
    d You meet young people from around the world.
  4 How did Lisa and Ian react to their punishment?
    a They agreed it was appropriate.
    b They were quite unhappy.
    c They wanted to change it.
    d They thought it was hard work.

4 🔊 8.9 Study the Vocabulary box. Find more adjectives with negative prefixes in the article and write the missing words. How do these prefixes change the meaning of an adjective?

VOCABULARY — Word building: negative adjectives

Prefix	Examples
un-	unhappy, uninteresting, unimportant, uncomfortable, unkind, unfair, _____
im-	impatient, _____
il-	illogical, _____
ir-	irregular, _____

A fair punishment

Imagine that you're a police officer. What would you do if you saw some teenagers shoplifting? A kind police officer's decision helped Lisa and her brother Ian out of a difficult situation.

When Lisa was fifteen and Ian was seventeen, they were arrested for stealing from a shop. The police officer who caught them did an unusual thing: he gave them a choice. Did they want to go to a normal court, where an adult judge would decide their punishment? Or did they want to go to a youth court, where a group of young people would decide their punishment?

For Lisa and Ian, the answer was easy. They knew they had done something illegal and it was impossible to avoid punishment, but they hoped young judges might understand their situation better. That's why they chose to go to a youth court.

But what is a youth court? It's a place where the jury – the group of people who make decisions – is made up of people aged 12–19. Young people who are in trouble with the law have a chance to explain their story, be judged and get back on the 'right track'. There are now thousands of these courts around the world, including Europe, Asia and the USA. Of course, normal courts still deal with serious crimes.

At the court, Lisa and Ian, who were very nervous, were given three punishments. First, they both had to write an apology to the shop owner. Then they had to do forty hours of 'community service'. In other words, they had to help other people in their local area. Finally, they had to volunteer at the youth court themselves. The brother and sister both felt this was fair. They didn't want to be irresponsible any more. As volunteers, they have learned how the court works. They have both helped to choose fair punishments for other young people too.

YOUR WORLD

5 Do you think youth courts are a good idea? Why?/Why not?

8.4 Grammar
have/get something done

VIDEO ▶ A NEW LOOK

Abe: They're the photos for the poster for our film.
Eren: Wow! They're great. Is that Carla?
Abe: Yes.
Eren: So, who's that?
Abe: It's Carla too!
Eren: No way!
Abe: Yes, she wore a wig and make-up. In the film she's accused of a crime she didn't commit and she's on the run from the police. So, she changes her look. She gets her hair cut short. She has it dyed blonde. She has her eyebrows shaped and then she gets her fingernails and her make-up done.
Eren: How come her eyes have changed colour?
Abe: She put in coloured contact lenses.
Eren: She's so different! She looks like a rock star!
Abe: OK, I'm ready. Let's go to the park.
Eren: I've changed my mind. Let's go to the centre.
Abe: Why?
Eren: I want to change my look, to get my hair cut.

1 Look at the photo. What do you think Abe and Eren are doing?

2 ▶ 40 ◀) 8.10 Watch or listen and check your ideas from Exercise 1. Why does Carla's character in the film change her look?

3 Do you like to change your appearance? What do you usually change – your hairstyle or your clothes?

4 Study the Grammar box. Find more examples of *have/get something done* in the dialogue.

> **GRAMMAR** *have/get something done*
>
> She *has her eyebrows shaped*.
> I want to *get my hair cut*.
> Are you *going to get your hair dyed*?

GRAMMAR TIME > PAGE 134

⚠ WATCH OUT!
We use possessive adjectives (*my, your, his, her*, etc.) to talk about body parts.
I got *my* hair cut. NOT ~~I got the hair cut.~~

5 Match the sentence halves.
1 ☐ The burglar broke the window
2 ☐ He took a photo of the suspect
3 ☐ If you put money in your back pocket,
4 ☐ Your crime drawings are so good
5 ☐ It would be a good idea
6 ☐ After she got out of prison,

a you'll get it stolen.
b she had her name changed.
c you should have them published.
d to get a burglar alarm installed.
e so we had to get it fixed.
f and had it photocopied.

6 Complete the sentences with the correct form of *have something done*.
1 I *had my hair cut* (my hair/cut) last week.
2 I _____ (my eyes/not test) for ages.
3 I _____ (already/my photo/print) in the local paper twice.
4 I don't want to _____ (my bike/steal), so I always lock it up.
5 I'd love to _____ (my bedroom/clean), but I have to do it myself.

YOUR WORLD

7 In pairs, say if the sentences in Exercise 6 are true for you. Correct the false sentences.

> *I didn't have my hair cut last week. I had it cut about a month ago.*

Unit 8 104 I can use the construction *have/get something done*.

8.5 Listening and Vocabulary
Crimes and criminals

1 In pairs, describe the photo. How can social media help the police solve a crime like this? What about other crimes?

2 ◆)) 8.11 **WORD FRIENDS** Match the verbs with the nouns to make phrases about investigating crimes. Listen and check.

1. ☐ search   a a witness
2. ☐ arrest   b clues
3. ☐ interview   c the area
4. ☐ take   d fingerprints
5. ☐ look for   e a criminal

3 ◆)) 8.12 Listen to the first part of a podcast. What do you think happened?

4 ◆)) 8.13 Listen to the second part of the podcast and check your ideas from Exercise 3.

5 ◆)) 8.13 Listen again and number the events in the correct order.

a ☐ The police arrested the burglar.
b ☐ Katrina discovered her laptop was missing.
c ☐ A friend told Katrina about a conversation in the park.
d ☐ The police looked for clues in and near the house.
e ☐ Katrina called the police.
f ☐ Katrina and Mia started looking on social media.

6 ◆)) 8.14 Listen to the final part of the podcast and complete the notes.

Date of burglary: [1]_____
Time of burglary: between [2]_____ *and* _____ *p.m.*
Items still missing: [3]_____
Phone number: [4]_____
Reward: [5] £_____

VIDEO ▶ **WIDER WORLD**

7 ▶ 41 Watch five people answering the questions. What answers do they give?

What would you do if:
1. you had your phone stolen?
2. you saw someone shoplifting?
3. you saw someone vandalising something?

8 In pairs, ask and answer the questions in Exercise 7.

I'd call the phone company. Then I would tell all my friends and …

I can understand people talking about a crime.

8.6 Speaking
Keeping a conversation going

VIDEO ▶ IS SOMETHING WRONG?

Mum: It's so nice to go on a walk together. I love this park. You're quiet. Are you OK? Is something wrong?
Bea: I'm fine, Mum. Honestly.
Mum: Hmm … Come on, I can tell that you're worrying about something. It usually helps to talk.
Bea: I don't know.
Mum: Go on, tell me.
Bea: Well, some nasty comments were posted on my nature blog.
Mum: Really? What do you mean?
Bea: I shared my photo of that kingfisher we saw on the river. I thought it was amazing because it's hard to take good photos of birds when they're moving so fast.
Mum: Right …
Bea: Some people put nice comments like, 'So cute!'
Mum: That's nice!
Bea: But other people put things like 'Yawn. Boooring post!' Then one person said, 'A boring post by a boring person.' And I was really hurt.
Mum: Just ignore them! By the way, how many people liked your post?
Bea: I don't know, a few hundred?
Mum: Well, it seems to me most people agree with you.
Bea: Hmm, I see what you mean. 'Mum knows best', hey? After all, you're older and wiser … much older, in fact!
Mum: Hey! I'm not that old, OK?

SOUNDS GOOD! So cute! • Just ignore them! • By the way.

1 ▶ 42 🔊 8.15 Look at the photo. How do you think Bea feels? Watch or listen and check.

2 Do you think Bea's 'friends' showed respect in their online comments?

SET FOR LIFE

3 What can you do about negative comments on your social media? Discuss in pairs. Use these ideas to help you.
- ignore them
- block the person commenting
- if possible, speak to the 'commenter' in real life

4 Study the Speaking box. Find examples of the phrases in the dialogue.

SPEAKING Keeping a conversation going

Inviting
Are you OK?   Is something wrong?
Do you want to talk about it?   Go on, tell me.

Encouraging
What do you mean?   Really?   Then what happened?
I'm sure (you were/did).   Exactly.

Reassuring
Don't worry. I'm fine. Honestly.
Of course you can (do it).   Right.

Responding
Definitely!   Absolutely!   I don't know.

5 🔊 8.16 Complete the dialogues with one or two words in each gap. Listen and check.
1. A: I like social media, but sometimes it's bad.
   B: What do you _____?
   A: When people post negative comments it's bad. I try to post positive comments.
2. A: I think thirteen is the right age to use most social media sites.
   B: Yes, _____ ! I think twelve is too young.

6 Discuss the statement in pairs. How many phrases from the Speaking box can you include in your conversation?
All social media is bad for friendship.

YOUR WORLD

7 In pairs take turns to tell your partner about something you like or dislike about social media. Invite your partner to comment.

8.7 Writing

An opinion essay

1. Give examples of rubbish you see in your everyday environment. Do you think leaving litter is a crime?

2. Read the essay. What is the writer's main opinion? Do you agree?

> 'Rubbish is bad for the environment. People who leave litter outdoors should pay a fine.' Do you agree? Explain your ideas.

1 We all agree that litter is bad for the environment. But personally, I believe that stronger punishments are needed to deal with the problem of rubbish. For example, many riverbanks and beaches are littered with plastic bottles and bags. This is a serious problem for river wildlife as well as ocean animals, as the plastic is carried out to sea. As a result, many animals are hurt or killed by pieces of plastic.

2 On the one hand, we must punish people who don't clean up after themselves. For example, if you do not put your litter in a bin, you should have to clean up other people's rubbish too! On the other hand, are such punishments enough? In my opinion, people would stop dropping litter if they had to pay a fine every time.

3 However, I do not think small fines will solve the problem. Although fines can make people think about the environment, it may not be enough to make them change their habits. For this reason, I would like to see bigger fines, so as to put a stop to littering.

4 In conclusion, I agree with serious fines for people who continue to drop litter in order to keep the environment clean and safe.

3. Study the Writing box. Complete the gaps with words and phrases from the essay.

WRITING An opinion essay

1 Give your main reaction
 - In my opinion, …
 - Personally, _____ that …

2 Balance opinions
 - On the one hand, …
 - _____ , …

3 Add contrasting ideas
 - However, I think/do not think that …
 - _____ …

4 Summarise and conclude
 - Overall, …
 - In general, …
 - _____

4. Study the Language box. Find examples of the words and phrases in the essay.

LANGUAGE Connectors of purpose and result

Connectors of purpose: *to, in order to, so as to*
Connectors of result: *for this reason, as a result*

5. Rewrite the sentences using the words in brackets. Use the Language box to help you.
   1. People should take their litter home to protect the environment. (as)
   2. They had to pay a fine so they are more careful now. (result)
   3. Animals are important, so people need to think about them. (reason)
   4. I believe fines are useful to help us keep the law. (order)

WRITING TIME

6. Write an opinion essay on the following question: 'Littering is a serious problem. People who drop litter should do unpaid community work.' Do you agree? Explain your ideas.

1 Find ideas
 Make notes about:
 - litter in your local environment – think of examples
 - your opinion on community work. Is it a good punishment?
 - any other ideas to encourage people to behave responsibly
 - your conclusion

2 Plan
 Organise your ideas into paragraphs. Use the essay in Exercise 2 to help you.

3 Write and share
 - Write a draft essay. Use the Language box and the Writing box to help you.
 - Share your essay with another student for feedback.
 - Use the feedback from your partner and write the final version of your essay.

4 Check
 - Check language: did you use connectors correctly?
 - Check grammar: did you use the passive correctly?

I can write an opinion essay.

Vocabulary Activator

WORDLIST 🔊 8.17

Criminals
burglar (n)
pickpocket (n)
robber (n)
shoplifter (n)
thief (n)
vandal (n)

Word friends
(crime collocations)
break into homes
break the law
commit a crime
damage buildings
rob a bank
solve crimes
steal things

Word building
(crimes)
burglary (n)
pickpocketing (n)
robbery (n)
shoplifting (n)
theft (n)
vandalism (n)

Solving crimes
case (n)
clue (n)
detective (n)
fingerprint (n)
security camera (n)
suspect (n)
witness (n)

The law
court (n)
fine (n)
judge (n)
lawyer (n)
prison (n)
punishment (n)
reward (n)
sentence (n)

Word building
(negative adjectives)
illegal (adj)
illogical (adj)
impatient (adj)
impossible (adj)
irregular (adj)
uncomfortable (adj)

unfair (adj)
unhappy (adj)
unimportant (adj)
uninteresting (adj)
unkind (adj)
unusual (adj)

Word friends
(investigating crimes)
arrest a criminal
interview a witness
look for clues
search the area
take fingerprints

Extra words
accuse (v)
apology (n)
appear (v)
assistant (n)
author (n)
be in trouble with
catch (v)
chase (v)
choice (n)
community (n)
description (n)

elementary (adj)
engine (n)
eyebrow (n)
fair punishment
fingernail (n)
get away (v)
install (v)
investigate (v)
irresponsible (adj)
jewellery (n)
jury (n)
lie (v)
mind (n)
neighbourhood (n)
politician (n)
publish (v)
purse (n)
question (v)
quote (n)
recording (n)
series (n)
shop window (n)
stone (n)
street light (n)
swing (n)
wallet (n)

1 Use the wordlist to find these things.
1 two places where criminals are taken after they are arrested
2 five crimes that involve stealing something
3 three words for ways to pay for a crime
4 three jobs

2 Answer the quiz questions with words from the wordlist. Then write one more question. In pairs, ask and answer each other's questions.

Crime Quiz

1 What is someone who sees a crime and can describe what happened called? *witness*
2 Which crime involves people breaking objects which are not their own? _____
3 Who is a person who helps with legal problems? _____
4 Who is the person who decides the punishment for a criminal? _____
5 Where are criminals sent as a punishment for their crimes? _____
6 What can detectives look for to help them understand a case? _____

3 Match 1–8 with a–h to make phrases.
1 arrest the   a law
2 break the   b witness
3 commit a   c crime
4 interview a   d fingerprints
5 rob a   e criminal
6 search an   f area
7 take   g bank
8 steal   h things

4 In pairs, imagine you are detectives trying to find a criminal. Use your detective skills to suggest three things you could do. Use words from the wordlist.
We could look for clues.

5 🔊 8.18 **PRONUNCIATION** The underlined vowels in the suffixes of the words below are unstressed. Listen to their pronunciation (/ə/).

comfort**a**ble   import**a**nt   lawy**er**   logic**a**l
punishm**e**nt   regul**ar**

6 🔊 8.19 **PRONUNCIATION** Underline the vowels with the /ə/ sound in the suffixes of the words below. Listen and repeat.

assistant   burglar   impatient
impossible   robber

Unit 8

Revision

Vocabulary

1 Complete the second sentence so that it means the same as the first one. Use the correct form of the underlined word.
1. <u>Robbers</u> can go to prison for a long time.
   People who commit <u>robbery</u> can go to prison for a long time.
2. It isn't <u>possible</u> to read this book in one day.
   Reading this book in one day is _____ .
3. Police have arrested a <u>thief</u>.
   Police have arrested somebody for _____ .
4. We didn't feel <u>comfortable</u> in our new car's seats.
   Our new car's seats were _____ .
5. That woman has been a <u>burglar</u> in the past.
   That woman has committed _____ in the past.
6. I couldn't see the <u>logic</u> in the detective's ideas.
   The detective's ideas seemed _____ to me.

2 Complete the extract from a detective story with the words below.

> burglary case reward security
> suspect thief witness

Last week someone broke into another jewellery shop and stole the biggest diamond in London. It was only the latest crime in the most difficult ¹<u>case</u> I've ever had. Like the other crimes, the ² _____ left no clues at all, and there were no ³ _____ camera recordings to look at. But I got lucky: a ⁴ _____ came to see me! She was walking by the shop at the time of the ⁵ _____ and she described the person inside. But I still didn't have a ⁶ _____ . So I made a poster with an artist's drawing, offering a large ⁷ _____ for information.

3 Complete the news headlines with the Present Simple form of the correct verbs.

1. **Building workers d<u>amage</u> priceless painting in city art gallery**
2. **Detectives s_____ the crime of the century!**
3. **Armed men r_____ a bank and steal £1 million**
4. **Secret lives: the criminals who work by day and b_____ into homes by night**
5. **Police a_____ bank robbers after long car chase**

Grammar

4 Rewrite the sentences in the passive. Do not include the underlined subjects.
1. <u>They</u> investigated several internet crimes last year.
   Several internet crimes <u>were investigated last year</u>.
2. <u>We</u> don't use this building as a prison now.
   This building _____ .
3. <u>The city council</u> gave a lot of money to my neighbourhood to improve it.
   My neighbourhood _____ .
4. <u>People</u> don't play football very often in our park.
   Football _____ .
5. <u>Nobody</u> saw the burglar when she entered the building.
   The burglar _____ .

5 Complete the quiz questions with the Present Simple or Past Simple passive form of the verbs in brackets. Then match the answers below to the questions.

> Arthur Conan Doyle   dogs   Robin Hood
> Socrates   Washington D.C.

1. Which ancient Greek philosopher (give) a death sentence? <u>was given</u>
2. Who (the Sherlock Holmes books/write) by?
3. Which American city (FBI headquarters/locate) in?
4. Which famous British thief (play) by Russell Crowe in a 2010 film?
5. What animals (use) to find illegal substances in airports?

6 Complete the dialogues with the correct form of *have something done* and the verbs in brackets.
1. A: Your hair looks great! When ¹<u>did you have it dyed</u> (you/it/dye)?
   B: Yesterday.
2. A: The security camera isn't working.
   B: I know, we ² _____ (it/fix) soon.
3. A: Why do you keep your phone in your bag?
   B: I don't want to ³ _____ (it/steal).
4. A: Who printed the crime photos? They're great!
   B: I ⁴ _____ (not/them/print). I did them myself.
5. A: Your detective stories are really good!
   ⁵ _____ (you/any of them/publish)?
   B: Not yet, but I'd like to.

Speaking

7 In pairs, turn to page 137 and follow the instructions to role play a dialogue. Then swap roles.

Dictation

8 🔊 8.20 Listen. Then listen again and write down what you hear.

SET FOR LIFE

You decide!

Should I play in the match instead of going to Elsa's birthday lunch?

For
- ☐ The team has never chosen me for a match before – it's fantastic that they asked me.
- ☐ They might be annoyed with me if I say 'no'.

Against
- ☐ I might play badly and that will be embarrassing.
- ☐ I don't know the people in the team very well.
- ☐ It's my best friend's birthday and she'll be sad if I don't celebrate her birthday with her.
- ☐ Everyone will talk about her birthday lunch the next day, and I'll feel bad that I wasn't there.

1 Read Harry's for and against lists. What would you do if you were in his situation?

2 In pairs, discuss the questions.
1. What short-term decisions have you made today/this week/this year?
2. What long-term decisions will you have to make in your life?
3. Have you ever had to make a difficult decision? What was the situation? Why was it hard to decide what to do?

3 In pairs, look at the statements. Do you think they are T (true) or F (false)?
1. ☐ Humans have adult brains from the age of about fourteen.
2. ☐ Adults and teenagers make decisions in the same way.
3. ☐ It's important for teenagers to think about the long term when they make decisions.

4 🔊 8.21 Listen to an expert's talk on making decisions and check your answers in Exercise 3.

5 🔊 8.22 Listen to the next part of the talk and choose the correct option.
1. Before you make a decision, make sure you know all the *people / facts*.
2. In a list of reasons for and against a decision, include *short-term / good* reasons and *long-term / bad* reasons.
3. There isn't always only one right *reason / decision*.
4. You won't always have the *result / decision* that you hoped for.

6 Look again at Harry's lists in Exercise 1. Has he written down long-term (L) reasons or short-term (S) reasons?

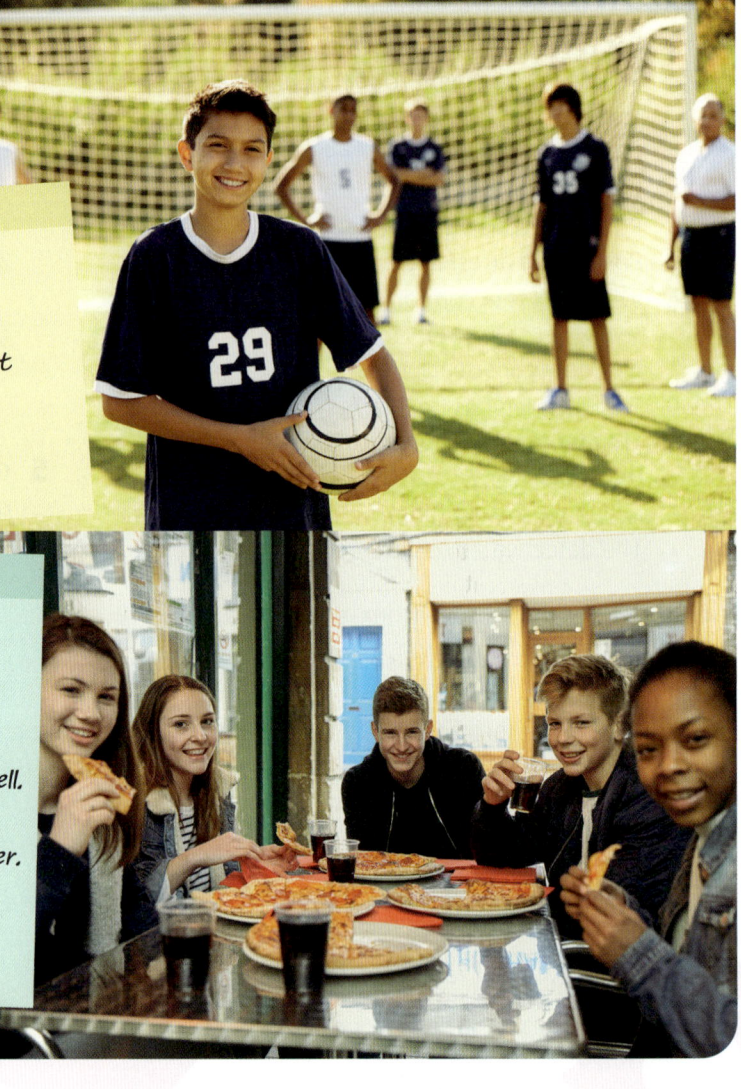

Units 7–8   I can make responsible decisions.

Make a decision

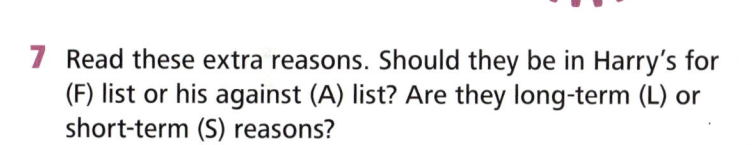

7 Read these extra reasons. Should they be in Harry's for (F) list or his against (A) list? Are they long-term (L) or short-term (S) reasons?

1	I've trained with the team for months, so I've worked hard for the opportunity.
2	If I don't agree to play in the match this time, they may not ask me again.
3	It's Ethan's birthday next month, and then Elsa's birthday will be old news.
4	It's good for my well-being and health to play a sport.
5	I'll get to know my teammates more quickly if I play in matches with them.
6	People don't stay friends if they don't make the effort to celebrate their birthdays together.
7	I want to get better at my sport and it's hard to do that if I don't play in matches.

8 Give each of Harry's reasons in Exercises 1 and Exercise 7 a score from 1 (not at all important) to 10 (extremely important). Then compare the total score for all the 'for' reasons and all the 'against' reasons. What do you think Harry should do?

9 Read the Useful Phrases. Imagine you have to make a decision. In pairs, choose one topic and discuss some reasons for and against.
1 Should I give up my hobby so that I can spend more time studying?
2 Should I tell my friend's parents that he sometimes shoplifts?
3 Should I miss three months of school to be in a film?

10 Read the Useful Tips. Do you think these ideas will help you to make better decisions in the future? Why?/Why not?

SET FOR LIFE

11 In pairs, make a decision. Remember to think about short-term and long-term reasons. Follow these steps.

1 Choose one of the situations in Exercise 9 or think of your own ideas.

2 Write two lists, with reasons for and against. Use expressions from the Useful Phrases box to discuss your reasons.

3 Give each reason a score from 1 (not at all important) to 10 (extremely important). Use the total scores to help you make the decision.

4 Present your decision and reasons to the class.

USEFUL TIPS

When you make decisions, it's important to consider short-term and long-term reasons, and make the best decision with the information available.

- Make sure you know all the facts before you decide.
- Make lists of reasons for and against.
- Think about both long-term and short-term reasons.
- Choose the decision with the more important reasons.

USEFUL PHRASES

Reasons for and against
One long-term/short-term advantage is that …
In the long/short term, it's (not) a good idea because …
If you (didn't) … , you would(n't) …

What should influence a decision
That's a very important point.
That's the biggest reason for … -ing.
I don't think that should influence the decision very much.
That doesn't matter very much because …
I think … is a bigger issue than …

Lessons in life

9

VOCABULARY
School subjects | Describing students | Learning and assessment | Collocations with *make* and *take* | Phrasal verbs

GRAMMAR
Reported speech: statements | Word order in questions

Top five coolest lessons?

Do you ever want to learn outside the classroom? Would you enjoy studying subjects where you take a practical exam, not a written test?

If the answer is 'yes', you might like to move to Australia and Hawaii! In these places, it's important for pupils to be confident in water, so surfing lessons are a normal part of the school curriculum. As well as Language, Maths and History, many countries also have special lessons in subjects which they believe are important. In Scotland, traditional dance lessons are often offered to high school pupils. In some schools in the UK, it's possible to learn unusual new skills like bee-keeping or to have IT lessons in cyber security! And in the USA, some students spend one year creating a science discovery project.

Such a variety of choices is great for students, preparing them for either the world of work or further study.

9.1 Vocabulary
Education

1 Read the article and find the five 'cool' lessons. Then, in pairs, answer the questions.
1. Do you agree that all these lessons are cool?
2. Which would you add to your school curriculum? Why?
3. Which would you not add? Why?

2 🔊 9.1 Study Vocabulary box A. What do you think of these subjects? What are your favourite subjects? In pairs, discuss your ideas.

> **VOCABULARY A** School subjects
>
> Art Biology Chemistry Cooking D&T (Design and Technology) Drama Economics Geography History IT (Information Technology) Languages Literature Maths Music PE (Physical Education) Physics

3 Add the subjects from Vocabulary box A to the correct category in the spidergram. Can you add any more subjects?

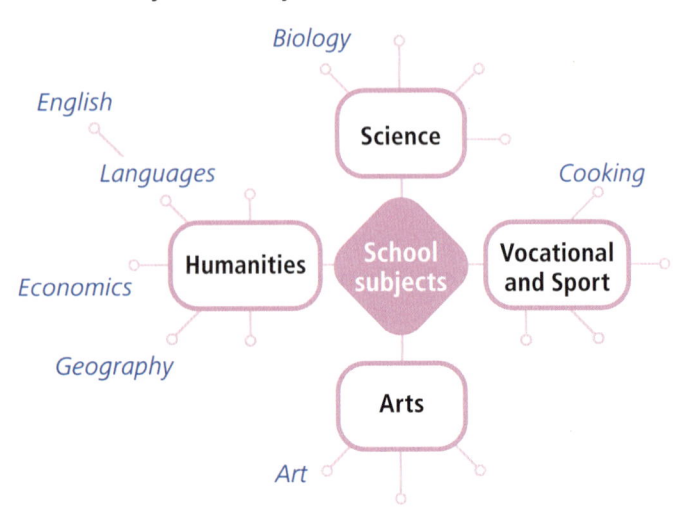

Biology
English
Languages
Economics
Geography
Art
Cooking

School subjects: Science | Humanities | Vocational and Sport | Arts

Unit 9 112

4 Which subjects from Vocabulary box A are taught in your school? Would you add any of the skills below to the curriculum?

> Fashion design   Film-making   Gardening
> Karate   Photography

5 **I KNOW!** In pairs, make your own spidergram about School. Add the three categories below, and the examples. How many words can you add to each category?
1 Types of schools: *primary school*
2 People at school: *head teacher*
3 Places at school: *library*

6 Do you ever use spidergrams to learn facts? Which subjects do you think they are best for?

7 🔊 9.2 Study Vocabulary box B. Can you add more words describing students?

VOCABULARY B — Describing students

Qualities of a good student: confident   creative   hard-working   intelligent   talented
Skills: critical thinking   general knowledge   problem-solving   teamwork

8 🔊 9.3 Complete the sentences with words from Vocabulary box B. Listen and check.
1 Students who are able to learn and understand things easily are *intelligent*.
2 It's useful to know information about the world around you. This is called _____.
3 If you believe you can do things successfully, you are _____, which helps you to do well.
4 Students who are _____ can use their imagination to find ideas in science subjects as well as arts.
5 _____ is a useful skill because it teaches you to think clearly and ask the right questions.
6 If you are doing a task and can find a solution, you are good at _____.
7 Students who are _____ are never lazy and always try to do their best. This can help them do well in any future job.
8 If you can work well with others, you've learned the secret of _____. This is one of the most important skills you can have in life.

9 Read texts (1–3) quickly ignoring the gaps. Match the texts with photos A–C.

1 ☐ My favourite lesson is IT. I love ¹*learning* about how computers work and how to fix problems. We also find out about the future of computers. Last term, we did a ² _____ about robots – we worked together and built our own robot.

2 ☐ I enjoy studying Geography because our teacher makes the lessons fun. Although we have to ³ _____ a lot of information, the classes are really interesting. There's one thing I don't enjoy: giving ⁴ _____ ! It's hard to stand up and talk in front of the class.

3 ☐ I enjoy Food Preparation classes because I like the mix of science and cooking. We have written exams at the end of the course, and we also have ⁵ _____ exams, where we make food using a recipe.

10 🔊 9.4 Study Vocabulary box C. Complete the texts in Exercise 9 with the correct form of the words from the box. Listen and check.

VOCABULARY C — Learning and assessment

Learning
learn   memorise   revise   study   curriculum

Types of assessment
online test   practical exam   presentation   project   speaking exam   written exam

YOUR WORLD

11 Which class activities and types of assessment are the most suitable for different subjects and learners? Discuss in pairs and give reasons.

I can talk about school life.   **113**   Unit 9

9.2 Grammar
Reported speech: statements

1 Look at the posts. What is a debating club?

Debating Club

- Jack: We're **starting** a debating club.
- Daisy: I'**m looking for** some good topics to discuss.
- Mrs Walker: That'**s** a great idea!
- Tom: We **need** to advertise it.

2 🔊 9.5 Listen to Daisy talking about the debating club and look at the posts in Exercise 1 again. What do you notice about the verbs in bold above and the verbs in the recording?

3 🔊 9.6 Read the interview quickly. What topics are chosen for the debates?

MILL HOUSE SCHOOL NEWS BY KATE BRANDON

'New Debating Club!'
Interview with Peter Brown, Year 11 student.

Tell us about the new debating club. How did it all start?
Last term the pupils of Year 11 told their teachers that they wanted to start a debating club. The teachers said that they liked the idea, so now each week we run a debate.

What are the rules?
One team has to agree and the other team has to disagree. Then the audience decide which team is the winner.

What about the topics of debates?
The teachers said we needed interesting topics, so we made a list. We have a mix of serious and silly topics. Last week the audience said they wanted to discuss something lighter.

So, what topic did you choose?
'Pasta or Pizza: which is best?' Our teachers told us to research our speeches. The audience can ask us difficult questions, so it's important to have a good plan and … stay calm.

How can you join the club?
Just come to our debate. The teachers told us that we could have as many members as we wanted. 'The more members, the more interesting debates!' they said. So, join us!

4 Study the Grammar box. Find more examples of reported speech in the interview. Then change the reported statements to direct speech: what were each person's exact words?

GRAMMAR | **Reported speech: statements**

Present Simple → Past Simple
'You need a list of interesting topics.'
Teachers said (that) we needed a list of interesting topics.

Present Continuous → Past Continuous
'We're starting a debating club.'
Pupils told their teachers (that) they were starting a debating club.

GRAMMAR TIME ▶ PAGE 134

WATCH OUT!
We use *said* (*that*) or *told me/you*/etc. (*that*) to report someone's words.

5 🔊 9.7 Choose the correct option. Listen and check.

Max told Sara that he ¹*is planning / was planning* to join the debating club. Sara said that she ²*doesn't want / didn't want* to join. She said that she ³*wasn't / isn't* keen on speaking in public and then added, 'I ⁴*can't / couldn't* come anyway because I ⁵*went / go* to dance classes on Tuesday.' Then Max said that the next debate ⁶ *is / was* 'Pasta or Pizza'. Sara said that it ⁷*sounds / sounded* a lot of fun and she told him she ⁸*wanted / want* to give it a try.

6 Complete the reported statements.
1. 'Uniforms aren't important.'
   Nicola said uniforms _weren't_ important.
2. 'I disagree.'
   Jared said he _____.
3. We don't want to discuss sports.
   They told me they _____ to discuss sports.
4. I'm planning a speech about pasta.
   Ethan said he _____ a speech about pasta.
5. Julia doesn't know what pizza to order.
   Mum said Julia _____ what pizza to order.
6. I'm not coming to the debate on Friday.
   I told them I _____ to the debate on Friday.

7 **YOUR WORLD** Write a sentence that someone has said in the past week. In pairs, take turns to report what that person said. Use *said* or *told*.

Unit 9 — I can report what people say.

9.3 Reading and Vocabulary
Learning effectively

How to train your brain!

In our Citizenship class, Mrs Jones told us there were seven secret ways to become confident students. First of all, she said students needed to 'think like teachers'. [1]____ A researcher gave the same information to two different groups of students. The first group had to learn the information for a test. The second group had to learn the information to teach it to someone else. I was surprised that the second group learned best. [2]____ Because they knew how to explain it clearly.

Secondly, Mrs Jones said that we had to write down some things we remembered after each lesson. Then we had to make more notes in the evening.

Mrs Jones said that the third secret was taking tests. Tests aren't really the end goal of learning. [3]____ And after a few tests you should be able to see that you've made some progress.

Secret four is called 'spaced practice'. One researcher told students to study a topic in short sections, for half an hour or one hour. Your brain can store this information easily! This means you need to take regular breaks from studying.

The fifth secret is strange: 'Don't focus!' Researchers think it's good to mix things up. If you move between different parts of topics, you will see connections and the whole topic will hopefully start to make sense.

However, my favourite secret is number six. [4]____ Mrs Jones said that students who usually worked in the same place needed to move. Your brain makes a connection between the place and the topic you're learning. So sitting in a fresh place makes a topic easier to remember.

And finally, secret seven is good for learning vocabulary. When you're not sure of the meaning of a word on your list, don't check it. Try to understand the meaning from the context in which the word is used. [5]____ Your brain remembers things better when it has to work hard.

1 Do you think people can change their intelligence? Why/Why not?

2 Read the article quickly and answer the questions.
   1 Who do you think is the writer?
   2 What is the writer's purpose?
   3 Sum up each of the seven secrets.

3 🔊 9.8 Read the text again. Complete the gaps with a sentence from the list. There is one extra sentence.
   a Think of things that are related to it.
   b It's 'study in different places'.
   c She told us about an interesting experiment.
   d Many people forget the next rule.
   e They're actually a good way for us to learn!
   f Why did they remember the information so well?

4 In pairs, write two questions about the article and ask the class.

5 🔊 9.9 **WORD FRIENDS** Complete the phrases with *make* or *take*. Sometimes both are possible. Listen and check.
   1 *take* a test/an exam
   2 _____ sense
   3 _____ notes
   4 _____ progress
   5 _____ a connection
   6 _____ a break

6 Which of the seven secrets in the article is the best? Will you try any of these ideas? Discuss in pairs.

YOUR WORLD

I can understand an article about effective learning.

9.4 Grammar
Word order in questions

VIDEO ▶ AN INTERVIEW

Bea: Thanks for letting me interview you.
Carla: No problem. I know you need articles for the school news blog.
Bea: So, I've got a list of questions about your Portuguese course. Is it OK to record the interview?
Carla: Of course. Go ahead.
Bea: OK then. Have you done any online courses?
Carla: Yes, I've just finished an eight-week course in Portuguese.
Bea: That's so cool! Why did you choose to learn Portuguese?
Carla: Well, I know some Portuguese, but I wanted to practise speaking. We're going to Brazil in the summer, so I'd like to chat with my cousins.
Bea: Lucky you! Er, who was your tutor?
Carla: She was my dad's friend. She helped me a lot.
Bea: Was it easy to learn a language online?
Carla: Yes, and the lessons were interesting. I learned some salsa moves and I made things. Just a minute … How cool is this?
Bea: Wow! That headdress is amazing!
Carla: Can I ask you a question now? Why do you ask so many questions?

Bea: Because I'd like to be a journalist one day. Do you want to listen to the interview?
Carla: Sure.
Bea: Oh no! I don't believe it! I forgot to press 'Record'!
Carla: Really?

1 ▶ 43 ◀ 9.10 Look at the photo. What do you think is happening in the photo? Watch or listen and check.

2 Study the Grammar box. Find more examples of questions in the dialogue.

GRAMMAR ▶ Word order in questions

Yes/No questions
It is OK. → Is it OK?
You have done some online courses. → Have you done any online courses?
You enjoyed it. → Did you enjoy it?

Wh- questions
Why are you laughing?
Why do you ask so many questions?

Subject questions
A: Who studied with you? B: Lee studied with me.

Object questions
A: Who did you study with? B: I studied with Lee.

GRAMMAR TIME ▶ PAGE 135

3 Write questions for these answers.
1 Yes, I had pasta for dinner last night.
   Did you have a hot meal for dinner last night?
2 No, I left home early this morning, not late.
3 Yes, we're going to Brazil for our summer holidays.
4 Yes, I saw two films at the cinema last week.
5 No, I'm not going to do anything for my birthday.

4 Write two questions for each answer. Make questions about the underlined words.
1 The fire started in the Science lab.
   What happened in the Science lab?
   Where did the fire start?
2 Class 12D had a Maths test this morning.
3 Everyone in my class has read this book.
4 The teacher saw me when I was at the bus stop.
5 All my friends are going to see that new film.

YOUR WORLD

5 In pairs, ask and answer the questions you wrote in Exercise 3. Some of your answers can be false. Guess if your partner's answers are true.

Unit 9 — I can make questions with the correct word order.

9.5 Listening and Vocabulary
Conversations in the classroom

1 Teachers ask 300–400 questions every day! Do your teachers ask any of these questions? What other questions do they ask?
- Did you understand everything?
- What does … mean?
- What do you think about … ?

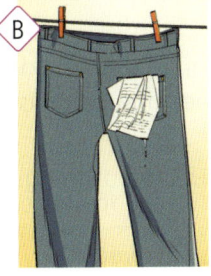

2 🔊 9.11 Listen to four dialogues and choose the correct answer.
  1 What does the teacher want the girl to do before the test?
  2 Where are all the other students now?
  3 What happened to the boy's form?
  4 What were the students doing?

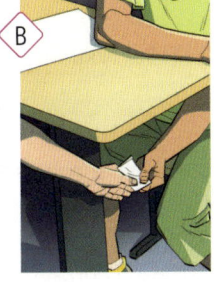

3 🔊 9.11 Listen again. Which teacher asked the most questions? Why do you think he/she did that?

4 🔊 9.12 Study the Vocabulary box and complete the sentences below with the phrasal verbs. Listen and check.

VOCABULARY — Phrasal verbs

calm down   fill in (a form)   get on   hand in/out
look over   look up   miss out

1 The teacher asked us all to *hand in* our homework on time.
2 Pupils who finish early should _____ with some extra reading.
3 I'm definitely coming to the end-of-term party – I don't want to _____ on all the fun!
4 Make sure you _____ all your answers before you finish.
5 You can _____ any words you don't know in a dictionary.
6 We have to _____ this form with our name and phone number.
7 Ella was so nervous before her exam, so I told her to _____ and take a deep breath.

5 🔊 9.13 Choose the most appropriate answer to each question. Listen and check.
  1 Who's ready to hand in their essay?
     a Yes, I will.   b I've just finished it.
     c No, it wasn't difficult.
  2 Are we going to look over the test results now?
     a Yes, I will.   b No, it isn't.
     c Yes, we are.
  3 Did the students get on quietly with their projects?
     a No, they didn't.   b No, there weren't.
     c Where were they?
  4 Can everybody calm down, please?
     a Yes, Miss.   b No, he can't.
     c Thank you, Miss.

VIDEO — **WIDER WORLD**

6 ▶ 44 Watch five people talking about their first school and first teacher. Note down one thing each person remembers about the school, and one about his/her teacher.

7 Write a few sentences about a memory from your primary school. In pairs share your memories.

I can understand short classroom conversations.

9.6 Speaking
Exchanging information

VIDEO ▶ **WHAT A COINCIDENCE!**

Bea: I can't believe it's the last week of term. I can't wait to go on holiday.
Abe: Last week of the semester, you mean. And go on vacation!
Miyu: Excuse me? Would you mind … ?
Abe: Do you want me to take your photo?
Miyu: Thank you so much. Awesome! Maybe just one more.
Bea: Hey, I'm Bea. Have you been in England before?
Miyu: Hi, I'm Miyu. Well, this is my first time, but I've been here for a month now.
Abe: Really? Where are you from? Your accent sounds American.
Miyu: Yeah, you guessed it. I'm from the USA.
Abe: Me too! Which part of the States are you from?
Miyu: New York.
Bea: I'd love to go to New York City.
Miyu: Oh no, I'm not from New York City. I'm from a town in upstate New York, Syracuse.
Abe: No way! That's where I'm from!
Bea: That's so funny. How long are you staying for, Miyu?
Miyu: My brother and I are staying with a lovely host family for the summer because we're doing a Drama course at Grove College.
Bea: I don't believe it! That's where my mum works!
Miyu: What a coincidence!
Abe: What do you think of the UK?
Miyu: I really like it. Look, what are you guys doing right now? Would you like to get an ice cream?

SOUNDS GOOD! • I can't wait! • You guessed it. • What a coincidence!

1 Have you ever met a tourist in your area? Did he/she ask you for any help?

2 ▶ 45 🔊 9.14 Watch or listen and answer the questions.
  1 Why does Miyu speak to Abe and Bea?
  2 Why do Abe and Bea ask a lot of questions?
  3 What do Abe and Miyu have in common?

3 Do you think Miyu felt welcome when she met Abe and Bea? Why?/Why not?

SET FOR LIFE
4 Work in pairs. Imagine you have just met a visitor from another country. What friendly things can you say? Make a list.

5 Study the Speaking box. Match the questions with responses in the dialogue.

SPEAKING | **Exchanging information**

Past experience
Have you been in England before?

Present situation
Where are you from? How long are you staying for?
What do you think of the UK?

Future plans
What are you (guys) doing now/later?
Would you like to get an ice cream?

6 🔊 9.15 Complete the dialogues with phrases from the Speaking box. Listen and check.
  1 A: _____
    B: Yes. That would be great. Let's go.
  2 A: _____
    B: Just a few weeks.
  3 A: _____
    B: Well, it's interesting, but I miss home.
  4 A: _____
    B: Yes, I have. I love it here.

YOUR WORLD
7 In groups of three, role play the situation below.
Students A and B, you are friends. You meet Student C, who is a friend of Student A. Have a conversation using phrases from the Speaking box and Exercise 6.

Unit 9 | I can exchange information in a conversation.

9.7 Writing
A formal letter asking for information

1 Read the advert. Which course would you choose? Why?

Summer Courses
- English Revision
- English for Science
- English for Arts
- English for Humanities
- English for Vocational Studies

Would you like to improve your language skills this summer? Write to us explaining which course you are interested in and why. Let us know if you have any questions about our courses.

2 Read Georgia's letter in response to the advert in Exercise 1. What two things does she want to know?

3 Study the Writing box. Add more phrases from Georgia's letter.

WRITING | A formal letter asking for information

Greeting
1. Dear Mr/Mrs/Ms/Miss (surname),
   _____

Say why you are writing
2. I am writing to ask for/about …
   _____

Ask for information
3. Would you mind … (+-ing)?
   _____

Give information
4. My teacher said that …   My plan is to …
   She also told me that …   I would like to …
   _____

Before you finish
5. I look forward to your reply.
   _____

End your letter
6. Yours sincerely, (if you know the person's name)
   _____ (if you used Dear Sir/Madam)

4 Study the Language box. Find examples of the phrases in the letter. Then complete the sentences about you.

LANGUAGE | Talking about learning goals

- My aim is to (study/work on) …
- My plan is to (learn/stay) …
- I hope to (learn more about/find out about) …
- I would like to (improve/practise) …

---

33 Alexiou Street, Athens 104 36, Greece
20th October

1. Dear Sir/Madam,

2. I am writing to say that I am interested in the English for Science summer course. My aim is to study Science at university and this course will help me.

3. Please could you send me more information about the topics that are covered in the course? Also, would you mind telling me more about the accommodation with a host family – in particular, the price?

4. My English teacher said that my language skills were suitable for this course. However, she told me that I needed to improve my speaking skills. My plan is to stay with a host family as I would like to practise speaking every day. I also hope to learn more about British culture while I am staying there.

5. I look forward to hearing from you soon.

6. Yours faithfully,
Georgia Kallas

WRITING TIME

5 Look at the advert in Exercise 1 again and choose a course. Write a letter in response to the advert, asking for information.

1 Find ideas
Make notes about:
- questions you would like to ask.
- information you will give.
- your learning goals.

2 Plan
Organise your ideas into paragraphs. Use Georgia's letter to help you.

3 Write and share
- Write a draft letter. Use the Language box and the Writing box to help you.
- Share your letter with another student for feedback.
- Use the feedback from your partner and write the final version of your letter.

4 Check
- Check language: did you use a range of phrases to talk about your learning goals?
- Check grammar: is the word order in questions correct?

I can write a formal letter asking for information.

Vocabulary Activator

WORDLIST 🔊 9.16

School subjects
Art (n)
Biology (n)
Chemistry (n)
Cooking (n)
Drama (n)
D&T (Design and Technology) (n)
Economics (n)
Geography (n)
History (n)
IT (Information Technology) (n)
Languages (n)
Literature (n)
Maths (n)
Music (n)
PE (Physical Education) (n)
Physics (n)

Describing students
(qualities of a good student)
confident (adj)
creative (adj)
hard-working (adj)
intelligent (adj)
talented (adj)

(skills)
critical thinking (n)

general knowledge (n)
problem-solving (n)
teamwork (n)

Learning
curriculum (n)
learn (v)
memorise (v)
revise (v)
study (v)

Types of assessment
online test (n)
practical exam (n)
presentation (n)
project (n)
speaking exam (n)
written exam (n)

Word friends
(learning)
make a connection
make/take notes
make progress
make sense
take a break
take a test
take an exam

Phrasal verbs
calm down (v)
fill in (a form) (v)
get on (v)
hand in (v)
hand out (v)
look over (v)
look up (v)
miss out (v)

Extra words
aim (n)
bee-keeping (n)
Citizenship (n)
classroom (n)
club president (n)
course (n)
culture (n)
cyber security (n)
debate (n)
discovery (n)
driving (n)
environment (n)
fashion design (n)
final term (n)
food preparation (n)
fresh place (n)

gardening (n)
goal (n)
head teacher (n)
high school (n)
host family (n)
Humanities (n)
karate (n)
look forward to (v)
member (n)
option (n)
photograph (n)
popular (adj)
pupil (n)
research (n)
Science (n)
special lesson (n)
speech (n)
spidergram (n)
stay calm
store information
suitable (adj)
surfing (n)
traditional dance (n)
university (n)
vocational (adj)

---

1 Complete the sentences with words from the wordlist.
This subject teaches you to:
1 draw beautiful pictures. *Art*
2 play a character in a film. _____
3 use a computer well. _____
4 understand how money works. _____
5 prepare food. _____
6 enjoy sport and stay fit. _____

2 Choose two school subjects from the wordlist. In pairs, take turns to say why you are interested in these subjects.

3 Complete the sentences with words from the wordlist. Then change the sentences to make them true for you. In pairs, compare your learning routine.
1 I *take* a break from my homework every fifteen minutes.
2 I have excellent _____ knowledge: I know lots of facts about different things.
3 At school, I have _____ exams in Music, which means I have to play the piano.
4 I've made _____ this year in History. I'm much better at it.
5 I _____ tidy notes in lessons because I study well from them later.

4 Find words from the wordlist which match descriptions of the students. Then, in pairs, decide which three qualities are most important for good students.
1 He's really good at looking at information and making sense of it. *critical thinking*
2 She believes in herself and is not afraid to try. _____
3 She's great at thinking of new ideas and she also loves Art lessons. _____
4 He always works very hard! _____
5 She works very well with other students in a group. _____
6 He understands even difficult things really well. _____

5 🔊 9.17 **PRONUNCIATION** Listen to the sentences and underline the main stress in the phrasal verbs in bold.
1 Can you **look over** your work please?
2 **Calm down**! Everything will be OK.
3 Please **hand in** your work.
4 **Look up** that word in the dictionary.
5 Please **get on with** your homework!

6 🔊 9.17 **PRONUNCIATION** Listen again and repeat.

Unit 9

Revision

Vocabulary

1 Choose the correct option.
1. My sister is very good *in / at* Chemistry: she's the best in her class.
2. Most people hate giving a *project / presentation* in front of other people.
3. My brother is *revising / studying* Medicine at university.
4. Could you fill *in / up* this form, please?
5. You've worked hard! Do you want to *take / make* a break?

2 Write the correct word for each definition.
1. A school subject where you learn to plan and build things. D*&T (Design and Technology)*
2. All the subjects that students study at school. c_____
3. A subject where you learn about great books. L_____
4. A test where you show your skills by doing tasks in real-life situations. p_____ e_____
5. A school subject where you learn about animals and plants. B_____
6. Assessment where you write and upload answers by computer. o_____ t_____

3 Complete the text with the words below. Which tips would you follow?

> look   make   memorise   miss   ~~revise~~   take (x2)

How to survive a test!

- Start to ¹*revise* a few days before, not the night before!
- Maybe the notes you made two months ago don't ²_____ sense. Write your notes again and use diagrams and colour to help you understand and ³_____ the information.
- Always ⁴_____ regular breaks when studying for a test.
- When you ⁵_____ a test, don't go too fast! You might make a mistake, or ⁶_____ out something.
- Try to leave five minutes at the end so you can ⁷_____ over your answers one more time.

Grammar

4 Read the dialogues and complete the sentences.
1. Mum: I'm cooking and I need some help.
   Lisa: I'm doing my homework. John is free: he can help.

> Mum said she ¹*was cooking* and needed help. Lisa said that she ²_____ her homework, but that John ³_____ free and that he ⁴_____ help.

2. Jo: I'm enjoying Geography lessons this term. They are interesting.
   Tom: I agree. I'm making a lot of progress. But the teacher gives a lot of homework!

> Jo said she ⁵_____ Geography lessons that term and that they ⁶_____ interesting. Tom agreed and said that he ⁷_____ a lot of progress, but that the teacher ⁸_____ a lot of homework.

5 Make questions with the words in brackets. Then, in pairs, answer the questions.
1. why / ancient Egyptians / build / pyramids / ?
2. where / polar bears / live / ?
3. who / discover / radium / ?
4. Rio de Janeiro / the capital of Brazil / ?
5. which countries / send / manned spacecraft into space now / ?
6. how / Hannibal / cross / the Alps and beat the Romans in battle?

6 Write questions to which the underlined words are the answers.
1. <u>My sister Emily</u> plays football.
2. <u>I revised for my Maths exam</u> last night.
3. I saw <u>Graham</u> at Sandra's birthday party.
4. The Geography lesson finished <u>at half past two</u>.
5. <u>It started raining</u> when we went outside.
6. <u>Everyone</u> is going to visit the zoo this weekend.

Speaking

7 Work in pairs. Student A: turn to page 137, Student B: turn to page 143, and follow the instructions to role play a dialogue. Then swap roles.

Dictation

8 🔊 9.18 Listen. Then listen again and write down what you hear.

BBC CULTURE

Different forms of education

Anna's school

I go to an alternative school which is different from the traditional schools my friends go to. First of all, our learning is more creative and interactive. We don't just sit in class and remember facts; we do a lot of practical stuff.

For example, today we had a Science lesson. We learned all about robots and then we built a model car on our own. It was fun – I enjoyed working alone because I could focus better. Then we took it in turns to choose a topic and give a presentation. We often do group work so we can learn from each other. It's fun, but the noise doesn't let me think sometimes.

Anyway, it's great that we have the freedom to do lots of practical activities. And the other interesting thing is that there are no tests – we just revise the material in our own time!

We only do academic subjects for a few hours a day. The rest of the day we do gardening, creative arts and crafts. Today we had singing and dancing – my favourites! We also have interesting discussions on different problems our world has and think of ways to help to make our world better in the future. One thing that they discourage at my school is using the computer. We aren't allowed to sit in front of a screen for a long time unless we're looking for information for a project. I don't like this, but I understand the reasons – we can do that at home.

Here the teachers are great – they are your friends. They don't just instruct you; they help you achieve your potential. I love that. I actually look forward to going to school!

achieve (v) succeed in doing something
discourage (v) try to make someone want to do something less often
in our own time (phr) – outside normal school hours
take it in turns (phr) one after another

1 🔊 9.19 **VISIBLE THINKING** In pairs, follow these steps.
   YOUR VIEWPOINT
   1 Look at the photos. How are the students learning in each one?
   2 How do you like to learn? Do you prefer working in groups or alone?
   THE WRITER'S VIEWPOINT
   3 Read the article and answer the questions.
      a What does Anna think about learning on her own?
      b What doesn't she enjoy about working in groups?
   WHAT DO YOU THINK NOW?
   4 Which is better: group work or working on your own?

2 Read the article again and answer the questions.
   1 What type of schools do Anna's friends go to?
   2 Why did she find her Science lesson fun?
   3 Who chose the topics of the presentations?
   4 When can the students use computers at Anna's school?
   5 How does Anna see her teachers?

3 In pairs, discuss these questions.
   1 What do you think about tests?
   2 How traditional do you think your school is? Why?
   3 Would you like to go to a school like Anna's? Why?/Why not?

BBC ▶ Learning goals

4 Look at the photo. What kind of alternative school do you think it is? Discuss in pairs.

5 ▶ 46 Watch the video and check your answers to Exercise 4.

6 ▶ 46 Watch the video again and answer the questions.
  1 Do the students at Ian's school work hard?
  2 What do they do after the lessons finish?
  3 What time does Ian get home?
  4 Why does he go to bed right after dinner?

7 How is Ian's alternative school different from Anna's?

8 In pairs, discuss the questions.
  1 The video says, 'Ian knows that you have to work hard if you want to be the best. But when you have a passion and a talent, you don't mind doing a little bit extra.' Do you agree? Why?/Why not?
  2 Would you like to attend an alternative school? Why?/Why not?

PROJECT TIME

9 In groups of four, create a website for a new school. Follow these steps.

1 **In groups, think about what information to include. Decide who can prepare this information.**
  - what students will learn at the school
  - what the timetable will be
  - what students will do after the lessons
  - a day in the life of a student at the school

2 **Individually, create your part of the website.**
  - Think about what information you want to give and write your text.
  - Find or draw pictures to illustrate your section of the website.

3 **In your group, put together your website. You can use a website template.**
  - Decide on a title, the layout and a logo.
  - Position the text, the logo and the pictures.
  - Check and edit your website.

4 **Share your website with the class.**
  - Answer other students' questions.
  - Look at the other websites. Ask questions.

Progress Check Units 1–9

Vocabulary and Grammar

1 Complete the sentences with words formed from the words in brackets.
1 The new husband of my mother is my *stepfather* (FATHER).
2 The internet is very _____ (HELP) for students who need to find information for homework.
3 Police think there was a _____ (THIEF) in this office because important papers are missing.
4 You can be arrested if you do something that's _____ (LEGAL).
5 The _____ (MANAGE) of the transport company were sorry about the bus problems.
6 It doesn't help to be _____ (PATIENT) if you have to wait a long time for something.

2 Complete the text with one word in each gap.

Last year none of us could think ¹ *of* an idea for Grandma's eightieth birthday. Then one evening when we ² _____ watching television, my sister surprised us. She stood in front of the TV and said, 'I've ³ _____ thought of the perfect thing for Grandma!' Grandma loves rabbits, so we decided to ⁴ _____ a cake made in the shape of a rabbit. I knew a cake shop ⁵ _____ they designed cakes. Grandma said, 'It's ⁶ _____ best cake in the world!'

3 Choose the correct answer.

My friend Gail and I ¹ ___ together at the weekend because we are doing an online course about preparing meals with healthy ² ___ . Students don't take tests, but teachers assess your ³ ___ on the course from the work you do. We had to prepare our own recipe and ⁴ ___ it for the other students, ⁵ ___ would then cook and taste it! I knew I would do this task better if I ⁶ ___ with someone else. Online courses are interesting and ⁷ ___ of them are free.

1 a meet   b bring   c get
2 a flavours   b parts   c ingredients
3 a description b performance c exam
4 a follow   b connect   c upload
5 a who   b which   c that
6 a work   b will work   c worked
7 a much   b a lot   c a little

Speaking

4 Match 1–7 with a–g to make a dialogue.
1 ☐ A: Hi! My name's Juanita. What's yours?
2 ☐ A: Have you stayed at this camp before?
3 ☐ A: Where are you from?
4 ☐ A: I'm from Spain. So, how long are you staying for?
5 ☐ A: And what are your plans after the camp?
6 ☐ A: That sounds interesting. So, the sports here are good. Do you agree?
7 ☐ A: Let's meet up later. Would you prefer to meet in the games room or here?

a B: Definitely!
b B: No, this is my first time.
c B: Two weeks.
d B: Olga. Nice to meet you!
e B: I'm going on holiday with my family.
f B: I'd rather meet in the games room.
g B: Turkey, and you?

5 In pairs, do the speaking task. Go to page 143.

Listening

6 You are going to hear a police officer talking to school students about the crimes below. In pairs, discuss the questions.

(burglary   pickpocketing   shoplifting)

1 Which of the crimes is the easiest to stop happening?
2 For which crime is it the easiest to catch the criminal?

7 🔊 PC1–9.1 Listen to the police officer and write his answers to the questions in Exercise 6.

8 🔊 PC1–9.1 Listen again and choose the correct answer.
1 Shoplifting is an easy crime to commit because
  a nobody ever looks at you in a shop.
  b shoplifters can easily take things and leave.
  c shop security is often not good enough.
2 The best way for shops to stay safe from shoplifters is to
  a record a video of people in the shop.
  b tell the police if there was a shoplifter.
  c watch people in the shop at all times.
3 It is difficult for police to catch burglars because
  a burglars make a mess in the house.
  b the police don't take fingerprints.
  c burglars are very careful during the burglary.

4 You should tell police about a stranger near your house because
   a your house might not have strong enough security.
   b this person might be a burglar who is studying the house.
   c this person might tell a burglar about your house.
5 One of the few ways to catch a pickpocket is to
   a notice the pickpocket committing the crime.
   b think of a good plan to catch the pickpocket.
   c call for help after the crime.
6 It's easy to stay safe from pickpockets if you
   a stay near other people who can help you.
   b keep your personal things close to you.
   c stay away from someone who might be a pickpocket.

Reading

9 You are going to read an article about an environmentally friendly school. Look at the photo and the name of the school. In pairs, discuss what it might be like to go to this school.

10 PC1–9.2 Read the article about an environmentally friendly school. Complete the gaps with sentences a–f. There is one extra sentence. Listen and check.
   a One of these is project work, which is very important at Green School.
   b It's a tropical island with beautiful beaches.
   c Another example of a project managed by students is the 'Bio Bus'.
   d They look different to any classes I've ever seen before.
   e The results also find their way onto the school lunch menu.
   f This is a daily reality for students at Green School.
   g We hope they will agree and offer to show us around.

11 Would you like to be a student at Green School? Why?/Why not? Discuss in pairs.

Green School, Bali

1 Imagine what it would be like if your school were right next to a tropical forest! As you're listening to the teacher's instructions, you hear the sounds of wildlife such as exotic birds and insects. ^{1} _____ The school opened in 2008 in Bali, part of the Indonesian archipelago between the Pacific and Indian Oceans. ^{2} _____ My wife and I, like many Australians, love to have our holiday there.

2 We are teachers, so we're interested in knowing more about the school. On this year's holiday to Bali we hope to take some time away from the beaches to see it. We are going to write to the school to ask about the possibility of a visit. ^{3} _____ The classrooms are made from local plants like bamboo, which are all found right there on the island. ^{4} _____ There are large open spaces between them, and windows open to the outside on all sides.

3 Many of the subjects at Green School are the same ones which are taught in many schools around the world. But the curriculum gives special attention to certain types of learning. ^{5} _____ The school believes that children should learn by studying about different, interesting topics. For example, students grow fresh fruit and vegetables in the school's gardens and then describe what they've done. ^{6} _____ It started in 2015 and it's the school's environmentally friendly local transport. Students at Green School experience a different way of learning, and I do hope we can visit it!

Writing

12 Go to page 143. Think about your answers to the questions. Then, in pairs, discuss your answers. Give reasons.

13 Write an opinion essay (100–150 words) on the following question: 'Students should decide what they learn.' Do you agree? Use the paragraph plan below to help you.
   • Paragraph 1: Introduce the topic and give your opinion.
   • Paragraph 2: Present some ideas which support students deciding what they learn.
   • Paragraph 3: Present some possible problems with students deciding what they learn.
   • Paragraph 4: Summarise your opinion.

Grammar Time

1.2

Present Simple and Present Continuous, state verbs

Present Simple
We use the Present Simple for facts, permanent situations and routines.
They sing in a band.
She doesn't use her tablet every day.

Time expressions
every day/week/month/year
once/twice/three times a month
on Mondays/weekdays/holiday
always/usually/often/sometimes/rarely/never

Present Continuous
We use the Present Continuous for actions that are happening at or around the moment of speaking.
They're playing a computer game now.
I'm recording songs this week.

Time expressions
now, at the moment, this morning/afternoon, this year, these days

State verbs
State verbs often express opinions, preferences, mental states and perception. Some common state verbs are: love, like, hate, prefer, want, need, understand, think, feel, hear, see.

We don't normally use state verbs in continuous tenses, even if they refer to the moment of speaking.
I don't need any help at the moment, thank you.

1 Complete the text with the Present Simple or Present Continuous form of the verbs in brackets.

Kids my age ¹*love* (love) watching music videos on YouTube, and so do I. One of my favourites is *What Does The Fox Say?* by Ylvis. It's not a new song, but I ² _____ (think) it's really cool. The music is great, and the video is fun to watch. In the video, there's a fancy dress party and all the people ³ _____ (wear) animal costumes. They are in a forest, and they ⁴ _____ (dance) and making strange animal sounds. If you ⁵ _____ (not know) the song, look for it on YouTube. It's great!
Unlike me, my sister ⁶ _____ (not like) music videos. She ⁷ _____ (prefer) videos about shopping, where people ⁸ _____ (buy) things and then ⁹ _____ (show) the viewers what's in their shopping bags. In fact, she ¹⁰ _____ (watch) one at the moment – on my laptop!

2 Write a short text about your favourite music video. What's in it? Why do you like it? Use the text in Exercise 1 to help you.

1.4

Verb + -ing, verb + to-infinitive

Verb + -ing
After: avoid, can't stand, enjoy, finish, look forward to, (not) mind, miss, practise, stop
You can go out when you finish tidying your room.
We also use the -ing form after prepositions.
Don't leave without saying goodbye to your friends.

Verb + to-infinitive
After: agree, allow, ask, choose, decide, forget, hope, learn, need, offer, plan, remember, try, want, would like/love
Remember to call your parents when you arrive.

Verb + -ing or to-infinitive
After: like, love, hate, prefer, start
I love taking/love to take photos of cats.

1 Complete the sentences with the correct form of the verbs in brackets.
1 Martha's parents often allow her *to stay up* (stay up) late at night.
2 I would love _____ (buy) a new tablet – this one's too old.
3 Don't worry about me – I don't mind _____ (wait).
4 Why don't you practise _____ (play) this song again?
5 Please try _____ (stay) calm.

2 Choose the correct option.
Ella: What are you planning ¹*to do / doing* at the weekend?
Josh: I don't know. I need ²*to write / writing* the French essay – finish ³*to write / writing* it, in fact.
Ella: That doesn't sound very exciting.
Josh: I know! I can't stand ⁴*to write / writing* essays! What about your weekend, then?
Ella: Well, I'm trying ⁵*to earn / earning* some money, so I'm helping my uncle in his garden. He offers ⁶*to pay / paying* me five pounds an hour. In fact, he wants me ⁷*to bring / bringing* a friend to help us plant some trees. Would you like ⁸*to join / join* us?
Josh: Really? Yes, I'd love ⁹*to join / join* you!

3 In pairs, practise the dialogue in Exercise 2. Then make a similar dialogue using your own ideas. Try to use some of the verbs in the Grammar box above.

2.2

Past Simple: regular and irregular verbs

We use the Past Simple to talk about actions and situations that started and finished in the past. We often mention when these actions/situations happened.

Regular verbs
Regular verbs form the Past Simple with the ending -ed.
It snowed last night.
It didn't snow last night.
Did it snow last night?

Irregular verbs
Irregular verbs do not form the Past Simple with -ed.
Each verb has its own form. For a list of irregular verbs, see page 136.
We saw a storm yesterday.
We didn't see the storm.
Did you see the storm?

Time expressions
yesterday, two hours/days/weeks/years ago, in 2020, last week/year/night.

1 Complete the sentences with the Past Simple form of the verbs in brackets.
 1 I *visited* (visit) my aunt in August.
 2 I last _____ (see) the rainbow two weeks ago.
 3 It _____ (rain) a lot last summer.
 4 We _____ (take) many photos during the holidays.
 5 Lisa _____ (study) for the Maths test last night.
 6 I _____ (have) fried eggs for breakfast yesterday.

2 Make questions in the Past Simple. Use the time expressions below. Then, in pairs, ask and answer the questions.

> yesterday   the day before yesterday
> last Monday/Friday/Saturday   last month   last summer
> a year ago   two years ago   five years ago

 1 what / you / have / for lunch / ?
 2 what films / you / see / ?
 3 where / you / go / on holiday / ?
 4 what sports / you / do / ?
 5 what video games / you / play / ?
 6 what mobile phone / you / have / ?

 A: *What did you have for lunch the day before yesterday?*
 B: *I had a chicken sandwich and an apple.*

3 Write five true sentences about yourself. Use the Past Simple and five different time expressions.

2.4

Past Continuous and Past Simple

We use the Past Continuous to describe an activity that was in progress at a particular time in the past. We also use it to describe a scene (e.g. in a story).
At six o'clock I was talking to friends online.
It was midnight. Outside, it was snowing.

She was doing her homework. She wasn't playing games.
They were swimming. They weren't running.
Was she sleeping? Yes, she was./No, she wasn't.

Past Continuous and Past Simple
We often use the Past Simple with the Past Continuous to talk about an action that happened while another one was in progress. We use the Past Continuous for the longer action that was in progress and the Past Simple for the shorter action.
I was walking in the forest when I saw a bear.
Anne called me while I was doing the Maths homework.

1 Complete the sentences with the Past Simple or Past Continuous form of the verbs in brackets.
 1 When you *called* (call), I _____ (take) a shower.
 2 It was a beautiful day. The sun _____ (shine) and the birds _____ (sing).
 3 A: What _____ (you/do) at 10.00 p.m. on Wednesday?
    B: I'm not sure. I _____ (not sleep). I think I _____ (watch) a film on TV.
 4 A: _____ (you/play) games on your phone when the teacher _____ (come) into the classroom?
    B: No, I _____ ! I _____ (look) for some information about Asia on the internet.

2 Complete the text with the Past Simple or Past Continuous form of the verbs below.

> appear   break   come   fall   hear
> hike   run   shout   try

Last winter I ¹*was hiking* in the mountains with my friend Jake when we ² _____ a strange sound. We were quite scared. There was lots of snow on the top of the mountain and it ³ _____ down on us really quickly. It was an avalanche! 'Run!' Jake ⁴ _____ . We ⁵ _____ when we both ⁶ _____ down the slope and Jake ⁷ _____ his leg! I ⁸ _____ to call my dad on my mobile when a helicopter ⁹ _____ in the sky. We were saved!

Grammar Time

3.2

Present Perfect with *ever*, *never*, *just*, *already* and *yet*

We form the Present Perfect with *have/has* + the past participle of the main verb. For regular verbs, the past participle is the same as the Past Simple form. For irregular verbs, it is different. For a list of irregular verbs, see page 136.

We use the Present Perfect to talk about:
- life experiences, often with *ever* (in questions) and *never* (in negative sentences).
  Have you ever tried Mexican food?
  I've never eaten sushi.
- actions that finished a very short time ago, often with *just*.
  I'm not hungry. I've just had a sandwich.
- actions that were (or were expected to be) completed at an unspecified time with the past. We often use *already* in affirmative sentences and *yet* in negative sentences and questions.
  I've already cooked lunch.
  I haven't cooked lunch yet.
  Have you cooked lunch yet?

1 Complete the sentences with the correct form of the verbs in brackets.
1. Our pizza <u>has just arrived</u> (just/arrive). Let's eat!
2. Dave _____ (already/wash) the dishes, so we can relax.
3. A: _____ (you/have) lunch yet, boys?
   B: No, we _____ .
4. A: _____ (Lee/do) the shopping yet?
   B: Yes, she _____ (just/return) from the shops.
5. I _____ (never/try) Indian food.
6. Ian and Eva started making dinner two hours ago and they _____ (not finish) yet.

2 In pairs, ask and answer questions about the things below. Use the Present Perfect with *ever*.
1. try snails
2. cook a family dinner
3. make a cake
4. be to an expensive restaurant
5. upload a video on YouTube
6. watch a horror film

A: *Have you ever tried snails?* B: *Yes, I have.*

3 You are organising a party with a friend. Write him/her a note to say what you have already done and what you haven't done yet.

Hi Mark! I've already bought some crisps and nuts, but I haven't bought any soft drinks yet. …

3.4

Present Perfect with *for* and *since* | Present Perfect and Past Simple

Present Perfect with *for* and *since*
We often use the Present Perfect with *for* and *since* to talk about an action or situation that started in the past and still continues.

We use *for* to say how long something has continued, e.g. with *a week, a month, a year, a long time.*
They've owned this restaurant for two years.

We use *since* to say when something started, e.g. with *2019, March, last Tuesday, the day we met.*
I've had this laptop since February.

Present Perfect and Past Simple
We use the Past Simple when we say when a past action happened.
I went to this pizzeria last Sunday.

With the Present Perfect, we don't use a time reference. We are talking about things that have happened in our lives up to now.
I've been to this restaurant. It's really nice.

Be careful: when we want to give more details about an experience, we use the Past Simple.
I've been to this restaurant. I went there with my cousins last week.

1 Complete the sentences with *for* or *since*.
1. I've lived in this house <u>since</u> I was born.
2. I've known Tim _____ ten years.
3. I've had this bike _____ two months.
4. I haven't seen Jo _____ yesterday.

2 Make sentences using the correct form of the verbs.
1. Maria / get / her mobile phone / two years ago
   Maria got her mobile phone two years ago.
2. she / win / her skis in a skiing competition / last year
   _____
3. she / make / her jumper herself / last winter
   _____
4. she / find / her favourite book in a park / three weeks ago
   _____

3 How long has Maria had her things? Look at Exercise 2 again and write sentences using *for* or *since*.

Maria has had her mobile phone for two years.

4.2

Comparatives and superlatives, *too/not enough*, *(not) as … as …*

Comparative
To compare two people, things, places, etc., we use the comparative form of the adjective (+ *than*).
His first film was *funnier than* the second one.
The book is *more interesting than* the film.

Superlative
To compare one person, thing, place, etc. in a group with the rest, we use *the* + the superlative form of the adjective.
Coming 2 America is *the funniest* film I've seen.
This is *the most interesting* book I've read.

too/(not) enough
We use:
- *too* + adjective to mean 'more than you need'.
  The screen is *too dark*. (= It's darker than it should be.)
- adjective + *enough* to mean 'just right'.
  The screen is *bright enough*. (= It's OK.)
- *not* + adjective + *enough* to mean 'less than you need'.
  The screen is*n't bright enough*. (= It should be brighter.)

(not) as … as
We can also use *not as* + adjective + *as* to compare two people, things, places, etc.
The film is *as good as* the book.
The cinema is*n't as exciting as* the theatre.

1 Write the comparative and superlative forms of the adjectives below. Then choose three comparative forms and three superlative forms and write true sentences.

> amusing   bad   big   difficult
> heavy   large   sad   strange

2 Complete the text with the words below.

> as comfortable as   bigger   cheaper   ~~closer~~
> comfortable enough   more expensive   the best
> the biggest   too expensive

I often go to the cinema and here are my three favourites. Multi-Film and MacroMovie are two typical multiplex cinemas. MacroMovie is ¹*closer* to the city centre and it has ² _____ screens (probably ³ _____ in the city), but it's also ⁴ _____ than the other cinemas, so I don't go there so often. The tickets are ⁵ _____ if you ask me … The seats in Multi-Film are ⁶ _____ the seats in MacroMovie, but the tickets are ⁷ _____ . I often choose Chaplin Cinema; maybe the chairs there aren't ⁸ _____ , but it's got ⁹ _____ sound quality.

3 In pairs, talk about three films you know. Use Exercise 1 to help you.

A: I think … is the funniest.
B: Yes, and it also has the best special effects.

4 Write a short paragraph comparing two actors or two TV programmes.

4.4

Quantifiers: *some, any, much, many, (a) few, (a) little, a lot of, lots of*

Countable and uncountable nouns
We use quantifiers with nouns to talk about quantity. Countable nouns refer to things we can count, e.g. *a bracelet, three bracelets*. Uncountable nouns refer to things we cannot count, e.g. substances and liquids (*rice, milk*), groups of things (*furniture, jewellery*) and abstract ideas (*love, peace*).

a lot/lots of, *much* and *many*
We use *a lot/lots of* with all nouns in affirmative sentences.
There's *lots of* cola for everyone.
I've got *a lot of* T-shirts.
We use *much* with uncountable and *many* with countable nouns, usually in negative sentences and questions.

How many T-shirts have you got?   *How much* cola is there?
I haven't got *many* T-shirts.   There isn't *much* cola.

some and *any*
We use *some* and *any* with countable and uncountable nouns. We use *some* in affirmative sentences and *any* in negative sentences and questions.

I've got *some* T-shirts.   There's *some* cola.
Have you got *any* T-shirts?   Is there *any* cola?
I haven't got *any* T-shirts.   There isn't *any* cola.

a few, few, a little, little
We use *a few* and *few* with countable nouns, and *a little* and *little* with uncountable nouns. The article *a* changes the meaning.

I've got *a few* T-shirts. (= some T-shirts)
I've got *few* T-shirts. (= not many T-shirts)
There's *a little* cola. (= some cola)
There's *little* cola. (= not much cola)

Grammar Time   **129**

Grammar Time

1 Read the texts and choose the correct answers.

I only wear sports clothes, so in my wardrobe there aren't ¹*any* smart dresses. I've got ² _____ T-shirts and ³ _____ hoodies. I haven't got ⁴ _____ jewellery – only ⁵ _____ bracelets.

I like smart clothes, so in my wardobe there are ⁶ _____ suits and ⁷ _____ white shirts. I haven't got ⁸ _____ trainers – I hate sports shoes!

1	a **any**	b some	c much
2	a lots of	b a lot	c much
3	a a little	b a few	c any
4	a much	b many	c any
5	a a little	b little	c a few
6	a a few	b few	c any
7	a some	b any	c much
8	a much	b few	c any

2 Write a short paragraph about clothes and accessories you have got. Try to use different quantifiers from the Grammar box above.

5.2

Future forms: *will*, *be going to*, Present Continuous, Present Simple

Will
We use *will* for predictions or decisions made at the moment of speaking.
I don't think he'll win the competition.
Wait, I'll help you.

Be going to
We use *be going to* for plans and intentions, and for predictions based on things we know now.
I'm going to take up kayaking.
Look at the sky: it's going to rain.

Present Continuous
We use the Present Continuous to talk about fixed arrangements.
We're having a competition next month.

Present Simple
We use the Present Simple to talk about timetables and schedules.
My basketball training starts in October.

1 Choose the best option.
1. *I'm going to / I'll* buy a new tennis racket, so I'm looking for some offers online.
2. I'm sorry, I can't come with you on Tuesday. *We're visiting / We'll visit* my grandparents.
3. In our school, all extra-curricular classes *are starting / start* in October.
4. Susan looks really pale. She *isn't going to finish / doesn't finish* the race.
5. I've arranged an interview with Mr Saunders for our school magazine. He's *coming / going to come* tomorrow at 6.30.
6. A: I'm starving.
   B: *I'm going to / I'll* make you a sandwich.

2 Complete the questions with the words below. Then, in pairs, ask and answer the questions.

going (x2)   having   meeting   will (x2)

1. What do think the weather *will* be like tomorrow?
2. Are you _____ to get a summer job during the holidays?
3. Are you _____ any extra-curricular classes tomorrow?
4. Are you _____ your friends in the evening?
5. Do you think e-books _____ replace 'real' books in the future?
6. Are you _____ to organise a birthday party any time soon?

A: What do you think the weather will be like tomorrow?
B: I think it will be rainy and windy.

5.4

First Conditional with *if* and *unless*

We use the First Conditional (*if* + Present Simple, *will*) to talk about something that may happen in the future as a result of an action or situation.

The *if* clause can come at the beginning of the sentence or after the main clause. When it is at the beginning, we use a comma between the two clauses.
If you like gymnastics, you'll love slacklining.
You'll love slacklining if you like gymnastics.

Unless
We can also use *unless* in First Conditional sentences. It means 'if not'.
You won't be good at slacklining if you don't practise.
You won't be good at slacklining unless you practise.

Time clauses with *when*
Notice the difference between a First Conditional sentence and a time clause with *when*.
I'll tell Jack about the competition if he comes. (Jack may or may not come.)
I'll tell Jack about the competition when he comes. (Jack will come and then I will tell him.)

1 Complete the First Conditional sentences with the correct form of the verbs in brackets.
1 We _will go_ (go) skiing at the weekend if it _____ (snow).
2 If she _____ (come) round, I _____ (show) her some skateboarding tricks.
3 Your team _____ (not win) the match if they _____ (not change) a few players.
4 If the train _____ (not be) late, the footballers _____ (arrive) at Brighton at 5 p.m.
5 The training _____ (not start) if the coach _____ (be) ill.
6 If the rain _____ (stop), I _____ (go) jogging.

2 Rewrite the sentences. Use _if_ or _unless_.
1 You won't get better unless you practise.
   You'll get better if you practise.
2 If we don't win, our coach will be very disappointed.
3 Unless Joe feels better, he won't come to basketball practice.
4 They won't choose her for the team if she isn't really good.
5 I won't join the gym unless I have more free time in the summer.

6.2

Modal verbs: must, have to, ought to, should

Obligation and prohibition
We use _must_ and _have to_ to express obligation. We use _must_ when the speaker feels that something is necessary. We use _have to_ when something is necessary because there is a rule or because another person says so (e.g. a teacher, a manager).
I _must go_ now. I don't want to be late.
We _have to_ wear a uniform at school.

We use _mustn't_ to expresses prohibition.
You _mustn't_ use your mobile phone during the flight.

Advice
We use _should/shouldn't_ and _ought to_ to give advice. The negative form of _ought to_ is not very common.
You _should/shouldn't_ take the train.
You _ought to_ pack your bag now.

Lack of obligation
To say that something is not necessary, we use _don't have to_.
She _doesn't have to_ work in July.

Notes on form
Must, _should_ and _ought to_ are modal verbs. They have the same form in all persons, singular and plural. To form questions, we use inversion. We don't normally use _ought to_ in questions.
She _must/should/ought to_ leave now.
Must/Should we leave now?
You _mustn't/shouldn't_ leave now.

Have to has different forms (I/you/we/they have to; he/she/it has to). To form questions and negative sentences, we use _do/does_ and _don't/doesn't_.
You _have to_ wait here.
She _doesn't have to_ work hard.
_Do_ we _have to_ go now?

1 Complete the second sentence so that it means the same as the first one. Use the verbs in brackets.
1 It is necessary for Joanna to wear a suit in the office.
   Joanna _has to wear a suit_ in the office. (has)
2 Is it a good idea for us to check out before breakfast?
   _____ before breakfast? (should)
3 Don't take your passport – it's not necessary.
   You _____ passport. (have)
4 You should buy new sunglasses.
   You _____ sunglasses. (ought)
5 Using a dictionary is not allowed in the exam.
   You _____ in the exam. (mustn't)
6 Is it necessary for Abe to take a sleeping bag?
   _____ a sleeping bag? (does)

2 Choose the correct option.
1 Betty _____ clean her room today because she did it yesterday.
   a has to   b mustn't   c doesn't have to
2 My teacher says I _____ read books in English to learn new words.
   a should   b mustn't   c don't have to
3 We _____ to leave right now if we don't want to be late.
   a must   b should   c ought
4 Football players _____ touch the ball with their hands.
   a shouldn't   b mustn't   c have to

Grammar Time **131**

Grammar Time

6.4

Modal verbs: *must, could, may/might, can't* (speculation)

We can use the modal verbs *must, could, may/might* and *can't* to speculate about the present or future. We use:

- *must* when we strongly believe that something is true.
  She *must* feel exhausted after the trip. (= I'm sure she feels exhausted.)
- *may/might* or *could* when we think that something is possibly true.
  It *may/might/could* be cold at night in the mountains. (= It's possible that it's cold.)
- *can't* when we strongly believe that something is not true.
  This rucksack *can't* weigh more than ten kilos – it's so small! (= I'm sure it doesn't weigh more than ten kilos.)

1 Complete the dialogues with the words below.

> might   can't   ~~must~~

A: Joe had a shower and went straight to bed. He ¹*must* be exhausted after his football practice.
B: He ²_____ be exhausted. He didn't go to football practice today, and he got up at 11 a.m.
A: Oh. Well, he ³_____ want to get some rest before his next football practice, then!

> can't   must   could

A: The water ⁴_____ be freezing – look, nobody's swimming.
B: No, it ⁵_____ be freezing – not with this sunny weather. The water is always quite warm here.
A: I'm not going anyway. It ⁶_____ be muddy or full of seaweed … Brr!

2 Complete the modal verbs in the email.

✉

Hi Mark,

I'm writing about the cruise. I've thought about it, and I think it ¹*may* not be the best idea. First of all, the cruise in the Mediterranean ²m_____ cost a fortune – I'm sure we can't afford it. It ³c_____ also be a bit boring because we get to the harbour in the evening, and it's too late to go sightseeing. Just looking at the sea ⁴c_____ be very exciting!

Let's go sailing instead. I think it's more exciting – and it ⁵m_____ be healthier too! Let me know what you think.

Martha

7.2

Second Conditional

We use the Second Conditional (*if* + Past Simple, *would*) to talk about:

- unreal or imaginary situations in the present or future.
  If dogs *had* wings, they *would fly*. (= Dogs don't have wings, and they don't fly.)
- situations in the present or future that are not very likely.
  If I *had* some money, I *would buy* a new bike.
  (= I probably won't have money, and I probably won't buy a bike.)

We often use the phrase *If I were you* to give advice.
If I were you, I would ask someone for help.

We can use *were* instead of *was* in Second Conditional sentences.
If she *was/were* taller, she'd join the basketball team.

1 Complete the Second Conditional sentences about friendship with the correct form of the verbs in brackets.

A good friend:
1 *would help* (help) me if I _____ (be) in trouble.
2 _____ (give) me some money if I _____ (not have) any.
3 _____ (try) to help me feel better if I _____ (be) ill.
4 _____ (not be) angry with me if I _____ (do) something wrong.
5 _____ (not complain) if I _____ (not be) in a good mood.

2 Make Second Conditional sentences.
1 how / you / behave / if / you / be / me / ?
  How would you behave if you were me?
2 Chris / not feel / so sad / if / his classmates / not laugh / at him
  _____
3 if / I / win / the match / my parents / be / very proud of me
  _____
4 Sarah / be / very disappointed / if / we / miss / her birthday party
  _____
5 if / you / work / harder / you / not fail / all your exams
  _____

7.4

Relative clauses

We use relative clauses to give information about people, things and places. We use *who* to refer to people, *which* to refer to things and *where* to refer to places.

Defining relative clauses

With defining relative clauses, the information we give is important and necessary. The sentence is not complete without it.
This is the woman who asked about you.
I ate the sandwich which was in the fridge.
This is the town where my dad grew up.

In defining relative clauses, we can use *that* instead of *who* and *which*.
This is the woman that asked about you.
I ate the sandwich that was in the fridge.

Non-defining relative clauses

With non-defining relative clauses, we give extra information. This information is not essential to identify the person, thing or place we are talking about. The sentence is still complete without it.
I saw Ed Davies, who lives in my street.
We saw Arrival, which is my favourite film.
He comes from Cornwall, where my mum grew up.

We use commas to separate the non-defining relative clause from the main clause.
Maria Kennel, who lives next door, is in my class.

1 Join the sentences using defining relative clauses. Which relative pronouns can be replaced with *that*?

1 That's the hospital. I was born there.
   That's the hospital where I was born.
2 This is the teacher. He teaches German at my brother's school.
3 Where's the pen? It was on my desk.
4 We visited the house. Shakespeare lived there.
5 Is that the tablet? Did your dad give it to you for your birthday?

2 Join the sentences using non-defining relative clauses.

1 Ian's house is on West Street. My school is there.
   Ian's house is on West Street, where my school is.
2 Fiona told me about Heath's birthday party. It was a surprise.
3 Mark's cousin went to our school. He is a doctor now.
4 The President Hotel is the oldest building in the town. We stayed there.
5 My great-grandmother lived in a village near Edinburgh. Edinburgh is the capital of Scotland.

8.2

Present and Past Simple passive

We use the passive:
- when we think that an action is more important than who does it.
- when we don't know who did the action that we are talking about.

Present Simple passive

We form the Present Simple passive with *am/is/are* + past participle.
The play is based on Agatha Christie's crime novel.
Shoplifters aren't always caught.
Where are these security cameras made?

Past Simple passive

We form the Past Simple passive with *was/were* + past participle.
The witness was interviewed yesterday.
He wasn't found guilty.
When were the criminals arrested?

If we want to say who did the action, we use *by*.
Shoplifters aren't always caught by store owners.
The witness was interviewed by Detective Bower.

1 Rewrite the sentences in the passive.

1 Someone damaged the school gate last night.
   The school gate *was damaged last night*.
2 People don't use CCTV cameras just for fun.
   CCTV cameras _____ .
3 Someone saw the suspect in Hyde Park on Sunday.
   The suspect _____ .
4 Did the police arrest the robbers?
   Were _____ .
5 Do people find fingerprints on food and clothes?
   Are _____ .
6 Someone stole my aunt's bag this morning.
   My aunt's bag _____ .
7 The police caught the criminals yesterday.
   The criminals _____ .
8 The thieves hid the stolen painting in the garage.
   The stolen painting _____ .

Grammar Time

8.4

Have/get something done

We use *have something* done to talk about things that we don't do ourselves but somebody else (usually a professional) does for us. The form is: subject + *have* + object + past participle.
I made my costume. (= I made it myself.)
I had my costume made. (= Somebody else made it for me.)
We can use *get something done* in the same way. It is more informal and we often use it in spoken English.
I got my costume made.

1 Complete the questions with the correct form of *have something done*. Then, in pairs, ask and answer the questions.
   1 How often *do you have your hair cut* (you/your hair/cut)?
   2 _____ (you/ever/your photo/take) by a professional photographer?
   3 When was the last time you _____ (your computer or phone/service)?
   4 Would you ever _____ (your hair/dye) blue or green?
   5 _____ (your room/paint) in the near future?
   6 Should _____ (people/their houses/clean) or should they clean them themselves?

2 Complete the email with the phrases below.

| it styled   ~~my dress made~~   my hair cut |
| my nails painted   some photos taken   them repaired |

✉

Hi Jessie,

How are you? How are the preparations for the end-of-year party going? I've already had ¹*my dress made*. I'm really lucky as my aunt works in a little clothing company and I had a discount. The dress is red and it's got little red roses at the front. I'm going to wear my red shoes. They are the same colour as the dress and I had ² _____ last week. Anyway, I don't want to have ³ _____ although it's a bit long now … My mum says it brings bad luck before the exams! I'm only going to have ⁴ _____ before the party. And I'm not going to have ⁵ _____ – I'll paint them myself. By the way, don't forget we're having ⁶ _____ on Monday for the album. Do you know what we should wear then?

Best,
Pam

9.2

Reported speech: statements

We use reported speech to say what someone has said. When we report someone's words:
• we use *said* or *told*.
  'I'm tired,' he told me. →
  He *told me*/He *said (that)* he was tired.
• we change the pronouns and possessive adjectives.
  'We're waiting for *our* friends,' they said. →
  They said (that) *they* were waiting for *their* friends.
• we change the tense of the main verb in this way:
  Present Simple → Past Simple.
  'I *want* to study Biology,' she said. →
  She said (that) she *wanted* to study Biology.
  Present Continuous → Past Continuous.
  'I'*m working* on my project,' he said. →
  He said (that) he *was working* on his project.

1 Rewrite the sentences in reported speech.
   1 'I'm writing an essay,' Ken said.
      Ken said (that) he was writing an essay.
   2 'We don't have to wear a uniform at my school,' Mia said.
      _____
   3 'We want to start a school debating club,' the students said.
      _____
   4 'Our Geography teacher gives us a lot of homework,' Ollie said.
      _____
   5 'I'm never late for class,' Nadia said.
      _____

2 Rewrite the sentences in direct speech.
   1 Fred said he needed help with his homework.
      '*I need help with my homework*,' Fred said.
   2 Mr Green said lessons always started at 9.00.
      '_____,'
      Mr Green said.
   3 Pete and Anna said they were thinking about joining the theatre club.
      '_____,'
      Pete and Anna said.
   4 I said I didn't know what was for homework.
      '_____,'
      I said.
   5 Jim said he was making a vlog about his town.
      '_____,'
      Jim said.

9.4

Word order in questions

Yes/No questions

- Yes/No questions begin with an auxiliary verb (e.g. *be*, *have*) or a modal verb (e.g. *can*, *should*). To form questions, we use inversion: we put the auxiliary/modal verb before the subject.
  He *is* talented. → *Is* he talented?
  He *can* help us. → *Can* he help us?
- With verb forms that already have an auxiliary verb (e.g. Present and Past Continuous, Present Perfect, *be going to*, *will*), we simply change the order of the subject and the auxiliary.
  They*'re* leaving. → *Are they* leaving?
  She*'s* going to stay. → *Is she* going to stay?
- With the Present and Past Simple, we add an auxiliary verb (*do/does, did*) to form the question.
  He studies abroad. → *Does he study* abroad?
  They passed the test. → *Did they pass* the test?

Wh- questions

Wh- questions begin with a question word (e.g. *what*, *where*, *when*, *how*). After the question word, the word order is the same as in yes/no questions.
They are going to the park. → *Where are they* going?
He bought a laptop. → *What did he buy*?

Subject questions

Questions with *who* or *what* can be about the subject or object of the answer.

When they are about the subject, we use the same word order as in affirmative sentences. We don't use auxiliary verbs. Compare:
Who saw David? → Nick *saw* David. (Our question is about Nick. Nick is the subject.)
Who did Nick *see*? → Nick saw *David*. (Our question is about David. David is the object.)

1 Order the words to make questions. Then, in pairs, ask and answer the questions.

1 do / most useful / what / subjects / you / find / ?
  What subjects do you find most useful?
2 last month / you / how many / take / tests / did / ?
  _____
3 doing / at 5 p.m. / yesterday / what / you / were / ?
  _____
4 any homework / you / to / are / do / this evening / going / ?
  _____
5 cheated / in a test / you / have / ever / ?
  _____

2 Write two questions for each answer. Use the question words in brackets.

1 My dad has bought me a new tablet. (who, what)
  Who has bought you a new tablet?
  What has your dad bought you?
2 Jessica is going to take a French exam next week. (who, when)
  _____
  _____
3 Mark wants to study in Belgium. (who, where)
  _____
  _____
4 The accident happened in the Science lab. (what, where)
  _____
  _____
5 Emily won the writing competition. (who, what)
  _____
  _____

Irregular Verbs

🔊 10.1

Infinitive	Past Simple	Past Participle	Infinitive	Past Simple	Past Participle
be	was | were	been	lay	laid	laid
become	became	become	learn	learned/learnt	learned/learnt
begin	began	begun	leave	left	left
break	broke	broken	lend	lent	lent
bring	brought	brought	let	let	let
build	built	built	lie	lay	lain
burn	burned/burnt	burned/burnt	lose	lost	lost
buy	bought	bought	make	made	made
can	could	been able to	meet	met	met
catch	caught	caught	pay	paid	paid
choose	chose	chosen	put	put	put
come	came	come	read	read	read
cost	cost	cost	ride	rode	ridden
cut	cut	cut	ring	rang	rung
do	did	done	run	ran	run
draw	drew	drawn	say	said	said
dream	dreamed/dreamt	dreamed/dreamt	see	saw	seen
drink	drank	drunk	sell	sold	sold
drive	drove	driven	send	sent	sent
eat	ate	eaten	set	set	set
fall	fell	fallen	shine	shone	shone
feed	fed	fed	show	showed	shown
feel	felt	felt	sing	sang	sung
fight	fought	fought	sit	sat	sat
find	found	found	sleep	slept	slept
fly	flew	flown	speak	spoke	spoken
forget	forgot	forgotten	spell	spelled/spelt	spelled/spelt
forgive	forgave	forgiven	spend	spent	spent
get	got	got	stand	stood	stood
give	gave	given	steal	stole	stolen
go	went	gone	sweep	swept	swept
grow	grew	grown	swim	swam	swum
hang	hung	hung	take	took	taken
have	had	had	teach	taught	taught
hear	heard	heard	tell	told	told
hide	hid	hidden	think	thought	thought
hit	hit	hit	understand	understood	understood
hold	held	held	wake	woke	woken
hurt	hurt	hurt	wear	wore	worn
keep	kept	kept	win	won	won
know	knew	known	write	wrote	written

Student Activities

Unit 5 Revision Exercise 7

Student A

- this evening: work on History project; then: watch TV
- tomorrow: play football; after that: meet friends
- next Saturday: go shopping; later: help my grandparents

Unit 6 Lesson 6.6 Exercise 7

Student A

You're at the train station and your train is late. Call your friend and explain what's happening.

A: Hi, It's me. I'm at …

Student B

Your friend calls from the station but it's noisy. You want to know what time she is arriving.

A: Hi, It's me. I'm at …

Unit 6 Revision Exercise 7

- **Student A:** Ask, 'Do you like the Mediterranean?'
- **Student B:** You didn't hear 'Mediterranean' very well. Ask for clarification.
- **Student A:** Clarify what you said.
- **Student B:** Thank Student A, say you understand and answer his/her question.

Then swap roles and role play a different situation where you ask for and give clarification.

Unit 9 Revision Exercise 7

Student A

You are an activity leader at a summer camp. You ask Student B questions about the things below because to help you to plan groups for social activities.

- personal details (name, nationality, etc.)
- present situation (school, interests, etc.)
- past experience (travel, films seen, etc.)
- future plans (study, work, etc.)

Unit 7 Lesson 7.6 Exercise 5

Student A

Describe a person in the photo below. Follow the instructions. Then swap roles.
- Choose a person in your photo to describe.
- Your partner/group should ask you questions.
- Answer the questions with one piece of information at a time.

A: Who are you thinking of?
B: A person who looks/is wearing …
A: Where is this person?
B: He's/She's behind/in front of …

Unit 7 Revision Exercise 7

Student A

Unit 8 Revision Exercise 7

You are friends. Student B looks a bit sad and isn't saying much.
- **Student A:** Check if Student B is OK.
- **Student B:** Say you are fine.
- **Student A:** Encourage Student B to speak.
- **Student B:** Explain your problem.
- **Student A:** Respond to the problem and reassure Student B.
- **Student B:** Thank Student B.
- **Student A:** Ask Student B if they feel better.
- **Student B:** Reassure Student A that you feel fine now.

Student Activities

SCIENCE

CLIL 1

Cooking and science

Heston Blumenthal is an English chef. He is important because he has made people think about the science of cooking. Heston uses complicated scientific techniques all the time in his cooking, and some of the equipment that he uses in his kitchen is from a science laboratory!

Science is part of all cooking. Every time we cook something, there is a chemical change. A chemical change means that we create a new substance. The process is irreversible – the ingredient cannot change back. To do this, we need energy – in cooking that means a high temperature. When we use heat during cooking, we change both the taste and the texture of the ingredients.

Here are some examples of chemical changes that happen when we cook. A cake looks and tastes very different before and after cooking. With the heat of the oven, it rises. This is because the baking powder ($NaHCO_3$) in the mixture changes at a high temperature. It produces carbon dioxide (CO_2) and the cake grows. But there was no CO_2 in the cake before! Another example is when we toast bread. The carbohydrates in the bread break to form carbon (C). This makes the bread brown and hard, a change in texture and colour. Proteins in meat and eggs change too. The protein molecules take the energy from the heat and change shape. The meat gets harder and red meat becomes brown. Clear egg whites become solid and white.

Chefs like Heston Blumenthal use their knowledge about chemical changes in food to create new tastes and textures. Heston's famous bacon-and-egg ice cream is made using liquid nitrogen!

A science laboratory **B** protein molecule

C high temperature **D** liquid nitrogen

1 In pairs, discuss the questions.
1 Look at photos A–D. What do they show? How do you think they are linked to cooking?
2 Why do you think some people say cooking is an art and others say it is a science?

2 🔊 10.2 Read the article and answer the questions.
1 Who is Heston Blumenthal and why is he important?
2 What does 'a chemical change' mean?
3 What happens to make a cake rise?
4 What happens when bread becomes toast?
5 What happens when we cook meat and eggs?
6 Which of Heston's dishes is made using liquid nitrogen?

3 In pairs, discuss the questions.
1 What did you find most interesting in the article? Why?
2 What other everyday activities can science help us with?

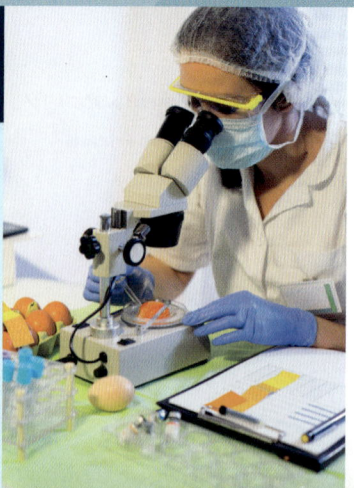

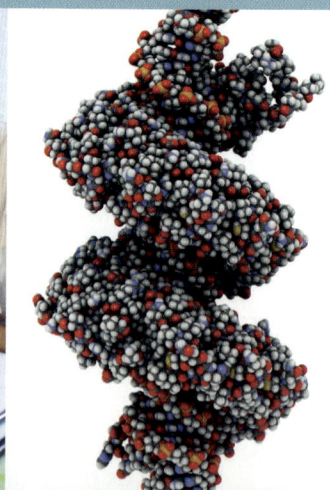

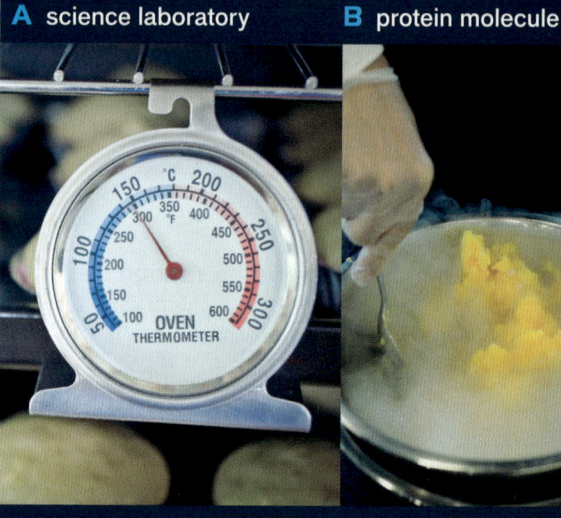

4 Think of a raw ingredient which changes when we cook it. Then, in pairs, take turns to describe the ingredient before and after cooking. Can your partner guess what it is?

A: *Before cooking they're round, white and hard. After cooking at a high temperature they're light, brown and break easily.*
B: *Potato slices which become crisps!*

5 (GO ONLINE) Use the internet to research another chemical change that happens to food during cooking. Make notes about these things.
- what happens and why
- examples of meals where this happens
- any other interesting information

6 (SHARE IT) Prepare a short presentation. Write a paragraph about the chemical change. Add pictures and diagrams. Share your presentation with the class.

MUSIC

CLIL 2

David Bowie and space

1 David Bowie was one of England's greatest singers. He died in 2016, but for five decades, his music touched people all over the world. He was not only a singer, but also a songwriter and an actor. People remember him for his music, but also for the wonderful characters he created on stage, especially Ziggy Stardust. As a musician, he was always very imaginative and creative, and had his own unique style. He started singing pop songs, then rock, then glam rock and in the 2000s he even experimented with industrial and jungle styles.

2 One theme that Bowie used many times in his songs was space. His songs were often about going into space or aliens coming to visit Earth. Perhaps his most famous song about space is *Space Oddity*. It was released just before Apollo 11 landed on the moon on 20 July 1969. The lyrics of the song tell the story of a fictional astronaut, Major Tom, who goes on a space walk but loses contact with the astronauts in the space station and with the station on Earth.

3 *Space Oddity* became one of Bowie's signature songs. It also became famous again in 2013 for a very important reason. While on the International Space Station, the Canadian astronaut Chris Hadfield filmed himself singing *Space Oddity*. It was the first video ever shot in space. People remember Bowie for *Space Oddity*, but he also wrote many other space-themed songs, and they were very popular. Some of them are on his album *The Rise and Fall of Ziggy Stardust and the Spiders from Mars*.

1 Have you heard of David Bowie? What do you know about him? Do you know any of his songs?

2 Look at photos A–C. How do you think space and music might be connected?

3 🔊 10.3 Read the article quickly and check your ideas from Exercises 1 and 2. In which paragraphs (1–3) are photos A–C mentioned?
A ☐   B ☐   C ☐

4 Read the article again and complete the fact file.

David Bowie			
Born:	*1947*	Died: ¹ _____	
Famous character:	² _____		
Types of music:	³ _____		
Famous single:	⁴ _____	Released: ⁵ _____	
Famous album:	⁶ _____		

5 In pairs, read about two songs that were played in space. Student A, read text A. Student B, read text B. Take turns to tell your partner about your song. Then find and listen to the songs online. Which one is better? Why?

A *Across the Universe*, The Beatles
This was the first song that was sent into space as a radio message on 4 February 2008. It was sent from a seventy-metre dish at the Deep Space Network near Madrid. It celebrated the fortieth anniversary of the song, the forty-fifth anniversary of the DSN and the fiftieth anniversary of NASA.

B *Reach for the Stars*, will.i.am
On 28 August 2012, NASA sent this song from Mars to Earth using a special device. NASA and will.i.am wanted to encourage young people to study Science. The song travelled 300 million miles and was the first song ever sent to Earth from another planet.

6 **GO ONLINE** Use the internet to find out more about a famous singer/songwriter from your country. Make notes about these things.
- his/her career
- why he/she became famous
- any other interesting information

7 **SHARE IT** Prepare a digital presentation. Write a paragraph about the singer/songwriter. Add pictures and some of his/her music. Share your presentation with the class.

GEOGRAPHY

CLIL 3

The International Date Line

Tonga and Samoa are two islands in the South Pacific. They are 557 miles apart. If you flew from Tonga to Samoa, the journey would take you two hours, but you would arrive twenty-two hours before you left! It might be 5 November when you leave Tonga and 4 November when you arrive in Samoa. Why? Because you would cross the International Date Line (IDL). This can be confusing for travellers and cause problems with hotel bookings!

The IDL – an imaginary line, not a real one – goes from north to south. There are two other important imaginary lines across the Earth: the Equator, which divides the world into the northern and southern hemispheres, and the Prime Meridian (which goes through London), dividing the world into the western and eastern hemispheres. The IDL is on the opposite side of the world to the Prime Meridian. The world is always turning and as we travel around the world (east or west), our days become shorter or longer. The IDL tells all the countries in the world where the beginning of one day and the end of another come together.

The IDL starts at the North Pole and goes down to the South Pole, and crosses through the Pacific Ocean. But it isn't a straight line – it has several zigzags in it! This is so that it is the same date in one country. For example, the line zigzags east to go through the Bering Straits so that Alaska and Russia are on different sides. The country of Kiribati used to be on the eastern side, but it decided to change to the western side. It wanted to be the first country in the world to celebrate the new millennium in 2000!

1 When it is Friday 11th December in New York City, USA, it is Saturday 12th December in Sydney, Australia. Why do you think the dates are different?

2 🔊 10.4 Read the article quickly and check your answers in Exercise 1. Label A–C on the maps.

3 Read the article again and mark the sentences T (true) or F (false).
   1. ☐ It takes twenty-two hours to fly from Tonga to Samoa.
   2. ☐ The IDL is on the other side of the world from the Prime Meridian.
   3. ☐ The IDL goes in a straight line from north to south.
   4. ☐ It is the same time and day in Russia and Alaska.
   5. ☐ Kiribati is on the western side of the IDL.

4 What did you find most interesting in the article? Why?

5 Read about the history of the IDL. How was the problem of losing a day first discovered?

History of the IDL

In 1519 the explorer Ferdinand Magellan was the first person to sail round the world. During the journey, the crew kept careful records. When they got home, they discovered that they had lost a complete day. The date they had was a day behind the people in their country. This was the beginning of the idea of an international date line and in the seventeenth century it started to appear on maps. It became official in 1884, after an international meridian conference. However, there is still no law that says the IDL exists.

6 Why do you think the IDL is important? What would happen without it?

7 GO ONLINE Use the internet to find out about one of the other imaginary lines around the Earth. Make notes about these things.
   - where it goes
   - its purpose and when it was named
   - any other interesting information

8 SHARE IT Prepare a short presentation. Write a paragraph about the imaginary line you have chosen and add a map with labels. Share your presentation with the class.

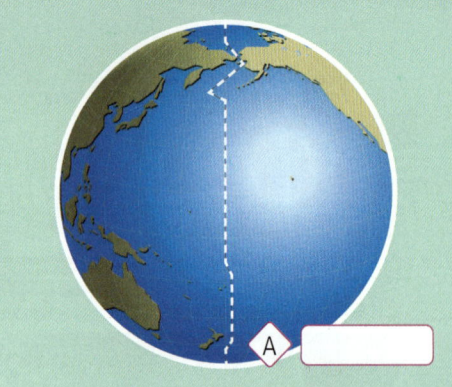

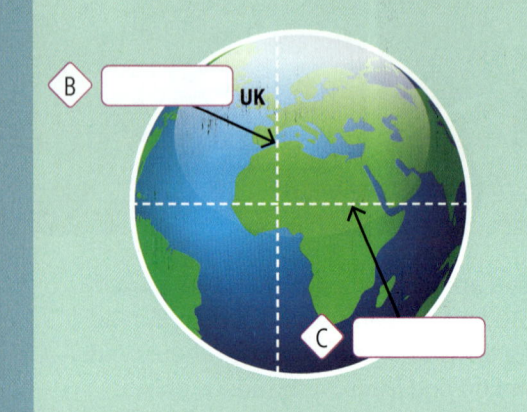

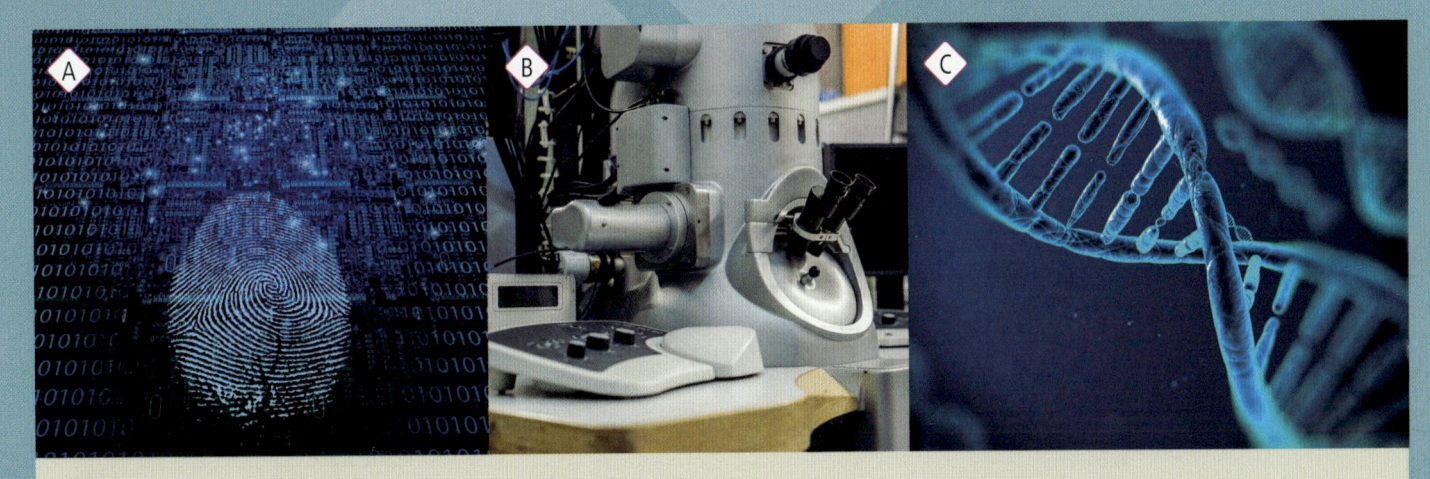

SCIENCE

CLIL 4

Forensics

The crime scene
When there is a crime, the police often use forensic scientists to help them to find the criminal. At nearly every crime scene there is some evidence that scientists can check. This might be blood, hair, fingerprints or other very small things that they can analyse. The forensic scientist uses special equipment in a police laboratory to carry out experiments. They use a powerful microscope (an electron microscope) to check both the evidence and samples from suspects. Forensic scientists also study dead bodies to find out how and when they died. This is called an autopsy, or post-mortem. All this information helps the police.

Fingerprints
Everyone has different fingerprints. These are the lines and circles on the tips of our fingers. When we touch something, we leave a print. Scientists can use special powder to copy these prints. These are compared to records of fingerprints to find out who left them.

DNA
DNA is like a genetic fingerprint. Everyone's DNA is different (apart from identical twins). So if a criminal leaves DNA at a crime scene, the forensic scientist can use it. DNA can be found in many things such as blood, hair, teeth, bone and saliva (from inside our mouths). We leave our DNA everywhere – on clothes and cups, in hairbrushes and on toothbrushes.

---

1 In pairs, discuss the questions.
  1 Look at photos A–C. What do they show? How do you think science can help detectives?
  2 What do you think a forensic scientist does?

2 🔊 10.5 Read the article quickly and check your answers in Exercise 1.

3 Read the article again and answer the questions.
  1 Where does a forensic scientist work?
  2 What can they find out about a dead person?
  3 What are fingerprints and how does a forensic scientist check them?
  4 What is DNA and where is it found?

4 In pairs, read the texts about evidence. Student A, read text A. Student B, read text B. Take turns to tell your partner about your text. How can the evidence you read about help forensic scientists?

> **A Hair** Our hair falls out all the time and a criminal often leaves hair at a crime scene. Scientists can analyse hair and find out if the colour is natural and if it is an animal or human hair. They can also get an idea of the age and gender of the person. There are many different things a hair can tell the scientist! If the hair has a root, it can also give DNA.

> **B Shoes** Shoes can leave prints. These can tell scientists about a criminal's size, the way they walk and the type of shoe that they wore. Shoes also leave dirt. Scientists can sometimes learn where the person lives or works, if they have pets, where they walk and even which field or path he/she has walked on.

5 Would you like to be a forensic scientist? Why?/Why not?

6 (GO ONLINE) Use the internet to find out how the police solved a famous crime using forensics. Make notes about the crime and the evidence.

7 (SHARE IT) Prepare a short presentation. Write a paragraph about the crime and the forensic work involved. Add pictures. Share your presentation with the class.

Student Activities

Unit 1 — Lesson 1.5 Exercise 2

Do you need a digital detox?
Results
- **Mostly a:** You're obviously busy with other things in life and that's great. Have fun and enjoy real time with your friends!
- **Mostly b:** You know your mobile is there when you need it, but technology isn't the most important thing in your life.
- **Mostly c:** You're internet crazy! You love being online and checking messages from friends. Make sure you take time to do other things too.

Unit 1 — Lesson 1.6 Exercise 5

Follow the instructions to role play a dialogue. Then swap roles.
- **Student A:** choose a situation from the list below. Then accept or reject Student B's solutions.
- **Student B:** listen to Student A and respond with a suitable suggestion.

- My QR code reader app doesn't work.
- I dropped my phone and it broke.
- There's no wi-fi signal in my room.
- My computer keeps crashing.

Unit 2 — Lesson 2.6 Exercise 6

- I copied my homework from a friend.
- I didn't buy my friend a birthday present.
- I spent a lot of money on a concert/sports ticket.

A: State the problem. Add extra information if possible.
B: Ask about your partner's actions.
A: Explain your reasons.
B: Give your opinion or say if you understand now.

Unit 2 — Revision Exercise 8

Follow the instructions to role play a dialogue. Then swap roles.
- **Student A:** Phone your friend. Apologise and say you don't want to go camping. Add extra information if possible.
- **Student B:** Accept your partner's apology and ask why they don't want to go camping.
- **Student A:** Explain your reasons. Add as many as you can.
- **Student B:** Accept your partner's explanation.

Unit 3 — Lesson 3.6 Exercise 6

Digby's Restaurant Menu

Starters
Nachos with cheese
Mini pizzas
Toast with olive oil, garlic and fresh tomatoes

Main courses
Salmon with sweet potatoes
Hamburger with fries
Pasta with mushroom sauce

Desserts
Fruit salad with fresh cream
Pumpkin pie with vanilla ice cream
Chocolate cake

Drinks
Cola • Carrot and pear smoothie • Apple juice

Unit 3 — Revision Exercise 8

SAM'S SNACKS MENU

SANDWICHES
Tuna • Salmon • Chicken •
Beef burger • Tofu burger

EXTRAS
Chips • Mushrooms •
Carrot and green pepper salad •
Olives • Pickles

DRINKS
Orange juice • Mango juice •
Pineapple juice • Mineral water • Tea

Progress Check Units 1–3 Exercise 5

1. You are on a walking trip in the mountains.
   - **Student A:** explain that you think you are lost. Apologise. It was your job to find the way, but the map app on your phone doesn't work.
   - **Student B:** respond to what Student A says.
   - Discuss a solution.

2. You are both at Student B's house. Student A is a guest. You are in the kitchen because you agreed to cook pizza.
   - **Student B:** explain that you have a problem with the recipe for the pizza. Explain the problem and apologise.
   - **Student A:** respond to what Student B says.
   - Discuss a solution.

Unit 5 Revision Exercise 7

Student B

- this evening: work out at gym; after that: cook dinner
- tomorrow: visit my uncle; then: do schoolwork
- next Saturday: watch football match; later: go to the cinema

Unit 7 Lesson 7.6 Exercise 5

Student B

Describe a person in the photo below. Follow the instructions. Then swap roles.

- Choose a person in your photo to describe.
- Your partner/group should ask you questions.
- Answer the questions with one piece of information at a time.

A: Who are you thinking of?
B: A person who looks/is wearing …
A: Where is this person?
B: He's/She's behind/in front of …

Unit 7 Revision Exercise 7

Student B

Unit 9 Revision Exercise 7

Student B

You are staying at the summer camp. Make up the information below about yourself and answer Student B's questions.

- personal details (name, nationality, etc.)
- present situation (school, interests, etc.)
- past experience (travel, films seen, etc.)
- future plans (study, work, etc.)

Progress Check Units 1–9 Exercise 5

1 In pairs, follow the instructions to role play a situation where you are making friends on a summer holiday course.
   - In pairs, decide where you are and what course you are doing.
   - Now work on your own. Imagine a new identity for yourself! Decide your new name and where you are from.
   - In pairs, talk about the holiday course experience and your future plans.

2 Think about your conversation. Did you:
   - listen carefully?
   - smile and show interest?
   - use a variety of different tenses correctly?
   - ask for clarification if you needed to?

3 Swap roles or work in new pairs and repeat the role play.

Progress Check Units 1–9 Exercise 12

	Yes	No	Maybe
1 Would you like to learn only by doing projects?	☐	☐	☐
2 Would you like to stop learning Maths?	☐	☐	☐
3 Would you like to learn outdoors?	☐	☐	☐
4 Would you like to learn to do creative and practical things with your hands?	☐	☐	☐
5 Would you like to decide what school subjects you learn?	☐	☐	☐

Student Activities

Pearson Education Limited
KAO Two
KAO Park
Hockham Way
Harlow, Essex
CM17 9SR
England
and Associated Companies throughout the world.

pearsonenglish.com/widerworld2e

© Pearson Education Limited 2022

All rights reserved; no part of this publication may be reproduced, stored in a retrieval system, or transmitted in any form or by any means, electronic, mechanical, photocopying, recording, or otherwise without the prior written permission of the Publishers

First published 2022

ISBN: 978-1-292-42274-9

Set in Frutiger Next Pro
Printed in Mexico

Acknowledgements
The Publishers would like to thank all the teachers and students around the world who contributed to the development of Wider World Second Edition: Milena Aleksić, Tuğba Arslantaş, Gülşah Aslan, Mahgol Baboorian, Katarzyna Beliniak, Burcu Candan, Seri Diri, Hanna Dudich, Sema Karapinar, Nadiia Kasianchuk, Duygu Kayhan, Iryna Kharchenko, Ana Krstić, Ilknur Manav, Fulya Mertoğlu, Ivana Nikolov, Banu Oflas, Duygu Özer, Jagoda Popović, Marija Šanjević, Karmen Irizar Segurola, Elif Sevinç, Ludmila Shengel, Ayşe Sönmez, Anna Standish, Natalia Tkachenko, Pamela Van Bers, Jelena Vračar, Agnieszka Woźnicka, Münevver Yanık.

The Publishers would like to thank the following people who commented on the Wider World Second Edition content: Milena Aleksi, Mahgol Baboorian, Hanna Dudich, Izabela Kołando, Karmen Irizar Segurola, Joanna Srokosz, Anna Zając.

We would also like to thank the authors of the first edition of Wider World whose work has been the basis for creating this adaptation: Kathryn Alevizos, Carolyn Barraclough, Catherine Bright, Sheila Dignen, Lynda Edwards, Rod Fricker, Suzanne Gaynor, Bob Hastings, Jennifer Heath, Liz Kilbey, Stuart McKinlay, Sarah Thorpe, Tasia Vassilatou, Damian Williams, Sandy Zervas.

Photo Acknowledgements
123RF.com: 41, Adam Borkowski 43, Andrey Safonov 34, Andrii Starunskyi 103, Andriy Popov 12, anyaberkut 100, auremar 78, bowie15 22, bracknell 55, Brent Hofacker 39, Cathy Yeulet 113, czarnybez 36, Dan Grytsku 19, denisfilm 74, dolgachov 143, elenathewise 45, Elizaveta Galitckaia 141, fazon 25, Fokke Baarssen 77, goodluz 137, Ian Allenden 122, 122, ibrester 138, Igor Salnikov 27, Ijupco 71, Iriana Shiyan 7, ismagilov 115, Jozef Polc 98, Katarzyna Białasiewicz 100, M Production 34, Matthew Benoit 41, natthanim 36, nitr 43, Olga Yastremska 36, 36, pixelrobot 100, Pop Nukoonrat 39, serezniy 12, Sergey Novikov 65, subbotina 39, Tatiana Epifanova 34, tatiana Gladskikh 41, Viacheslav Iakobchuk 91, vimart 12, yatomo 39, Yuliya Belenkova 25; **Alamy Stock Photo:** Douglas Lander 1, Matthias Scholz 24, Pacific Press Media Production Corp 51, Steve Speller 50, Universal Images Group North America LLC/DeAgostini 140; **BBC Studios:** 23, 47, 73, 99, 123; **Getty Images:** ©Hello Lovely/Corbis 60, Barcroft Media 24, bortonia/DigitalVision Vectors 37, Cameron Soencer/Getty Images AsiaPac 72, CasarsaGuru 65, Caspar Benson 34, Corbis/VCG/Corbis 65, fotografixx/E+ 66, Gary S Chapman/Photographer's Choice RF 93, Guerilla 110, Image Source/DigitalVision 62, JohnnyGreig/E+ 74, kali9/E+ 74, Karl Tapales/Moment 43, Michael Putland/Hulton Archive 139, Michael Regan/Getty Images Europe 67, ShutterWorx/E+ 119, Thomas Barwick/Stone 15, Tim Robberts/Stone 53, Westend61 74, 105; **Jubilee Sailing Trust:** 79; **Pearson Education Ltd:** 28, 30, Ian Wedgewood 113, Jon Barlow 6, 8, 9, 10, 11, 16, 18, 38, 42, 54, 56, 64, 68, 76, 80, 90, 94, 104, 106, 116, 118, Studio 8 114; **Sean Ebsworth Barnes:** 57; **Shutterstock.com:** 52, 78, 78, 89, 110, 114, adriaticfoto 138, Aleksandra Duda 100, AlohaHawaii 93, Anton Chernov 43, Arcady 140, Artur Bogacki 25, Billion Photos 92, Bruce Rolff 141, Castleski 139, christianpinillo 26, Cookie Studio 74, daseaford 29, David Prado Perucha 137, Djent 13, Dusan Zidar 36, Erika J Mitchell 60, Fotos593 31, gladcov 13, 13, 13, 13, Gorodenkoff 60, Graphic design 55, Hendrika Koerts 55, I Wei Huang 46, ictor Moussa 102, Image Source Trading Ltd 40, Izf 14, javarman 36, joyfull 98, Kuzma 107, Lukas Gojda 62, makuromi 138, mauricioalvesfotos 55, molekuul_be 138, Moneca 114, NASA 139, North Devon Photography 112, pajtica 63, Paul Prescott 125, Pavlo S 2, 3, Photo Spirit 78, Photo Volcano 33, Picsfive 39, pornpan chaiu-dom 81, Sergey Zaykov 29, Sopotnicki 25, SpeedKingz 100, Stephen Coburn 103, stockphoto-graf 62, theerasakj 78, Timolina 36, Tom Wang 74, UfaBizPhoto 60, vitstudio 141, wavebreakmedia 113, 143, WAYHOME studio 114, Wildlife World 48

Illustrated by Gergley Fórizs (Beehive) 77, 88; Maguma AKA Marcos Guardiola Martin (IllustrationX) 35, 61, 85, 111; Dina Ruzha 84; Rupert Van Wyk (Beehive) 17.
All other images © Pearson Education

Cover photo © Front: **Alamy Stock Photo:** Sara Winter

Wider World

SECOND EDITION

Set for learning, set for life in the real world

Wider World Second Edition prepares teenagers for their life ahead: it equips them with the future skills they will need to enjoy their social lives, pursue their studies and succeed in their careers as citizens of the world.

New BBC videos cover the huge diversity of life and culture, expose learners to authentic English, inspire them to develop their language skills, build communicative competence, and fire curiosity in the world outside the classroom.

Comprehensive teacher support and resources make teaching intuitive, with minimal preparation. They enable teachers to adapt to the needs of individual students, so every student can achieve their highest potential and flourish in their lives ahead.

Student's Book with eBook
- The eBook brings the Student's Book to life with interactive activities with instant marking, video and audio.

Wider World Second Edition is fully accessible on your computer, tablet and mobile phone so that you can enjoy the full functionality of your course wherever you are.

pearsonenglish.com/widerworld2e

Also available
- Student's Book with Online Practice & eBook
- Student's eBook Access Code
- Student's eBook with Online Practice Access Code
- Workbook
- Workbook with Online Practice
- Online Practice Access Code

Learning English with Pearson? Access English language materials to support your learning journey.

Ready to prove your English skills? Get exclusive preparation materials for Pearson English exams. pearsonenglish.com/exams-offer

	GSE	CEFR	Pearson English International Certificate	Benchmark	Cambridge
Starter	10-25	<A1/A1		Benchmark YL Learners Level 1	
Level 1	24-34	A1/A2	Levels A1/1	Benchmark YL Learners Level 2	A2 Key for Schools
Level 2	32-42	A2/A2+	Level 1	Benchmark YL Learners Levels 3/4 Benchmark Test A	A2 Key for Schools
Level 3	40-50	A2+/B1	Levels 1/2	Benchmark YL Learners Levels 4/5 Benchmark Tests A/B1	A2 Key for Schools B1 Preliminary for Schools
Level 4	45-55	B1/B1+	Level 2	Benchmark YL Learners Levels 5/6 Benchmark Test B1	B1 Preliminary for Schools

ISBN 978-1-292-42274-9

¡Nos vemos!

Paso a paso 5

Libro del alumno A2.3

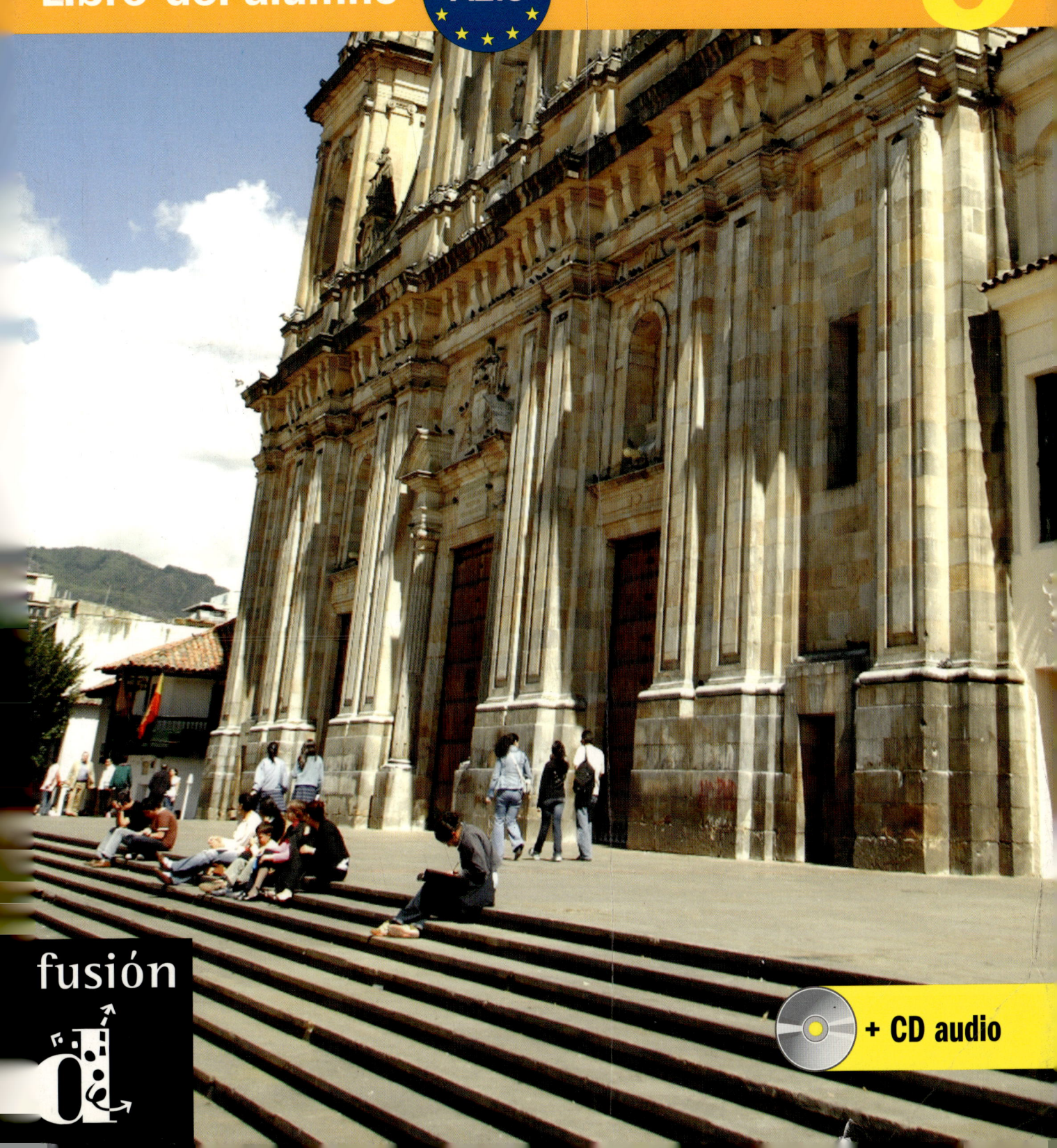

fusión

+ CD audio